Business Guides on the Go

"Business Guides on the Go" presents cutting-edge insights from practice on particular topics within the fields of business, management, and finance. Written by practitioners and experts in a concise and accessible form the series provides professionals with a general understanding and a first practical approach to latest developments in business strategy, leadership, operations, HR management, innovation and technology management, marketing or digitalization. Students of business administration or management will also benefit from these practical guides for their future occupation/careers.

These Guides suit the needs of today's fast reader.

Vanessa Miller • Jens U. Pätzmann

Archetypical Roles in Startups

Eight Personality Traits You Need in Your Founding Team

Springer

Vanessa Miller
Neu-Ulm University of Applied Sciences
Neu-Ulm, Germany

Jens U. Pätzmann
Neu-Ulm University of Applied Sciences
Neu-Ulm, Germany

ISSN 2731-4758 ISSN 2731-4766 (electronic)
Business Guides on the Go
ISBN 978-3-031-22252-8 ISBN 978-3-031-22253-5 (eBook)
https://doi.org/10.1007/978-3-031-22253-5

This Springer imprint is published by the registered company Springer Nature Switzerland AG.
The registered company address is: Gewerbestrasse 11, 6330 Cham, Switzerland

Preface

The composition of the team is just as crucial as the startup idea itself. Some investors even maintain that an excellent team with a mediocre idea is more promising than a mediocre team with an excellent idea. Diverse teams seem to have advantages over very homogeneous ones. For example, a team of five made up exclusively of creative minds is missing key contributors like the seller, the resource guard, and the implementor. Throughout the startup journey, complementary and at times even contradictory skills are needed.

Nevertheless, it is the most common case that friends, not strangers, join forces to found a startup. Friendships are usually built for shared interests, attitudes, and values. A team consisting of friends tends to be homogeneous. Investors have recognized this and favor groups with diverse skills and characteristics, in order to ensure that the right team members can take on responsibility for the various functions—different personalities are needed for marketing, finance, organization, product development, and so on.

Most investors and mentors focus on technical skills, experience, and qualifications, because assessing team composition in terms of personalities is a challenge. However, evaluating potential founding teams' personality setup can be a worthwhile effort because there is often a lack of self-awareness and mutual understanding. A personality test, designed as a self-test, can be a useful tool. The market for personality assessment tools, including those that measure motifs and emotions, is varied and growing. And yet their application for startup teams is little explored.

The authors of this book suggest that an adaptation of archetype theory inspired by C. G. Jung can generate useful insights into the social dynamics within startup teams. Archetype theory is not without controversy. In particular, scientists wonder whether the approach is empirically sound. At least it can be proven beyond doubt that there are certain structures within the human psyche that have universal validity. In a so-called blockbuster analysis, Pätzmann and Hartwig (2018) analyzed fifty internationally successful cinema movies and grouped the roles that appeared in them into archetypes and anti-archetypes.

This was followed by publications on archetypes and how they can be applied for storytelling (2019), customer insights (2020), and employer branding (2020). Parallel to this book, publications on colors and archetypes (2023) and the emotionalization of business models through archetypes (2023) are planned. All publications aim to contribute to practical application.

Neu-Ulm University of Applied Sciences, where the two authors work, sees itself as an international business school for innovation, sustainable entrepreneurship, and digital transformation. All activities in research and teaching aim to solve burning practical problems in a global context. This is what we want to achieve with this book. It is intended to be a practical book based on sound research. We address founders, incubators, mentors, investors, business angels, and entrepreneurs in an international environment. We also target bachelor's and master's students in the fields of Entrepreneurship, Business Administration, and Business Psychology. This book intends to help start a business by successful teamwork.

We want to thank our international experts who helped us to gain insights about archetypical team roles in startup teams—Germany: Prof. Dr. Daniel Schallmo, Michael Reichert, Prof. Dr. Thomas Bayer, Prof. Dr. Tobias Engelhard; Israel: Tal Berman, Brian Steinberg, Itai Mendelsohn, Dr. Jaime Amsel, Nimrod Katz; Kenya: Pamela Mbae, Dr. George Kosimbei, Benjamin Barwa, Dr. Anncarol Karanja, Martin Irungu, Simon Ndirangu.

Special thanks to Prof. Dr. Vered Holzmann, Academic College of Tel Aviv-Yaffo. She advised us intensively and is our coauthor on several publications on entrepreneurship.

Thanks also to Barbara Bethke of Springer Nature, who convinced us that this book series was the right one for our project.

Neu-Ulm, Germany
October 2022

Vanessa Miller
Jens U. Pätzmann

Contents

About the Authors

Vanessa Miller is a Research Associate for Circular Economy and Entrepreneurship at the Neu-Ulm University of Applied Sciences (HNU). She holds a Bachelor of Arts in Interdisciplinary American Studies from the University of Tübingen and an executive Master of Business Administration from HNU. She has lived in the USA and Kenya and has work experience in international education. At HNU, she is responsible for collaborative projects with African partner universities, among others for the joint development of a Master's degree in Circular Agro-Economy at the University of Rwanda. Her research interests include circular economy, sustainable entrepreneurship, entrepreneurial teams, and intersections of culture and business models.

Jens U. Pätzmann teaches Marketing, Branding, and Strategy for startups at the Neu-Ulm University of Applied Sciences. He received his doctorate from the Faculty of Communication Sciences, Freie Universität Berlin. Jens U. Pätzmann is a co-director of the Institute for Entrepreneurship and is one of few researchers investigating archetypes and their relevance to the startup ecosystem. Also, he is a member of the Africa Institute. His international activities focus on Europe, Israel, and Kenya. Jens U. Pätzmann has been applying archetypes to the practice for twelve years and has published extensively on exploiting archetypes for marketing, branding, and organizational behavior.

Part I

Team Roles in Startups

The implementing team behind a business idea is the decisive factor for its success. Choosing the right teammates is a founder's most vital decision and a critical point for investors, mentors, and other stakeholders. Not only hard skills and experience are important, but it is critical to have different yet complementary personality types within a team. Chapter 1 provides an introduction to the topic and proposes Jungian archetype theory as an untraditional approach to personalities in startup teams. Chapter 2 presents insights into social interactions in startup teams and which team member compositions are the most successful. Chapter 3 provides an overview of the development of archetype theory and which practical application fields modernized archetypical models have today.

1

Introduction

1.1 Relevance of the Topic

The creation of new firms is of broad economic relevance. It mitigates fluctuation of bankrupt ventures (Foo et al., 2006, p. 389), creates new jobs (Gopalkrishnan, 2017, p. 9), and functions as a coping mechanism in times of rising unemployment (Barba-Sánchez & Atienza-Sahuquillo, 2017, p. 1098). Moreover, entrepreneurship brings about change and innovation in old and new industries (Gopalkrishnan, 2017, p. 9) and can breathe life into developing economies much more effectively than foreign aid can (Christensen et al., 2019). Entrepreneurial ventures have therefore been termed "the lifeblood of most economies" (Klotz et al., 2013, p. 250). A newly founded company's statistical likelihood of success, however, is dishearteningly low. Failure rates are estimated between 40 and 90% (*Must-Know Startup Statistics*, 2021; Cerdeira & Kotashev, 2021; de Mol et al., 2015; Gopalkrishnan, 2017, p. 9; Kozusznik et al., 2020, p. 393 f; *20 Factors That Predict Startup Failure*, 2018).

Next to product-market-fit issues and insufficient funding, organizational and environmental factors have been blamed for the low chances of success (Vanaelst et al., 2006, p. xxii). Research on success factors

V. Miller, J. U. Pätzmann, *Archetypical Roles in Startups*, Business Guides on the Go,
https://doi.org/10.1007/978-3-031-22253-5_1

identified the characteristics of the founder(s) as a key aspect. Researchers at first concentrated on solo entrepreneurs; yet, more entrepreneurs operate in teams rather than alone (Klotz et al., 2013, p. 226). Teams of founders are not only more common than solo entrepreneurs but also more successful (Vanaelst et al., 2006, p. xxii). Therefore, researchers' attention shifted to the characteristics of and interactions between startup team members (Muñoz-Bullon et al., 2015, p. 3).

Founding teams have a significant impact on new venture outcomes (Kollmann et al., 2017, p. 845). Upper echelons theory states that the top management team profoundly impacts the whole organization and it has been confirmed for startup teams, indicating that the founding teams' impact is even greater in nascent ventures than in established ones (Jin et al., 2017, p. 745). Hence, the founding team is crucial in convincing an investor to believe not only in the idea, but also in its successful implementation (Brattström, 2019, p. 10; Coe, 2019, p. 51). Weak founding teams are cited as one of the main causes of startup failure (Wasserman, 2012, p. 3). Much emphasis has been placed on teams' demographics, prior experience, technical skills, and other hard factors. However, the compatibility of founding team members' personalities and interpersonal processes play a significant role as well (Brattström et al., 2020; de Mol et al., 2015; Kakarika, 2013, p. 32; Klotz et al., 2013; Kollmann et al., 2017; Kozusznik et al., 2020; Lechler, 2001; West III, 2007). Founders and investors have high stakes in working with balanced and effective startup teams. Founding teams weakened by mismatching personalities and dysfunctional conflicts can lead to failures of otherwise promising business ideas.

Therefore, much research has been conducted on team composition in startup teams: for example, on members' previous experience in industry and with startups (Muñoz-Bullon et al., 2015), new member addition (Forbes et al., 2006), team conflict in startup teams (Klotz et al., 2013, p. 240), and other factors. It has been proven that interpersonal conflicts, as opposed to cognitive conflicts, in startup teams hamper firm success most severely (Klotz et al., 2013, p. 242). Complementarity of hard skills is not sufficient to allow for effective teamwork. Social processes play an important role, too.

Human beings have a natural tendency to favor persons with similar characteristics, which often leads to rather homogeneous startup teams (Brattström, 2019, p. 6; Kakarika, 2013, p. 31). Yet, similar people do not always work well together. Collaborators should rather complement each other to form effective teams where each member can assume another responsibility that they are naturally inclined to (Belbin, 2010b, p. 64). Thus, even teams composed of highly capable individuals can be ineffective if members are overly alike (Belbin, 2010a, p. 23). The question of homophily versus diversity has received plenty of attention, whereby the emphasis has shifted from hard factors like demography and qualifications to diversity of personality, thinking style, and motivation (Kollmann et al., 2017).

Looking into personalities in startup teams and the compatibility of the members has been suggested as a promising field of research (Jin et al., 2017, p. 762; Klotz et al., 2013, pp. 230, 247; Kollmann et al., 2017, p. 855; Pitcher & Smith, 2001). Relevant findings can help identify suitable combinations of personalities to form more successful startup teams. This will enable startup founders to carefully select the right mix of team members, and help other stakeholders such as incubation mentors, business angels, and venture capitalists to evaluate a team's likelihood of success and give appropriate advice. The complexity of interpersonal relationships in a volatile startup environment requires a look beyond traditional business research (Brattström et al., 2020, p. 13).

Abundant practical and theoretical material on teams in the work environment is available. The literature has concentrated on areas such as team building, teamwork, team development, and different work contexts in which teams come together. In this general context, the question of team composition with regard to personalities has been examined (Bell et al., 2018). Team members do not only have functional roles based on their hard skills but also informal roles depending on their personality traits (Dick & West, 2005, p. 30). The work of Belbin (2010a, 2010b) has been very influential with regard to understanding how the mix of personalities in a team contributes to their success. Belbin (2010a, 2010b) has conducted expansive research on personality trait interaction in teams and created a model of nine specific team roles.

The context in which the team operates is significant for the demands that are posed on team personality composition (Bell et al., 2018, p. 354). Most of the aforementioned research focuses on teams working within established organizations. Yet, startup teams are operating under special conditions because they have limited resources, operate in uncertainty, are formed voluntarily, and face an entirely different set of challenges, low chances of survival, and evolving identities (Ambos & Birkinshaw, 2010, p. 1125; Brattström, 2019, p. 7; Klotz et al., 2013, p. 228). In short, they are fundamentally different, so that findings about teams in established organizations cannot simply be transferred to them (Brattström, 2019, p. 7; Klotz et al., 2013, p. 228). For this reason, more research on team member interactions specifically in startups is needed (Wright & Vanaelst, 2009, p. xxxvi).

1.2 Goals

This book responds to this need by reaching out to a concept developed in psychology and in the humanities: archetype theory based on the collective unconscious as conceptualized by the Swiss nineteenth-century psychiatrist Carl Gustav Jung. The concept of archetypes has been applied in management and organizational studies. In an investigation of archetypical themes in modern organizations, Kostera (2012) defines archetypes as "empty slots, ready to accommodate images, characters or plots important to culture and individual development" (p. 28). Archetypical roles and their practical relevance in human collaboration within a professional context have been empirically investigated by Moxnes and Moxnes (2016). Similarly, Ambos and Birkinshaw (2010) have applied the concept specifically to startup teams, using it to comprehend the nature of new ventures and the evolution they undergo over time. These examples show that archetype theory can be very helpful for the study of startup teams.

Pätzmann and Hartwig (2018) developed an empirically tested model of archetypes in contemporary language based on the study of internationally popular blockbusters. The model is based on Jung's theory of archetypes as well as Bischof's three fundamental motifs safety, excitement, and autonomy (Pätzmann & Hartwig, 2018, p. 3). It features 14 archetypes and 14 corresponding anti-archetypes, which are composed of both male and female figures and trigger human beings' motivational barriers and endorsers. The model has been applied to marketing and brand management (Pätzmann & Adamczyk, 2020; Pätzmann & Busch, 2019) and further developed into a personality test (Pätzmann & Genrich, 2020). Thus, the model has proven to be of high practical relevance. The work at hand takes up the suggestion by Pätzmann and Genrich (2020) to apply the archetypical personality test to startup teams (p. 36). The authors propose that this test can be used to generate practically relevant insights for founders, incubators, and venture capitalists in order to improve collaboration within startup teams.

This book pools a wealth of experience from German, Israeli, and Kenyan entrepreneurship experts, bringing together know-how from three very different entrepreneurship contexts. On the one end, Germany as one of the economic powerhouses in Europe represents an established, saturated economy in need of fluctuation and new innovations to defend its standing against upcoming economies, especially in innovation-intensive fields like artificial intelligence. As of 2020/2021, entrepreneurial activity is comparatively low in Germany (Bosma et al., 2021, p. 38). Israel, on the other end, has been labeled "the startup nation," with a government highly supportive of entrepreneurial endeavors and a vibrant high-tech startup scene (Almor & Heilbrunn, 2014). Kenya represents an emerging economy, one of the leading countries in Africa in terms of digital entrepreneurship, with its capital Nairobi being nicknamed the Silicon Savannah, and yet facing the challenges of a developing country (Mutuku, 2021). On the one hand, Kenya deals with rapid population growth and urbanization, youth unemployment, and a lack of basic infrastructure. On the other hand, it has a growing middle class and favorable economic outlooks (*Kenya GDP Annual Growth Rate*, n.d.). This creates huge market potential for bringing goods and services to the underserved (Christensen et al., 2019). These three countries represent diverse backgrounds where entrepreneurship fulfills different crucial roles. Expertise from those contexts can cross-pollinate and the innovation ecosystems can learn from each other.

In the present book, the authors suggest that the archetypical model developed by Pätzmann and Hartwig (2018) and the corresponding archetypical personality test by Pätzmann and Genrich (2020) can be a useful tool for startup teams. In the first step, a study was conducted to confirm the test's content validity. In the second step, the validated test was used as a research tool to identify the relevant archetypes for a startup team. In step three, in-depth expert interviews were employed to generate contextualized insights. With this mixed methods approach, we responded to the following research question, divided into five sub-questions:

Research question: Can archetypical roles be a useful instrument for startup team formation?

Sub-question 1: Which archetypes are most relevant for startup teams?

Sub-question 2: Which anti-archetypes are most tolerable in a startup team?

Sub-question 3: What is the role of the identified (anti-)archetypes in a startup team?

Sub-question 4: How do archetypical team roles interact within a startup?

Sub-question 5: Which practical relevance does the archetypical model have for the entrepreneurship ecosystem?

The quantitative survey identified seven (anti-)archetypes with special relevance for startup teams: mentor, leader, friend, artist, hero, rebel, and femme fatale. Those results were evaluated and deepened by means of semistructured in-depth interviews with 15 experts. Taken together, this generated seven profiles of archetypical roles specifically for startups and shed light on their interactions and their relevancy over the startup journey. Moreover, the manager was identified as an additional role of relevance for startup teams. Thereby, this work shows how the archetypical personality test can help to build more effective startup teams.

1.3 Concepts

Four central concepts run through this work: startup, startup team, archetype, and archetypical role. To understand the book, it is important to comprehend how it conceives and employs these terms. For this reason, the following section provides brief working definitions of the concepts. Thus, it becomes clear how these concepts were operationalized for the underlying studies.

1.3.1 Startup

Two different views on entrepreneurship can be distinguished: the following of new opportunities versus the creation of a new venture (Wright & Vanaelst, 2009, p. xi). In the broadest sense, entrepreneurship describes the pursuit of opportunities with insufficient resources (Wasserman, 2012, p. 332). Apart from that, researchers have formally defined entrepreneurial firms as any young businesses which have not exceeded a certain time since founding (Jin et al., 2017), are not yet officially registered (Ruef, 2010, p. 144), or below a certain maturity level in terms of branches, employees, revenues (*Must-Know Startup Statistics*, 2021), or positive cashflow (Muñoz-Bullon et al., 2015).

This book employs a very broad definition of *startups*. The focus is on the creation of independent new companies, allowing for a combination of both above-mentioned aspects and recognizing that not all newly founded businesses are characterized by an equal level of innovativeness. The novelty of a business' products and services has a great impact on the complexity it faces (Vanaelst et al., 2006, p. xxiv). This work does not limit itself to formalistic criteria of startups. It concentrates on business models with a certain level of novelty, but these can be incremental adaptations in established markets as well as disruptive high-tech innovations.

1.3.2 Startup Team

Teams, in general, are understood as a coherent group of individuals who depend on each other for a common goal and distinguish themselves from their environment (Afflerbach, 2020, p. 11). Yet, the term *startup team* is not clearly defined, and different operationalizations have been employed by researchers (Vanaelst et al., 2006, p. ix). Criteria for defining startup team members include mutual dependence and risk-sharing to build a common business, sharing strategic decision-making power and operational responsibility, significantly contributing to the main business idea, having financial interest and/or equity stakes, and joining the team early in the founding process (Brattström et al., 2020, p. 5; Chowdhury, 2005, p. 730; Francis & Sandberg, 2000, p. 9; Jin et al.,

2017, p. 744; Klotz et al., 2013, p. 227; Muñoz-Bullon et al., 2015, p. 2; Vanaelst et al., 2006, p. xi; Wasserman, 2012, p. 81).

The term *founder* also has considerable symbolic power and depends on the labels used by the team itself. Sometimes, members who join the venture later than others but have strategic decision-making power over a key aspect of business development are also referred to as founders (Wasserman, 2012, p. 84). In addition, it must be recognized that the definition of the *startup team* heavily depends on the stage of founding under consideration. The legal founding of a company can be the outcome of a long process preceded by team member turnover (Vanaelst et al., 2006, p. x), thus the term *team* must not be misunderstood as a static concept (Vanaelst et al., 2006, p. 250 f).

This book adopts the concept suggested by Ruef (2010) which emphasizes the porous boundaries of founding teams. It considers the startup as an emerging organization born through collective action. The founding of a startup is distinguished from self-employment by the intent to work with others, may it be in the function of "cofounders, employees, investors, advisors, or unpaid helpers" (Ruef, 2010, p. 7). Instead of mechanistically splitting individuals into discrete categories of entrepreneurs and non-entrepreneurs, this perspective considers entrepreneurship to range on a continuum that connects individuals to entrepreneurial groups based on their material and time investments, social networks, identities, and goals (Ruef, 2010, p. 7).

Ruef (2010) distinguishes contributions to a startup by two dimensions: contribution of financial resources and contribution of time and commitment. Owner-managers have the highest commitment: they have high financial stakes because they own equity, plus they invest a substantial amount of time. Investors share the financial risk, but dedicate little time. Employees dedicate their working hours, but own no equity. Other players in the entrepreneurial network have a lower time commitment and lower financial stake, but can still play a crucial role, like consultants, vendors, contact brokers, or even helpers from private circles. These roles are not static. They can change over time or be altogether absent from a given team. The boundaries are fluid (Ruef, 2010, pp. 61f).

The owner-managers of a startup usually create their own common identity to distinguish themselves as cofounders from the outside world and from less committed contributors. They form relationships to benefit from a business idea by building a company together (Brattström et al., 2020, p. 6). These boundaries can be purely mental or formalized and they are permeable, allowing for changes over time (Ruef, 2010, p. 85). Yet, when looking at the founding of a new venture as a social process, researchers must not overlook the extended social assistance network, which can make crucial contributions to the startup.

Definition In line with Ruef's perspective of the entrepreneurial team as a continuum, this book employs the following working definition: *Internal* team members are two or more individuals who choose to work together and to commit considerable investment (e.g., time, money, resources, contacts, and personal risk) with the common goal of forming an entrepreneurial venture. They have legal and/or financial stakes, share strategic decision-making power, and contribute a significant amount of time to operational tasks. *External* team members are those players in the entrepreneurial assistance network who contribute only a specific resource like funding, space, work, guidance, or expert knowledge. These can be mentors, investors, or other helpers, taking on various roles and functions. External helpers often commit themselves only part-time or temporarily. The status of *employees* is not fixed. Depending on the self-understanding of the founding team, employees can be considered internal or external team members (Ruef, 2010, p. 94). This book considers the composition of the team both pre-founding and after formal venture creation, recognizing the emergent nature of the group as well as team member turnover. This definition purposefully includes team members who leave the startup at some point in time or join later than others. Instead of looking only at owner-managers, this definition recognizes the pervious boundaries of the entrepreneurial team and conceptualizes it as a continuum—an individual can be part of the startup to a stronger or weaker extent. Permeable and flexible boundaries are very common for startup teams (Ruef, 2010, p. 105). An extent of flexibility is only given up when ownership and liability are defined in legal terms, which is often done very late in the founding process (Ruef, 2010, p. 105).

Thus, the entrepreneurial team under consideration in this book is not formalized with a compulsory common identity. The following research looks at the entire continuum of internal and external contributors. This broad definition helps to consider aspects of teamwork concerning the variety of stakeholders who play a role in the dynamic process of building a venture and does justice to the heterogeneity of contributions. It appreciates that even entrepreneurs who are formally considered solo founders depend on a network of non-owners who assist the building of the venture in one way or another (Ruef, 2010, p. 87).

1.3.3 Archetype

In this publication, we reach out to the concept of archetypes. The term *archetype* (αρχίτυπος) is composed of the two Greek words *arché* (αρχή) and *typos* (τύπος) (Marneros, 2018, p. 2). Both terms are polysemantic, that is they can take on different meanings. *Arché* refers to "the beginning," "the origin," or "the principle" among others. *Typos* denominates "the imprint," "the stamp," or "the type" (Marneros, 2018, p. 2; Ritter, 2008, p. 4). Thus, an archetype describes an "original form," "primal image," or "template" (Bacon, 2003, p. 89; Collin, 2012, p. 105).

Nowadays, the term archetype is used in two different ways: (1) anything that can be considered a generic type or structural pattern can be referred to as an archetype, for example, a product or phenomenon with defined characteristics or subject to a standardized interpretation scheme (Kostera, 2012; Marneros, 2018, p. 3); (2) a psychological understanding uses the term archetype as a manifestation of central themes in the collective unconscious of all human beings. This understanding finds wide usage in psychology, media, and management studies and borrows from the concepts of psychiatrist Carl Gustav Jung (1875–1961). It builds on classical and theological sources, including Greek, Roman, and Sanskrit philosophers (Mark & Pearson, 2001, p. 4).

The present work concentrates on the latter. Archetypes are deep-level, universal psychological structures in the collective unconscious, which Jung identified as a layer in the human psyche even below the personal unconscious (Carr, 2002, p. 478; Mark & Pearson, 2001, p. 4; Ritter,

2008, p. 4). Jung conceptualized archetypes as "[f]orms or images of a collective nature which occur practically all over the earth as constituents of myths and at the same time as individual products of unconscious origin" (cited by Mark & Pearson, 2001, p. 4). Thus, they can be understood as variable, yet stable "building blocks," or "empty slots" in the deepest psychological levels of all human beings (Kleine Wieskamp, 2019, p. 238; Kostera, 2012; Wertime, 2002, p. 61).

Archetypes manifest themselves in cultural products like myths, religion, literary storytelling, and artwork (Kostera, 2012; Mark & Pearson, 2001, p. 11); but also in individual dreams as well as interpersonal relationships where people can easily recognize archetypical patterns as familiar blueprints of human interaction (Bacon, 2003, p. 89). Archetypes influence human imagination and behavior (Ritter, 2008, p. 6), and have been compared to instincts in animals (Bacon, 2003, p. 89).

Jung distinguished between the archetype itself, the unconscious psychological pattern, and its concrete manifestation, which can take on diverse forms in different humans or cultures (Carr, 2002, p. 479). Jung described a number of such archetypical containers but as he constantly adapted his views, he did not leave a complete model (Kostera, 2012, p. 29). He differentiated two primary categories of archetypes: archetypes of transformation (e.g., individuation, sacred places, and plots) and personified archetypes, which are depicted as human characters (e.g., the mother, the sage, and the child). They are bipolar in nature, embodying both positive and negative aspects (Ritter, 2008, p. 15 f). Archetypes of personalities must be understood as idealized symbols which help the human psyche to emotionally order the figures and interpersonal processes around it (Czarniawska-Joerges & Wolff, 1991, p. 530).

1.3.4 Archetypical Role

This book works with personified archetypes, which appear in archetypical narrative plots like myths and fairy tales but also in contemporary storytelling like literature, film, and advertising. Organizational researchers have detected that these character blueprints are not only found in fiction but also steer human interactions in professional organizations like workplaces or classrooms. Drawing on the archetype concept by Carl Gustav Jung, the Norwegian psychologist Moxnes formulated a concept of 12 archetypical deep roles in organizational contexts (Moxnes, 1999, 2013; Moxnes & Moxnes, 2016). Moxnes "show[s] that archetypal themes on the level of human interaction are reflected in the roles of a primordial psychic template—a mental matrix of forms conveying *deep role* images" (Moxnes, 1999, p. 1439, original emphasis). He understands these archetypical deep roles as products of the collective mind, being "mental building blocks of organization" (Moxnes, 1999, p. 1440). They help to sort out judgments on members within one's own group or persons in other organizations (Moxnes, 2013, p. 1440; Moxnes & Moxnes, 2016, p. 1440).

At this point, it must be cautioned that these *archetypical roles* do not necessarily describe the *personality* of a person; they rather refer to the roles they *enact* or that are *ascribed to them* in a social setting. Moxnes (1999) asserts that "organizational deep roles [do] not show people as they 'are,' their 'personality.' Rather they are group-need oriented perceptions of people; they are as-if realities" (Moxnes, 1999, p. 1440). Accordingly, "[o]rganizational deep roles are such containers in which group members have sorted out and dumped stereotypical images and feelings" (ibid,, p. 1440). Moxnes and Moxnes (2016) use the language of family relations and fairy tales to show that archetypes powerfully act as attributions and projections of roles on members in an organizational context (p. 1520). Archetypical roles are understood "as unconscious mental forms filled with residues of primordial emotional life, which, in interaction with the environment, predispose individuals to respond with automatic thoughts, affects, and behaviors" (Moxnes & Moxnes, 2016, p. 1524). Similarly, this book uses the concept of archetypical roles not to conduct a deep psychological analysis of an individual's personality. Rather, it understands archetypes as a tool to describe roles enacted by or ascribed to members of a social construct.

On a macrolevel, the Polish–Swedish organizational researcher Czarniawska-Joerges and the German economist Wolff have made use of the archetypes of personalities to analyze the roles of leaders, managers, and entrepreneurs, "not in terms of organizational effectiveness, but as symbolic expressions of collective hopes and fears, played out ('performed') on the organizational stage" (Czarniawska-Joerges & Wolff, 1991, p. 529). They use the metaphor of the "organizational theater" for the professional world (ibid, p. 530), arguing that "the central organizational roles [leaders, managers, entrepreneurs] represent wishes and fears shared by organizational collectives; they are symbols which help to ascribe meaning to organizational events" (ibid, p. 530). On the same note, we argue that symbolic archetypical roles can help to better understand the interactions of different roles *within* an emerging organization, namely the startup team.

References

106 Must-Know Startup Statistics for 2021. (2021, Sep 30). *Embroker insurance services LLC*. Retrieved Dec 31 2021 from https://www.embroker.com/blog/startup-statistics/

Afflerbach, T. (2020). *Hybrid virtual teams in shared services organizations*. Springer International Publishing.

Almor, T., & Heilbrunn, S. (2014). Entrepreneurship in Israel: Theory and practice. *American Journal of Entrepreneurship, 6*, 16–36.

Ambos, T., & Birkinshaw, J. (2010). How do new ventures evolve? An inductive study of archetype changes in science-based ventures. *Organization Science, 21*(6), 1125–1140. https://doi.org/10.1287/orsc.1090.0504

Bacon, S. (2003). *Die Macht der Metaphern* (2nd ed.). ZIEL.

Barba-Sánchez, V., & Atienza-Sahuquillo, C. (2017). Entrepreneurial motivation and self-employment: Evidence from expectancy theory. *International Entrepreneurship and Management Journal, 13*, 1097–1115. https://doi.org/10.1007/s11365-017-0441-z

Belbin, R. M. (2010a). *Management teams* (3rd ed.). Routledge.

Belbin, R. M. (2010b). *Team roles at work* (2nd ed.). Routledge.

Bell, S., Brown, S., Colaneri, A., & Outland, N. (2018). Team composition and the ABCs of teamwork. *American Psychologist, 73*(4), 349–362. https://doi.org/10.1037/amp0000305

Bosma, N., Hill, S., Ionescu-Somers, A., Kelley, D., Guerrero, M., & Schott, T. (2021). 2020/2021 global report. *Global entrepreneurship monitor*. Retrieved Jan 22 2022 from https://www.gemconsortium.org/file/open?fileId=50691

Brattström, A. (2019). Working with startups? These are the three things you ought to know about startup teams. *Technology Innovation Management Review, 9*(11), 5–14. https://doi.org/10.22215/timreview/1279

Brattström, A., Delmar, F., Johnson, A. R., & Wennberg, K. (2020). A longitudinal project of new venture teamwork and outcomes. In *Research handbook on entrepreneurial behavior, practice and process* (pp. 309–334). Edward Elgar Publishing. https://doi.org/10.4337/9781788114523.00023.

Carr, A. (2002). Jung, archetypes and mirroring in organizational change management: Lessons from a longitudinal case study. *Journal of Organizational Change Management, 15*(5), 477–489.

Cerdeira, N., & Kotashev, K. (2021, March 25). *Startup failure rate: Ultimate report + infographic [2021]*. Failory. Retrieved Dec 31 2021 from https://www.failory.com/blog/startup-failure-rate

Chowdhury, S. (2005). Demographic diversity for building an effective entrepreneurial team: Is it important? *Journal of Business Venturing, 20*(6), 727–746.

Christensen, C. M., Ojomo, E., & Dillon, K. (2019). *The prosperity paradox* (1st ed.). Harper Business.

Coe, C. (2019). Building the startup dream team [Back page]. *Pharmaceutical Executive, 51*.

Collin, C. (2012). Das Psychologie-Buch.. Dorling Kindersley.

Czarniawska-Joerges, B., & Wolff, R. (1991). Leaders, managers, entrepreneurs on and off the organizational stage. *Organization Studies, 12*(4), 529–546.

de Mol, E., Khapova, S. N., & Elfring, T. (2015). Entrepreneurial team cognition: A review. *International Journal of Management Reviews, 17*, 232–255. https://doi.org/10.1111/ijmr.12055

Dick, R. V., & West, M. A. (2005). *Teamwork, Teamdiagnose, Teamentwicklung*. Hogrefe.

Foo, M.-D., Sin, H.-P., & Yiong, L.-P. (2006). Effects of team inputs and intrateam processes on perceptions of team viability and member satisfaction in nascent ventures. *Strategic Management Journal, 27*(4), 389–399.

Forbes, D. P., Borchert, P. S., Zellmer-Bruhn, M. E., & Sapienza, H. J. (2006). Entrepreneurial team formation: An exploration of new member addition. *Entrepreneurship Theory and Practice, 30*(2), 225–248.

Francis, D. H., & Sandberg, W. R. (2000). Friendship within entrepreneurial teams and its association with team and venture performance. *Entrepreneurship Theory and Practice, 25*(2), 5–26.

Gopalkrishnan, S. (2017). The role of humor in startup success: The mediating role of team performance. *Journal of Organizational Psychology, 17*(3), 9–23.

Jin, L., Madison, K., Kraiczy, N. D., Kellermanns, F. W., Crook, T. R., & Xi, J. (2017). Entrepreneurial team composition characteristics and new venture performance: A meta–analysis. *Entrepreneurship Theory and Practice, 41*(5), 743–771. https://doi.org/10.1111/etap.12232

Kakarika, M. (2013). Staffing an entrepreneurial team: Diversity breeds success. *Journal of Business Strategy, 34*(4), 31–38. https://doi.org/10.1108/JBS-06-2012-0020

Kenya GDP Annual Growth Rate. (n.d.). *Trading economics*. Retrieved Feb 10 2022 from https://tradingeconomics.com/kenya/gdp-growth-annual

Kleine Wieskamp, P. (2019). *Visual storytelling im business*. Hanser.

Klotz, A. C., Hmieleski, K. M., Bradley, B. H., & Busenitz, L. W. (2013). New venture teams: A review of the literature and roadmap for future research. *Journal of Management, 40*(1), 226–255. https://doi.org/10.1177/0149206313493325

Kollmann, T., Stöckmann, C., Meves, Y., & Kensbock, J. M. (2017). When members of entrepreneurial teams differ: Linking diversity in individual-level entrepreneurial orientation to team performance. *Small Business Economics, 48*, 843–859. https://doi.org/10.1007/s11187-016-9818-6

Kostera, M. (2012). *Organizations and archetypes*. Edward Elgar.

Kozusznik, M. W., Aaldering, H., & Euwema, M. C. (2020). Star(tup) wars: Decoupling task from relationship conflict. *International Journal of Conflict Management,31*(3),393–415.https://doi.org/10.1108/IJCMA-09-2019-0167

Lechler, T. (2001). Social interaction: A determinant of entrepreneurial team venture success. *Small Business Economics, 16*(4), 263–278.

Mark, M., & Pearson, C. S. (2001). *The hero and the outlaw*. McGraw-Hill.

Marneros, A. (2018). *Mein Bruder Sisyphos, mein Freund der Minotauros*. Springer.

Moxnes, P. (1999). Deep roles: Twelve primordial roles of mind and organization. *Human Relations, 52*(11), 1427–1444.

Moxnes, P. (2013). The Hero's dream and other primordial patterns of imagery archetypal influences on organisational fantasies and ideations. *Journal of Organizational Change Management, 26*(4), 638–653. https://doi.org/10.1108/JOCM-02-2013-0023

Moxnes, P., & Moxnes, A. (2016). Are we sucked into fairy tale roles? Role archetypes in imagination and organization. *Organization Studies, 37*(10), 1519–1539. https://doi.org/10.1177/0170840616634135

Muñoz-Bullon, F., Sanchez-Bueno, M. J., & Vos-Saz, A. (2015). Startup team contributions and new firm creation: The role of founding team experience. *Entrepreneurship & Regional Development, 27*(1), 80–105.

Mutuku, R. (2021, May 27). *The history of entrepreneurship in Kenya and its evolution. TUKO*. Retrieved Jan 22 2022 from https://www.tuko.co.ke/263846-history-of-entrepreneurship-kenya.html

A New Study Reveals the 20 Factors That Predict Startup Failure: Do Any Apply to You? (2018, Feb 05). Entrepreneur.com. Retrieved Jan 04 2022 from https://www.entrepreneur.com/article/308447

Pätzmann, J., & Adamczyk, Y. (2020). *Customer insights mit Archetypen*. Springer Gabler.

Pätzmann, J., & Busch, A. (2019). *Storytelling mit Archetypen*. Springer Gabler.

Pätzmann, J., & Genrich, R. (2020). *Employer branding mit Archetypen*. Springer Gabler.

Pätzmann, J., & Hartwig, J. (2018). *Markenführung mit Archetypen*. Springer Gabler.

Pitcher, P., & Smith, A. D. (2001). Top management team heterogeneity: Personality, power, and proxies. *Organization Science, 12*(1), 1–18.

Ritter, L. (2008). *Erfolgreich werben mit Archetypen–Helden und Narren in der Werbung*. VDM Verlag Dr.

Ruef, M. (2010). *The entrepreneurial group: Social identities, relations, and collective action*. Princeton University Press.

Vanaelst, I., Clarysse, B., Wright, M., Lockett, A., Moray, N., & S'Jergers, R. (2006). Entrepreneurial team development in academic spinouts: An examination of team heterogeneity. *Entrepreneurship Theory and Practice, 30*(2), 249–271.

Wasserman, N. (2012). *The founder's dilemmas: Anticipating and avoiding the pitfalls that can sink a startup*. Princeton University Press.

Wertime, K. (2002). *Building Brands & Believers*. Wiley.

West, G. P., III. (2007). Collective cognition: When entrepreneurial teams, not individuals, make decisions. *Entrepreneurship Theory and Practice, 31*(1), 77–102.

Wright, M., & Vanaelst, I. (2009). *Entrepreneurial teams and new business creation*. Edward Elgar.

2

What Is Known about Startup Founding Teams

This chapter gives an overview of what is already known about startup founding teams. Because of its economic significance, research on startup founding teams is a popular field. Research often follows an input-mediator-output framework. Popular areas for research are the team composition, social interaction and task performance within the team, and new venture success as a result of these interrelated inputs or processes, all embedded in the entrepreneurial context (Lechler, 2001, p. 275). Many of the presented insights are based on samples from the United States or European countries.

2.1 Why Startups Succeed or Fail

The chances for a new venture to survive the initial phases and to become an established company are astonishingly low. Failure rates within the early years have been estimated at 40 to over 90% (Must-Know Startup Statistics, 2021; Cerdeira & Kotashev, 2021; de Mol et al., 2015, p. 323; Gopalkrishnan, 2017, p. 9; Kozusznik et al., 2020, p. 393 f). Failure of a beloved startup project can present a learning experience for the involved

V. Miller, J. U. Pätzmann, *Archetypical Roles in Startups*, Business Guides on the Go,
https://doi.org/10.1007/978-3-031-22253-5_2

founders, but often it is discouraging and comes at a significant monetary and emotional price (Gopalkrishnan, 2017, p. 9).

Therefore, the reasons for these high failure rates have received considerable academic attention. External causes like the entrepreneurial environment, business idea, product market fit, financing issues, lack of resources, and so on have been researched extensively (Wasserman, 2012, p. 3). For very innovative startups, a high likelihood of failure is embedded within their DNA: "a startup is in essence a business experiment with potential," it tests an unknown business model based on assumptions (Cerdeira & Kotashev, 2021). The high risk of failure is a trade-off for high rewards in case of success:

> Paraphrasing Schumpeter's ideas in social constructionist terms, one can say that entrepreneurs are people who are the first to see a crack or a flaw in a social construction of economic reality, and to interpret it as an opportunity to actualize their ideas of what the world should look like. As long as this vision is not shared by others, they have to live with an individually constructed reality, which is a heavy burden to bear. What seem to be anecdotal stories of mad inventors and innovators might be actually quite true, in the sense that the unsuccessful inventors are people whose reality did not become socially confirmed. Those who succeeded, though, are the makers of our worlds. (Czarniawska-Joerges & Wolff, 1991, p. 534)

Hence, the high failure rates, particularly of innovative startups, are not surprising. In addition, an inconsistent execution of the strategy has been identified as one major risk factor (Gopalkrishnan, 2017, p. 12). Yet, it remains a puzzle which factors contribute to the successful implementation of a good idea.

Research suggests that the main drivers that make the difference between mad and ingenious ideas are internal: they rest within the founders themselves. Over 60% of failures are attributed to problems within the startup's management team (de Mol et al., 2015, p. 232; Kakarika, 2013, p. 31; Kinder, 2013, p. 5; Kotashev, 2019; Wasserman, 2012, p. 3). Next to hard factors like experience, qualifications, and social networks, interpersonal processes in teams are key. Turmoil and conflict can lead to ineffective decision-making and steer valuable energy away from more productive activities like product development and customer acquisition (Cerdeira & Kotashev, 2021; Kakarika, 2013, p. 31; Kozusznik et al., 2020, p. 394). Thus, venture capitalists pay careful attention to the founding team, and it is one of their top decision-making criteria (Brattström, 2019, p. 5; Franke et al., 2008; Kakarika, 2013, p. 31; Wasserman, 2012, p. 3). Some researchers focused on founders' prior relationships with each other, their motivations, and personality traits (Schippers et al., 2019, p. 2). Not everyone is apt to deal with the constant level of stress and uncertainty posed by a startup, whose survival is permanently at risk (Gopalkrishnan, 2017, p. 10). A weak, inexperienced, or conflict-ridden team is likely also the underlying cause of many secondary reasons for failure.

2.2 Why Entrepreneurs Form Teams

Following the popular myth of the entrepreneur as a lonesome hero, early entrepreneurship research focused on solo founders (Ruef, 2010, pp. 8, 12). This cult of individual heroic entrepreneurs has been replaced by a more nuanced picture of entrepreneurship as a social process driven primarily by teams (Belbin, 2010b, p. 137 f; Francis & Sandberg, 2000, p. 5; Vanaelst et al., 2006, p. 430). It has become clear that entrepreneurial teams are not only more common than solo founders (Brattström et al., 2020, p. 2; de Mol et al., 2015; Francis & Sandberg, 2000, p. 5; Klotz et al., 2013, p. 226; Kollmann et al., 2017; Muñoz-Bullon et al., 2015, p. 2; Schippers et al., 2019, p. 3; Steffens et al., 2012, p. 727), but also more successful (Foo et al., 2006, p. 389; Gopalkrishnan, 2017, p. 12; Lechler, 2001, p. 264; Muñoz-Bullon et al., 2015, p. 4). Thus, entrepreneurship research shifted its focus to the entrepreneurial group (Chowdhury, 2005; Lechler, 2001, p. 264; Muñoz-Bullon et al., 2015, p. 3; Wright & Vanaelst, 2009, p. ix), acknowledging the social nature of entrepreneurship, which "flourishes in ecosystems" (Gopalkrishnan, 2017, p. 10). Even if a startup only has one owner-manager, they are likely to depend on non-owners for additional resources and support (Ruef, 2010, p. 9; Steffens et al., 2012, p. 727).

Founding teams are even more important in innovative fields and in a VUCA world increasingly characterized by volatility, uncertainty, complexity, and ambiguity (Wright & Vanaelst, 2009, p. xii). Compared to solo entrepreneurs, founding teams have more valuable resources like a variety of skills, innovativeness, access to larger and more diverse social networks, and the capacity to emotionally support each other (Ruef et al., 2003, p. 202). Furthermore, developing economies show a great reliance on entrepreneurial groups, in the form of microcredit borrowing groups, rotating credit associations, and business groups; they spread the business risk, sometimes with legal independence, on several shoulders (Ruef, 2010, p. 216). In short, the more an entrepreneurial environment is characterized by risk, uncertainty, and information overload, the greater the significance of collaboration in teams becomes.

Teams composed of two or more internal members have been found to perform better than solo entrepreneurs (Gopalkrishnan, 2017, p. 12). The likelihood of success is increased even with just adding one cofounder, thanks to 30% more investment, three times faster customer growth, and by averting the danger of scaling too quickly (Mansfield, 2019). A single founder is unlikely to possess all the human, social, and financial capital necessary to build a viable venture; and attracting outside resources requires sacrifices in control or equity. Thus, adding a cofounder is a popular solution to recruit the necessary resources and to widen the scope of perspectives (Brattström et al., 2020, p. 3; Wasserman, 2012, p. 332). Core founders with a business idea in mind are especially likely to invite additional founders if they lack social, human, or financial capital, look into a fast-moving technology industry, or want to grow a big business (Wasserman, 2012, pp. 77, 83). Multiple founders are better able to process large amounts of information and to identify business opportunities in a complex environment.

Beyond the resource and complexity-processing perspectives, the social advantages of working with a team should not be underestimated. In teams with multiple members, tasks can be distributed according to preferences, it better suits those with a collaborative working style, and the cofounders can emotionally support each other throughout the challenging startup journey (Wasserman, 2012, p. 79 f). The process of starting a new business has aptly been described as an "emotional rollercoaster"

(Gopalkrishnan, 2017, p. 13). The mutual psychological support helps founders to deal with an environment characterized by uncertainty and a constant threat to survival (Brattström et al., 2020, p. 3; Lechler, 2001, p. 264), while on the other hand a critical second brain is sometimes needed to think through business ideas from different angles (Wasserman, 2012, p. 79 f). Truly innovative ideas often grow in social ecosystems, combining information from numerous sources and nurtured by diverse networks (Ruef, 2010, pp. 167, 183).

However, adding team members also comes at a cost. Each additional cofounder adds another level of complexity to the team, increases the likelihood of conflict and problems, and reduces the other founders' share of decision-making control and equity (Wasserman, 2012, p. 81). Larger founding teams complicate internal communication, coordination of tasks, and the issue of distributing incentives (Lechler, 2001, p. 266; Pearson et al., 2002; Schippers et al., 2019; Wasserman, 2012, p. 87). The costs of adding team members might explain why most entrepreneurial teams consist of few members only (Ruef, 2010, p. 39). Wasserman (2012) recommends adding another cofounder only if they bring something unique and significant to the startup and have a distinct role to take (p. 81).

2.3 How Startup Teams Differ from Those in Established Organizations

Entrepreneurial teams are fundamentally different from those in established organizations. Creating a startup company is a special task, which cannot simply be compared to tasks in existing companies. It presents its unique challenges and poses high demands to founders, which Stinchcombe famously termed the "liability of newness" in 1965 (p. 148). Building a startup inevitably means pursuing new opportunities with insufficient resources (Kozusznik et al., 2020, p. 394). As discussed before, uncertainty is at the heart of entrepreneurship. Therefore, entrepreneurship takes on a very special role in economies, drawing on unique personalities. Kostera (2012) maintains that "[a]n entrepreneur works best beyond the reach of rules, and enjoys shattering existing structures in order to construct new ones in their place" (p. 38). She characterizes an entrepreneur as "someone who builds a new order while simultaneously destroying the old one, who is the driving force of progress and transformation as they look for solutions outside the existing structures" (Kostera, 2012, p. 168). Dealing with unfamiliar contexts and creating new situations is the very nature of entrepreneurship (Czarniawska-Joerges & Wolff, 1991, p. 533). Managing uncertainty, creative destruction, challenge, risk taking, and adventure are the daily business of startup companies.

For this reason, the tasks and goals of a startup team are fundamentally different from the tasks and goals of teams in established companies preoccupied with managing existing resources. On the one hand, entrepreneurs are free-thinking, independent, strong-willed, determined, and self-initiated (Kostera, 2012, p. 170). They are characterized by above-average optimism, self-efficacy, autonomy, risk-tolerance, ambition, and an innovative mind (Barba-Sánchez & Atienza-Sahuquillo, 2017, p. 1099; Klotz et al., 2013, p. 249). High levels of proactiveness and innovativeness in startup teams are positively related to performance (Kollmann et al., 2017, p. 853). On the other hand, even though such personalities are not necessarily good team workers (Chowdhury, 2005, p. 734), entrepreneurs must be efficient cooperators and relationship managers (Kostera, 2012, p. 170). Managing intrapersonal processes is a critical skill for entrepreneurs.

Upper echelons theory has emphasized the impact of top management teams on organizations. This impact is even stronger in small and new organizations (Jin et al., 2017, p. 745) as well as in knowledge-intensive high-tech sectors (Brattström, 2019, p. 5). An owner-manager in a startup team enjoys great managerial discretion, without predefined norms, processes, budgets, and behavior patterns. A founder can lastingly shape their business (Jin et al., 2017, p. 747; Klotz et al., 2013, p. 228). The business model and products or services themselves undergo constant changes and iterative adaptions (Brattström et al., 2020, p. 5; Gopalkrishnan, 2017, p. 13). At the same time, the stress level is permanently high because resources are limited, the company's identity is fluid, and the chances of survival are low (Ambos & Birkinshaw, 2010, p. 1125;

Brattström et al., 2020, p. 5; Gopalkrishnan, 2017, p. 13). Entrepreneurs cannot rely on experience and routine problem-solving strategies as they are venturing into unexplored business opportunities and face dynamic, unpredictable, and fast-changing environments (Brattström et al., 2020, p. 5; Czarniawska-Joerges & Wolff, 1991, p. 533; Jin et al., 2017, p. 747; Kozusznik et al., 2020, p. 394). They have to cope with insufficient resources and are measured by reaching short-term goals like launching a product or securing funding for survival, rather than by profitability (Ambos & Birkinshaw, 2010, p. 1126).

In addition, startup team members are yet to define their common mode of working. At the same time, new team members might be added, and others may leave. Roles and jobs are not clearly defined, processes are not fixed, and the nature of the startup as well as its environment evolves constantly (de Mol et al., 2015, p. 233; Wright & Vanaelst, 2009, p. xxiii). The learning and defining of new roles lead to inefficiencies in any new organization; communication does not flow efficiently, and misunderstandings cause overlooking of tasks or duplication of work (Stinchcombe, 1965, p. 148). Consequently, launching a new business from zero is a much more demanding task than managing an existing one (Jin et al., 2017, p. 745). Following upper echelons theory, the impact of top management is more profound if the job demands are higher; consequently, the personal stamp a founding team can imprint on their company has much more weight than in an existing organization (Jin et al., 2017, p. 746; Pearson et al., 2002, p. 370). Findings relevant to teamwork in established organizations therefore cannot simply be transferred to startup teams.

2.4 Team Composition

Entrepreneurship researchers have sought to uncover the secret ingredients of a successful startup team. Popular research areas cover diversity, team size, prior ties among team members (Ruef, 2010, p. 19), and individuals' characteristics in terms of demography, qualification, experience, and social networks. Such hard factors are easily measurable and thus a grateful area of research. Yet, given the complexity of teamwork and entrepreneurial endeavors, there is no such secret recipe. It must be looked at in a more nuanced way (Klotz et al., 2013, p. 230). Hence, another research stream focuses on the structure and diversity of teams (Klotz et al., 2013, p. 230; Ruef et al., 2003, p. 195). The following section presents a selection of findings about favorable compositions of startup teams.

Breadth of resources in the form of a complementary skillset, diverse social networks, and suitable aggregated human capital have been identified as success factors (Muñoz-Bullon et al., 2015, p. 1). Franke et al. (2008) found out that a diverse educational background (i.e., a mix of engineering and management) enhances a startup's probability of success. Teams were more successful if at least some members had industry experience, some had a university degree, and some had leadership experience (Franke et al., 2008). High aggregated human capital and relevant experience tend to create better performing teams (de Mol, 2019; Jin et al., 2017, p. 759). Complementarity of skills and experiences are necessary to cover the diverse needs of an emerging company (Cerdeira & Kotashev, 2021; Kotashev, 2019).

Another important aspect is experience. On the one hand, industry experience provides founders with the right insider knowledge (Muñoz-Bullon et al., 2015, p. 1; Roure & Maidique, 1986, p. 295). On the other hand, life experiences also mold a person's character, helping them to deal with setbacks and to develop perseverance. Belbin (2010b) reported that life-changing events can lastingly influence an individual's working style and career path (p. 27). Previous founding experience also increases the likelihood of creating a viable business (Must-Know Startup Statistics, 2021; Muñoz-Bullon et al., 2015, p. 7). In line with the resource perspective, diverse experience among the team is beneficial (Ruef, 2010, p. 19). According to Steffens et al. (2012), experienced founders have a preference for teaming up with other startup veterans. However, serial founders are also more likely to leave the scaling business for a new challenge, which can have detrimental effects on the company in the long term (ibid, p. 741).

Regarding team size, the majority of startup teams are rather small, with two to four founders (Ruef, 2010, p. 39). This is in line with Belbin's (2010b) finding that smaller teams are more balanced, flexible, and successful (p. 102). Jin et al. (2017) found that moderately sized teams are at a disadvantage compared to small and large ones (p. 759). The reasoning is that small ones benefit from easy coordination processes and large ones enjoy enhanced information-processing capacity and broader resources, while midsized teams get the worst of both worlds (ibid, p. 760).

Yet, hard criteria like experiences and qualifications are often very weak predictors for job performance (Belbin, 2010b, p. 34), even more so when it comes to founding a startup. Correspondingly, de Mol et al. (2015) advise researchers against overly relying on composition measures (p. 251). Entrepreneurs' human capital does not simply add up in a team. The fit between the cofounders is decisive (Kollmann et al., 2017, p. 855), and a team's way of collaborating is more crucial than the pure team composition (Brattström et al., 2020, p. 4). Experienced venture capitalists tend to emphasize interpersonal dynamics of a startup team higher than novice venture capitalists, who are inclined to overemphasize qualifications (Franke et al., 2008, p. 476). Accordingly, researchers have shifted the focus away from analyzing hard factors like demographics and qualifications to personalities and social interactions within founding teams.

2.5 Prior Relationships

Cofounders' preceding relationships have received considerable attention. Possible cofounder sources can be family and friends, professional contacts, acquaintances, or strangers recruited through impersonal search processes (Wasserman, 2012, p. 89). Entrepreneurs tend to team up with persons they know well. Family, including romantic partners and relatives, friends, as well as former coworkers, are in fact the most common source of cofounders (Brattström, 2019, p. 7; Francis & Sandberg, 2000, p. 11; Lechler, 2001, p. 271; Ruef, 2010, p. 58; Wasserman, 2012, p. 100). The teaming up process can work in two modes: either, one core founder has a business idea and recruits cofounders to build an entrepreneurial team; or, a group teams up with the intention to build a company together, and then scouts for a suitable business opportunity (Francis & Sandberg, 2000, p. 11). Such teams are often built on strong mutual ties between the cofounders (ibid, p. 11). In general, the group formation process is heavily influenced by "social network constraints and in-group bias" (Brattström, 2019, p. 7).

Cofounding with family and friends has its advantages, especially in the early founding phase and in times of crisis, whereas it can also lead to conflict and team member turnover (Francis & Sandberg, 2000, p. 5). Recruiting them is easy and fast, and business ideas are likely to emerge in their numerous private interactions (Ruef, 2010, p. 75). Building a startup entails many crucial decision-making processes and personal risk bearing. Teams composed of family members or friends can already build on mutual trust and emotional support, which is vital in a risky startup environment (Ruef, 2010, p. 101). Trust is a central prerequisite in building new organizations: "trust that a stranger will do the job he says he will, that his promises to pay actually bind the resources he says they do, that the new goods he describes are something like what he says they are" (Stinchcombe, 1965, p. 149). Family and friends usually share similar views, values, and life experiences, so that they can easily be trusted and follow a common direction (Hellerstedt, 2009; Muñoz-Bullon et al., 2015, p. 5). Compared to working with strangers, the expectancies in long-term relationships minimize the risk of being betrayed by the partner or suffering from the free-rider problem, a lack of commitment in the expectation of nevertheless profiting from success (Ruef, 2010, p. 147). Furthermore, family and friends are also good sources of advice, resources, and uncomplicated help (Klotz et al., 2013, p. 237), especially in the early stages and in the form of external contributors from the assistance network.

Yet, cofounding with family and friends also harbors severe risks. The ease of recruitment comes with the possibility of working with people who are otherwise not apt for founding a company (Francis & Sandberg, 2000, p. 12). Knowing somebody in a private setting can mislead to a dangerous impression of knowing them in a business setting as well, but private and professional relationships are quite different (Wasserman, 2012, p. 100). Wasserman (2012) substantiates that cofounding with friends and family is the least effective, with former colleagues being the most effective type of cofounders and even groups of strangers beating friends and family (Wasserman, 2012, p. 101). The private relationship makes it more difficult to assign formal roles and to build a stable structure with the necessary hierarchy (Brattström, 2019, p. 7). Wasserman (2012) calls this core downside of founding with close relations the "playing-with-fire gap:" if a valued pre-existing social relationship is at risk, founders are less likely to verbalize uncomfortable topics like how to split equity fairly or how to deal with underperformers. This, in turn, can lead to detrimental business decisions and smoldering conflicts (p. 105 ff). Tragic stories of longstanding friendships being broken over a common startup are symptomatic. In addition, groups of friends are often characterized by similar characteristics, opinions, and perspectives, so the new business suffers from a lack of diversity of ideas and access to resources (Kakarika, 2013, p. 36; Ruef, 2010, p. 59). As friends and family usually move within similar social networks, they cannot bring a diverse set of valuable business contacts to the table (Muñoz-Bullon et al., 2015, p. 5).

The second category is professional contacts, especially former coworkers, which tend to form the most effective teams (Franke et al., 2008, p. 475; Roure & Maidique, 1986, p. 295; Wasserman, 2012, p. 101). Founding with former colleagues mitigates the tendency to build homogeneous startup teams (Hellerstedt, 2009), but it entails the risk of overlapping competences (Ruef, 2010, p. 76 f). The nature of the common joint work experience also makes a difference. Beckman (2006) discovered that cofounders who earlier worked in the same company are more likely to fully exploit an existing business model, while cofounders who previously worked in different companies tend to explore new fields. A mix of both settings further enhances the team (ibid). However, previous joint work experience also makes it more likely for a team member to exit (Hellerstedt, 2009).

The third category, cofounding with mere acquaintances or strangers recruited through impersonal channels, is uncommon but offers some perks (Ruef, 2010, pp. 66, 80). It is a great strategy to enhance diversity, add the missing skills and contacts, and establish a purely professional mode of collaboration. The downsides of founding with strangers or mere acquaintances are obvious from what is known about teamwork in general: at the beginning, much time and effort are spent in getting to know each other, building trust, and finding a shared way of working (Belbin, 2010b, p. 24). A common piece of advice for entrepreneurs is to know potential cofounders well, beyond their formal qualifications, by looking at their motivations, trustworthiness, and personality even in times of pressure (Kinder, 2013, p. 1).

Other than opting for founding with friends from the start, friendships are also likely to evolve in a startup environment that is characterized by a common goal, shared stress, and mutual interdependence (Francis & Sandberg, 2000, p. 12). Teams starting out as strangers who form close friendships in the course of doing business together benefit from both—the professionalism of founding with strangers and the mutual trust and appreciation of working with friends (Wasserman, 2012, p. 104).

2.6 Homogeneous Versus Heterogeneous Teams

The effects of heterogeneity can be both beneficial and detrimental for a startup team (Foo et al., 2006, p. 396; Kollmann et al., 2017, p. 846; Ruef, 2010, p. 80). Researchers have been trying to solve the puzzle of why so many entrepreneurs form homogeneous groups, although diversity can work in favor of the startup outcomes. For the most part, team diversity, the variance and mix of team members' characteristics, has been researched under a demographic and job-related lens, as these are easily measurable (Jin et al., 2017, p. 747; Kollmann et al., 2017, p. 845; Ruef, 2010, p. 71). Underlying is the assumption that visible demeanors of diversity in social identities influence team member interactions (Foo et al., 2006, p. 391; Ruef, 2010, p. 35). Results about the benefits or detriments of cofounder diversity are conflicting (Brattström et al., 2020, p. 11; Foo et al., 2006, p. 391; Jin et al., 2017, p. 747 f). On the one hand, more heterogeneous teams enjoy broader perspectives and information-processing capabilities; on the other hand, more homogeneous teams benefit from smoother intrateam social processes, that is fewer conflicts, better coordination, higher cohesion, and lower team member turnover, which in turn can lead to better performance (Chowdhury, 2005, p. 729; Jin et al., 2017, p. 747 f; Steffens et al., 2012,

p. 727). Thus, researchers follow two different perspectives, with some emphasizing the drawbacks of heterogeneity in terms of conflict, polarization, and poor social interaction; and others valuing the complementarity of human capital and views in heterogeneous teams (Kakarika, 2013, p. 32; Pitcher & Smith, 2001).

Similar to their preference to cofound with close relations, founders are also more likely to team up with people who have similar characteristics in terms of age, gender, ethnicity, education, work experience, and so on (Brattström, 2019, pp. 6, 10; Kakarika, 2013, p. 31; Ruef, 2010, p. 28; Ruef et al., 2003, p. 216; Steffens et al., 2012, p. 737; Wasserman, 2012, p. 91). For example, the age range between the cofounders usually does not exceed 10 years (Wasserman, 2012, p. 91). This tendency toward similarity–attraction is also well known in other contexts (Belbin, 2010a, p. 22; Bell et al., 2018, p. 351). Human beings are naturally attracted to and inclined to trust others with similar characteristics, from which they infer similar attitudes and values (Belbin, 2010a, p. 26; Brattström, 2019, p. 7; Jin et al., 2017, p. 748; Muñoz-Bullon et al., 2015, p. 5; Ruef, 2010, p. 36). In addition, occupational fields also attract similar personalities as they share common interests (Belbin, 2010a, p. 27).

Homophily seems to play an even stronger role in a turbulent startup environment, where teams are formed voluntarily and highly emphasize trustworthiness and familiarity (Brattström, 2019, p. 7; Kakarika, 2013, p. 31; Ruef, 2010, p. 99). Homogeneous startup teams benefit from more effective teamwork which is less conflict-ridden and hampered by misunderstandings, negative emotions, and distrust (Chowdhury, 2005, pp. 730, 733; Kakarika, 2013, p. 31; Kollmann et al., 2017, p. 846; Wasserman, 2012, p. 92; Wright & Vanaelst, 2009, p. xiii). In addition, it is easier and faster to build homogeneous teams, as humans move in social bubbles, whereby they are more likely to get in contact with others who share similar traits (Kakarika, 2013, p. 31; Wasserman, 2012, p. 92). Homogeneous teams are also more stable over time and suffer less from the turmoil of team member exits. Hellerstedt (2009) showed that individuals with deviating characteristics have the highest likelihood to leave a startup team. Vanaelst et al. (2006) found out that team member addition may lead to broader diversity of experience, but new members show a similar attitude to doing business, so that they do not disturb the team's primary direction (p. 249).

Hence, homogeneous teams enjoy great benefits of stability, familiarity, and easy communication, which help to survive the hazardous early stages (Ruef, 2010, pp. 209, 211). It has been suggested that homogeneity is more helpful in the short run, as it facilitates the building of an efficient team. In the long run, however, homogeneous teams might suffer from a lack of resources and broad perspectives (Steffens et al., 2012; Wasserman, 2012, p. 93). On the contrary, it can even lead to conflict because similar personalities may compete for the same roles (Wasserman, 2012, p. 92). Ruef (2010) also remarks that homophilous preferences might lead to teaming up with demographically similar cofounders on the mistaken belief that they have similar views, which in reality is not easily detectable (pp. 36, 71). Besides, teams composed of overly similar personality types can lead to extreme behaviors (Belbin, 2010a, p. 28).

Consequently, many researchers, as well as practitioners, have emphasized the benefits of diverse teams due to the advantages of broader resources, better capacity to process complex information, a wealth of ideas and opinions, and increased capability to innovate (Bell et al., 2018, p. 357; Coe, 2019, p. 51; Kakarika, 2013, p. 31; Ruef, 2010, p. 211; Wright & Vanaelst, 2009, p. xiii). Diverse teams are also likely to have access to a broad range of useful business contacts that do not overlap too much (Wasserman, 2012, p. 94). In addition, overly homogeneous teams are likely to fall into the trap of groupthink, where diverse ideas are not acknowledged or do not even emerge (Kakarika, 2013, p. 31). As entrepreneurial teams are usually small and do not have the resources to rely on a big workforce, it is crucial that the core founders bring critical competences and networks to the table (Foo et al., 2006, p. 391). Correspondingly, varied industry and entrepreneurial experiences have been related to better startup growth and survival rates (Kakarika, 2013, p. 31). The advantages of diversity are instrumental in dealing with non-routine challenges (Foo et al., 2006, p. 391; Jin et al., 2017, p. 748; Muñoz-Bullon et al., 2015, p. 17). The reasoning is that the benefits of diversity overweigh the costs because of the complex and fast-changing environment of a startup (Chowdhury, 2005, p. 730; Foo et al., 2006, p. 391; Jin et al., 2017; Wright & Vanaelst, 2009, p. xiii).

Nevertheless, purely demographic diversity does not seem to be related to favorable outcomes; attitudes, and personalities are a much more powerful influencer and cannot simply be deduced from hard facts (Bell et al., 2018, p. 357; Pitcher & Smith, 2001, p. 15). Diversity's effects depend on its type, the context, and how it is managed (Kollmann et al., 2017, p. 846). Apart from demographics, diversity in startup teams can occur in three different forms: (1) diversity of opinion, attitudes, and values, which shapes cofounders' views about the venture's direction; (2) diversity of expertise, in terms of education, functional background, and previous work experience; (3) diversity of power, which reflects the distribution of control and resources amongst the team members (Kakarika, 2013, p. 32 f). Kakarika (2013) found out that a moderate level of diversity of opinion is preferable, since high levels lead to conflicts and low levels cloud alternative views and opportunities (ibid, p. 34). Similarly, Wasserman (2012) cautions against teams with incompatible values and motivations (p. 96). Diversity of expertise is associated with purely positive effects: a wider range of social contacts, complementary knowledge and skills, greater capacity to innovate; while diversity of power only fuels conflicts connected to inequality as well as conformism (Foo et al., 2006; Kakarika, 2013, p. 35; Wasserman, 2012, p. 94). In fact, unequally distributed power can greatly undermine the positive effects of diverse personalities in management teams (Pitcher & Smith, 2001), and even lead to greater likelihood of team member turnover in startups (Hellerstedt, 2009).

The studying of diversity of demographics like gender, age, qualifications, and work experience must be understood as an imperfect proxy for what really makes the difference: variety of perspectives. For this reason, we turn to another sort of diversity in this book: diversity of personality, thinking style, and perspective, as suggested by Chowdhury (2005, p. 728). He discovered that demographic heterogeneity is irrelevant to startup outcomes, as it does not guarantee "team-level cognitive comprehensiveness" (ibid, p. 733). It is the breadth of opinions and viewpoints which makes all the difference; yet, diverse mindsets are not enough, the team must also develop a process that integrates the various ideas of all team members and still efficiently reaches decisions (ibid, p. 727).

Concentrating on this unobservable deep-level type of diversity, Kollmann et al. (2017) have researched variance of entrepreneurial orientation along the three dimensions of proactiveness, risk taking, and innovativeness. They found out that diversity in proactiveness and risk taking are unfavorable for team performance, whereas diversity of innovativeness is beneficial: both bold innovators and careful realists have their roles to play (Kollmann et al., 2017). Following this approach, this book looks at the setup of archetypical roles within a startup team instead of external indicators of diversity. We argue that unity of business vision can be complemented by diversity in thinking approaches and ideas, embodied in diverse archetypical roles.

2.7 Social Interaction in Startup Teams

As looking at the composition of startup teams in terms of hard facts has turned out to be only of limited use, entrepreneurship research increasingly started to investigate interpersonal issues like social processes and emergent states in founding teams to explain startup outcomes (Brattström et al., 2020, p. 9; Lechler, 2001, p. 263). Social interaction has many facets. It includes frequency and nature of communication, level, and type of conflict, founders' motivations and identities, their level of passion and commitment, and the teams' collective cognition as well as cohesion. Emergent states describe teams' properties which are dynamic in nature and underlie team processes, such as trust, confidence, cohesion, or identity (Brattström et al., 2020, p. 8; de Mol et al., 2015, p. 240). Team processes can be classified as task- or team-related processes. Whereas task-related processes refer to the team's actions, team-related processes describe interpersonal interactions (Brattström et al., 2020, p. 8; de Mol et al., 2015, p. 245). Team processes and emergent states mutually influence each other (Brattström et al., 2020, p. 8). For example, how a team deals with differing opinions on which business opportunity to pursue is influenced by the level of trust they pledge to one another, and subsequently affects the atmosphere in the team. Mediating factors are team members' psychological characteristics like personality, values, and attitudes (Bell et al., 2018, p. 351). Lechler

(2001) demonstrated the positive correlation of the quality of a startup team's social interaction to success indicators like competitive position and client satisfaction (p. 272). Stinchcombe (1965) also emphasized the benefits of effective teamwork for new organizations: "Such a disciplined and responsible work force, combined with social routines for letting them exercise initiative, greatly reduces the liability of newness" (p. 149). Therefore, the following section investigates available research about interpersonal processes in startup teams.

2.7.1 Cofounders' Motivations

The reasons why an individual embarks on the rocky road of launching a business differ widely. Next to financial goals, powerful entrepreneurial motivators are self-fulfillment, desire for autonomy, and the wish to make a social change (Ruef, 2010, p. 204). In a grounded theory study with founders of 49 firms in the Alpine sports industry, Fauchart and Gruber (2011) classified three distinct founder identities: Darwinians are primarily interested in economic rewards, communitarians are closely embedded in the sports community, and missionaries are motivated by "a particular cause for the benefit of society at large" (p. 936). The founders' identities significantly influence their firms, and divergent motivations among founding teams are a major source of conflict, often without the team being aware that fundamental motivational differences are the root of their issues (Fauchart & Gruber, 2011, p. 949). While it is probable that the three identities are specific to the study's region and industry, these findings permit the inference that deviating entrepreneurial motivations create considerable potential for dysfunctional conflict in all founding teams.

Research suggests that high levels of passion, commitment, and motivation beyond the hope for pecuniary rewards can be more crucial for startup success than technical qualifications. Entrepreneurial passion has turned out to be one key element: inexperienced but highly passionate and committed teams with a shared vision can outperform highly qualified teams with mediocre motivation or conflicting goals (de Mol, 2019). A shared strategic vision is what motivates team members to contribute their best (de Mol, 2019). Similarly, data from the United States show that those teams whose founders' primary goals are not self-interested or pecuniary in nature survive longer (Ruef, 2010, p. 201). Teams can only benefit from their members' assets if those are willing to make their insights, skills, and networks available for the team's shared purpose.

2.7.2 Collective Cognition

On the one hand, diversity of perspective is beneficial for the startup to identify opportunities, anticipate risks, understand customers, discover market segments, and come up with creative solutions. On the other hand, a common course of action is necessary. To balance these requirements, startups must build collective cognition which concerns "the knowledge architecture of the team" (de Mol et al., 2015). Collective cognition effectively "mediates between individual cognitions and firm actions and performance" (West III, 2007, p. 77). According to de Mol et al. (2015), "[e]ntrepreneurial team cognition is an emergent state that refers to the manner in which knowledge is mentally organized, represented and distributed within the team" (p. 243). It steers the team members' joint "problem-solving [...], assessments, judgments or decisions concerned with milestones and outcomes relevant to the entrepreneurial process" (ibid, p. 243). Effective collective cognition is a key prerequisite for successful teamwork (de Mol et al., 2015). West III (2007) found evidence that both overly consistent views as well as excessive oscillation between alternatives are detrimental to startup performance (p. 95). The necessary team synergy cannot be taken for granted (West III, 2007, p. 78). It is a long way to form a diverse pool of perspectives into a cohesive firm strategy, which every team member follows confidently.

2.7.3 Conflict

Conflict will inevitably arise among founders because startup teams frequently must take consequential decisions on the basis of insufficient information (Chowdhury, 2005, p. 734; Kozusznik et al., 2020, pp. 394,

407). Unresolvable conflicts have been cited as one of the primary causes of failure (Kozusznik et al., 2020, p. 394). For this reason, team conflict has received abundant academic attention (Klotz et al., 2013, p. 240; Lechler, 2001, p. 274; Pearson et al., 2002, p. 365). Not all conflicts must be detrimental, though. The effect of a conflict depends on its nature and the team's coping strategy. Conflicts occur in two guises: (1) as task-related or cognitive conflicts; (2) as affective or relational conflicts. Task-related conflicts indicate a difference of opinion about a given task and can have positive outcomes (Dick & West, 2005, p. 102; Francis & Sandberg, 2000, p. 13; Kozusznik et al., 2020, p. 394); whereas affective conflicts concern the interpersonal relationship between team members and are therefore detrimental (Francis & Sandberg, 2000, p. 13; Kozusznik et al., 2020, p. 394).

Affective conflict is purely dysfunctional in effect (Kozusznik et al., 2020, p. 394; Pearson et al., 2002, p. 368). It erodes a team's proactiveness and future orientation (Ruef, 2010, p. 21). The toxicity it causes can even diminish team members' willingness to continue working with one another (Francis & Sandberg, 2000, p. 11). Consequently, affective conflict is frequently connected to team member exit or even the dissolution of the entire founding team (Vanaelst et al., 2006, p. 265). A source of affective conflict can be founders' fundamentally different aspirations and strategic goals (Fauchart & Gruber, 2011, p. 952). Other causes are team member heterogeneity and the emotional strain of starting a business (Kollmann et al., 2017, p. 855). Entrepreneurs are encouraged to keep conflict purely functional and should not let it become personal (Kollmann et al., 2017, p. 855).

In spite of its dangers, conflict is an inevitable part of decision-making and creating shared cognition (Vanaelst et al., 2006, p. 252), and as such can even be healthy for the startup (Kozusznik et al., 2020, p. 394). Task-related conflicts can lead to improved results and a positive relation to profit, sales, and growth has been confirmed (de Mol et al., 2015, p. 246). Conflict related to strategic decision-making can increase the quality of the decisions because it prompts team members to critically question assumptions and opinions (Francis & Sandberg, 2000, p. 11). Conflict is a way of considering different perspectives while negotiating a common mindset. It evades the dangers of groupthink and broadens the viewpoints of all team members. Research suggests that startups are an environment where conflict can unfold its beneficial sides since small new ventures are not prone to intrigue and politics like large organizations, but on the contrary require fast decision-making (Ruef, 2010, p. 21).

Despite its good reputation, task-related conflict can easily turn into relationship conflict, which leads to a destructive conflict spiral (Kozusznik et al., 2020, pp. 393, 396). Kozusznik et al. (2020) studied the relationship between the two and demonstrated that the association between cognitive and affective conflict can be ameliorated by appropriate problem-solving strategies (p. 393). Individual disengagement and avoidance have been found to exacerbate the problem (ibid, p. 393). Consciously managing conflict, collaboratively solving the problem, and avoiding personalization can help startups to realize the positive effects of cognitive conflict. True collaboration and finding real solutions to arising issues stimulate creative problem solving (Dick & West, 2005, p. 103). This can even knit the team closer together (Kozusznik et al., 2020, p. 396).

2.7.4 Communication

Conflict-solving skills are closely related to intrateam communication. Open communication improves social interaction within a team and keeps disagreements from turning into toxic conflicts (Foo et al., 2006, p. 389). As a startup does not have set task allocations, formalized processes, and hierarchies, it is all the more important to communicate clearly (ibid, p. 391). However, the quality and openness of communication matters, not its frequency, as high communication frequency is correlated with conflict (ibid, p. 391). Openness of communication refers to the encouragement and tolerance of "frank expression of views," assumptions and motivations (ibid, p. 392). This increases the quality and speed of decision-making and avoids misunderstandings as well as loss of trust. Openness requires tolerating the articulation of deviating views, which counteracts the danger of groupthink (Pearson et al., 2002, p. 382).

Openness of communication requires special attention when founding with family and friends because they run a particularly high risk of evading sensitive issues like the distribution of roles and titles as well as rewards like equity shares, and often neglect putting agreements in writing (Wasserman, 2012, p. 200). These difficult decisions pose a special challenge to any founding team: "startup teams need to turn difficult though necessary discussions into qualitative and collective sensemaking exercises, rather than making them numbers-games where different individuals fight for a larger share of the pie" (Brattström, 2019, p. 9). The quality of communication about difficult decisions is decisive for efficient teamwork.

Effective communication also includes clear task allocation and responsibilities, which can be a challenge in an informal and free-spirited team which formed voluntarily (Foo et al., 2006). Consequently, startup teams often organize their workflows on a needs basis and lack clear management structures, processes, titles, and hierarchy (Klotz et al., 2013, p. 228). Nevertheless, having a clear structure is helpful to bring order into the chaos of startup life. Research indicates that clear job descriptions and distinct roles, which allow team members to work autonomously, are related to favorable startup outcomes (Brattström, 2019, p. 10; Klotz et al., 2013, p. 237). This includes unambiguous leadership since the desire for equal power can lead to confusion over decision-making control and responsibilities and hence cause power quarrels (Francis & Sandberg, 2000, p. 11; Wright & Vanaelst, 2009, p. xiv). Having a distinct leader, on the contrary, leads to higher satisfaction levels within the team because they streamline goals and expectations (Foo et al., 2006, p. 389).

2.7.5 Team Cohesion

In the end, it is emotions, not numbers, which weld a founding team together (Brattström, 2019, p. 9). If entrepreneurs are united by the passion for a common cause, they are set up to move mountains (de Mol, 2019; Fauchart & Gruber, 2011, p. 952; Foo et al., 2006, p. 392; Francis & Sandberg, 2000, p. 11). Team cohesion is another emergent state which has enjoyed significant scholarly attention. It describes how much affection team members have for each other and how dedicated they are to their shared tasks (Klotz et al., 2013, p. 243; Pearson et al., 2002,

p. 368). The quality of interpersonal relationships within a team enhances its performance (Pearson et al., 2002, p. 368). This is in line with findings about teamwork in general, where identification with the team leads to better cooperation (Afflerbach, 2020, p. 53). Team identification describes how an individual conceptualizes themselves in relation to the other team members with respect to their level of integration, interdependence, trust, and common goals (Afflerbach, 2020, p. 54).

Teams composed of highly committed and loyal members who value each other's unique contributions, create stronger collective cognition, and keep conflicts task-related, which in turn makes them more effective (Chowdhury, 2005, pp. 738, 742; Kozusznik et al., 2020, p. 396; Pearson et al., 2002, p. 368). Social integration denominates "social interaction, group pride, and spirit" (Foo et al., 2006, p. 392). This helps startup teams to better process information as they also enjoy higher levels of team cognition and team members are more willing to share their expertise (Foo et al., 2006, p. 392; Kakarika, 2013, p. 32). Emotionally identifying with a startup motivates the team to persevere even in difficult times (Brattström, 2019, p. 9; Foo et al., 2006, p. 389). The level of cooperativeness is enhanced by adding team members with personality traits which qualify them as good team workers, namely "agreeableness, extraversion, and emotional stability" (Bell et al., 2018, p. 355). Gopalkrishnan (2017) suggests that humor can deliberately be used to increase group cohesiveness, as common laughter bonds and helps to break the tension in difficult situations (p. 13). Sometimes, merely surviving a challenging time makes all the difference between having a good business idea and successfully launching it.

In liaison with open communication, the high level of mutual trust in cohesive teams mitigates the risk of affective conflict, allowing the team to benefit from the advantages of cognitive conflict (Pearson et al., 2002, pp. 365, 370). Closely bonded teams are also less likely to experience team member turnover (Pearson et al., 2002, p. 368). Concurringly, Franke et al. (2006) observed that experienced venture capitalists value team cohesion much more than inexperienced venture capitalists do, suggesting that experience shows team cohesion to be more significant than individual-level success indicators (p. 459).

Nevertheless, team cohesion also has its downsides. Closely knit teams may struggle to make difficult decisions that are uncomfortable to some team members but make sense business wise. This includes downgrading underperforming founders in managing positions when the scaling of the company outgrows them or laying off employees in difficult times (Wasserman, 2012, pp. 217, 222). Because “startups are often populated by people who value the mission and the camaraderie more than maximum profit” (ibid, p. 223), they sometimes find it difficult to keep a business hat on.

2.7.6 Team Roles in Startups

The use of psychological concepts in management studies is widespread. Foremost, it is personality tests that enjoy popularity in the business context, for example, the popular Myers-Briggs Type Indicator or tests based on the Big Five personality model. These personality tests are frequently used for hiring and coaching purposes. However, the use of personality tests has not yet been explored for the question of startup team composition. As expounded before, startup teams operate under fundamentally different circumstances from teams in established organizations. Personality concepts developed for established organizations should therefore not be transferred directly to startup teams. Personality tests are often too mechanistic to do justice to social interactions within a dynamic environment. Therefore, we postulate that a psychological analysis of individual personalities is not enough to explain the dynamics within a startup team.

Teamwork research discovered that human beings take on roles in teams, whereby functional roles must be discerned from informal roles (Belbin, 2010b, p. 24; Dick & West, 2005, p. 30). The functional role simply describes the task responsibilities ascribed to a team member. The informal role is covert and relates to the emotional and interpersonal components of teamwork. Ideally, the two roles are compatible, but this is not always given (Dick & West, 2005, p. 30). In comprehensive experiments, the influential teamwork researcher Belbin (2010a, 2010b) identified nine distinct team roles[1] based on their workstyle, task preferences, and interactions with others; whereby all roles are represented in an ideal team (Dick & West, 2005, p. 30). Human beings usually have a dominant preferred role with elements of further roles and can occupy two or more roles (Dick & West, 2005, p. 30). The team roles are influenced by personality, mental abilities, values and motivations, learnings and experience, and the social setting (Belbin, 2010b, p. 29). Eventually, roles are assumed based on both natural disposition and social expectations (ibid, p. 24).

Belbin (2010a) found out that a well-balanced team with complementary team roles can perform much better than a team composed purely of highly capable individuals who compete for the same team role (p. 14). Similarly, entrepreneurs also have preferences for specific entrepreneurial roles which match their personal identities (Fauchart & Gruber, 2011, p. 3). Cardon et al. (2009) discovered three entrepreneurial role identities: inventor, founder, and developer. They denote personal preferences for distinct phases and tasks in startup creation (p. 516). The remainder of this book is a deep dive into social roles important to startup teams, using archetype theory as a means to uncover hidden dynamics.

References

106 Must-Know Startup Statistics for 2021. (2021, Sep 30). *Embroker insurance services LLC*. Retrieved Dec 31 2021 from https://www.embroker.com/blog/startup-statistics/

Afflerbach, T. (2020). *Hybrid virtual teams in shared services organizations*. Springer International Publishing.

Ambos, T., & Birkinshaw, J. (2010). How do new ventures evolve? An inductive study of archetype changes in science-based ventures. *Organization Science, 21*(6), 1125–1140. https://doi.org/10.1287/orsc.1090.0504

Barba-Sánchez, V., & Atienza-Sahuquillo, C. (2017). Entrepreneurial motivation and self-employment: Evidence from expectancy theory. *International*

[1] The nine team roles according to Belbin (2010b) are: Plant, Resource Investigator, Co-ordinator, Shaper, Monitor Evaluator, Teamworker, Implementer, Completer Finisher, Specialist (p. 22).

Entrepreneurship and Management Journal, 13, 1097–1115. https://doi.org/10.1007/s11365-017-0441-z
Beckman, C. M. (2006). The influence of founding team company affiliations on firm behavior. *Academy of Management Journal, 49*(4), 741–758.
Belbin, R. M. (2010a). *Management Teams* (3rd ed.). Routledge.
Belbin, R. M. (2010b). *Team roles at work* (2nd ed.). Routledge.
Bell, S., Brown, S., Colaneri, A., & Outland, N. (2018). Team composition and the ABCs of teamwork. *American Psychologist, 73*(4), 349–362. https://doi.org/10.1037/amp0000305
Brattström, A. (2019). Working with startups? These are the three things you ought to know about startup teams. *Technology Innovation Management Review, 9*(11), 5–14. https://doi.org/10.22215/timreview/1279
Brattström, A., Delmar, F., Johnson, A. R., & Wennberg, K. (2020). A longitudinal project of new venture teamwork and outcomes. In *Research handbook on entrepreneurial behavior, practice and process* (pp. 309–334). Edward Elgar Publishing. doi:https://doi.org/10.4337/9781788114523.00023.
Cardon, M. S., Wincent, J., & Singh, J. (2009). The nature and experience of entrepreneurial passion. *Academy of Management Review, 34*(3), 511–532.
Cerdeira, N., & Kotashev, K. (2021, Mar 25). *Startup failure rate: Ultimate report + infographic [2021]. Failory*. Retrieved Dec 31 2021 from https://www.failory.com/blog/startup-failure-rate
Chowdhury, S. (2005). Demographic diversity for building an effective entrepreneurial team: Is it important? *Journal of Business Venturing, 20*(6), 727–746.
Coe, C. (2019). Building the startup dream team [Back page]. *Pharmaceutical Executive, 51*.
Czarniawska-Joerges, B., & Wolff, R. (1991). Leaders, managers, entrepreneurs on and off the organizational stage. *Organization Studies, 12*(4), 529–546.
de Mol, E. (2019, Mar 21). *What makes a successful startup team*. Harvard Business Publishing. Retrieved Jan 25 2021 from https://hbr.org/2019/03/what-makes-a-successful-startup-team
de Mol, E., Khapova, S. N., & Elfring, T. (2015). Entrepreneurial team cognition: A review. *International Journal of Management Reviews, 17*, 232–255. https://doi.org/10.1111/ijmr.12055
Dick, R. V., & West, M. A. (2005). *Teamwork, Teamdiagnose*. Hogrefe.
Fauchart, E., & Gruber, M. (2011). Darwinians, communitarians, and missionaries: The role of founder identity in entrepreneurship. *Academy of Management Journal, 54*(5), 935–957.

Foo, M.-D., Sin, H.-P., & Yiong, L.-P. (2006). Effects of team inputs and intrateam processes on perceptions of team viability and member satisfaction in nascent ventures. *Strategic Management Journal, 27*(4), 389–399.

Francis, D. H., & Sandberg, W. R. (2000). Friendship within entrepreneurial teams and its association with team and venture performance. *Entrepreneurship Theory and Practice, 25*(2), 5–26.

Franke, N., Gruber, M., Harhoff, D., & Henkel, J. (2008). Venture Capitalists' evaluations of start-up teams: Trade-offs, Knock-out criteria, and the impact of VC experience. *Entrepreneurship Theory and Practice, 32*(3), 459–483.

Franke, N., Harhoff, D., & Gruber, M. (2006). *What you are is what you like–similarity biases in venture capitalists' evaluations of start-up teams*. Elsevier.

Gopalkrishnan, S. (2017). The role of humor in startup success: The mediating role of team performance. *Journal of Organizational Psychology, 17*(3), 9–23.

Hellerstedt, K. (2009). *The composition of new venture teams: Its dynamics and consequences* (Publication Number 056) [Doctoral thesis, Jönköping University]. http://www.diva-portal.org/smash/record.jsf?pid=diva2%3A211307&dswid=-4921

Jin, L., Madison, K., Kraiczy, N. D., Kellermanns, F. W., Crook, T. R., & Xi, J. (2017). Entrepreneurial team composition characteristics and new venture performance: A meta–analysis. *Entrepreneurship Theory and Practice, 41*(5), 743–771. https://doi.org/10.1111/etap.12232

Kakarika, M. (2013). Staffing an entrepreneurial team: Diversity breeds success. *Journal of Business Strategy, 34*(4), 31–38. https://doi.org/10.1108/JBS-06-2012-0020

Kinder, P. (2013). Founding partners: How to assemble a winning startup team. (startup success). *Utah Business, 27*(3).

Klotz, A. C., Hmieleski, K. M., Bradley, B. H., & Busenitz, L. W. (2013). New venture teams: A review of the literature and roadmap for future research. *Journal of Management, 40*(1), 226–255. https://doi.org/10.1177/0149206313493325

Kollmann, T., Stöckmann, C., Meves, Y., & Kensbock, J. M. (2017). When members of entrepreneurial teams differ: Linking diversity in individual-level entrepreneurial orientation to team performance. *Small Business Economics, 48*, 843–859. https://doi.org/10.1007/s11187-016-9818-6

Kostera, M. (2012). *Organizations and archetypes*. Edward Elgar.

Kotashev, K. (2019, April 16). *Startup mistakes: First-hand lessons from 80+ Failed startups. Failory*. Retrieved Dec 31 2022 from https://www.failory.com/blog/startup-mistakes

Kozusznik, M. W., Aaldering, H., & Euwema, M. C. (2020). Star(tup) wars: Decoupling task from relationship conflict. *International Journal of Conflict Management, 31*(3), 393–415. https://doi.org/10.1108/IJCMA-09-2019-0167

Lechler, T. (2001). Social interaction: A determinant of entrepreneurial team venture success. *Small Business Economics, 16*(4), 263–278.

Mansfield, M. (2019, Dec 27). *Startup statistics–the numbers you need to know.* Small Business Trends. Retrieved Jan 23 2022 from https://smallbiztrends.com/2019/03/startup-statistics-small-business.html

Muñoz-Bullon, F., Sanchez-Bueno, M. J., & Vos-Saz, A. (2015). Startup team contributions and new firm creation: The role of founding team experience. *Entrepreneurship & Regional Development, 27*(1), 80–105.

Pearson, A. W., Ensley, M. D., & Amason, A. C. (2002). Understanding the dynamics of new venture top management teams: Cohesion, conflict, and new venture performance. *Journal of Business Venturing, 17*(4), 365–386.

Pitcher, P., & Smith, A. D. (2001). Top management team heterogeneity: Personality, power, and proxies. *Organization Science, 12*(1), 1–18.

Roure, J. B., & Maidique, M. A. (1986). Linking prefunding factors and high-technology venture success: An exploratory study. *Journal of Business Venturing, 1*(3), 295–306.

Ruef, M. (2010). *The entrepreneurial group: Social identities, relations, and collective action.* Princeton University Press.

Ruef, M., Aldrich, H. E., & Carter, N. M. (2003). The structure of founding teams: Homophily, strong ties, and isolation among U.S. *American Sociological Review, 68*(2), 195–222.

Schippers, M. C., Rauch, A., Belschak, F. D., & Hulsink, W. (2019). Entrepreneurial intentions of teams: Sub-dimensions of Machiavellianism interact with team resilience. *Frontiers in Psychology, 10.* https://doi.org/10.3389/fpsyg.2019.02607

Steffens, P., Terjesen, S., & Davidsson, P. (2012). Birds of a feather get lost together: New venture team composition and performance. *Small Business Economics, 39*, 727–743. https://doi.org/10.1007/s11187-011-9358-z

Stinchcombe, A. (1965). Social structure and organizations. In J. G. March (Ed.), *Handbook of organizations* (pp. 142–193). Rand McNally & Company.

Vanaelst, I., Clarysse, B., Wright, M., Lockett, A., Moray, N., & S'Jergers, R. (2006). Entrepreneurial team development in academic spinouts: An examination of team heterogeneity. *Entrepreneurship Theory and Practice, 30*(2), 249–271.

Wasserman, N. (2012). *The founder's dilemmas: Anticipating and avoiding the pitfalls that can sink a startup*. Princeton University Press.
West, G. P., III. (2007). Collective cognition: When entrepreneurial teams, not individuals, Make Decisions. *Entrepreneurship Theory and Practice, 31*(1), 77–102.
Wright, M., & Vanaelst, I. (2009). *Entrepreneurial teams and new business creation*. Edward Elgar.

3

Archetypical Roles in Social Interactions

Social interactions in startups are steered by deep psychological patterns. They happen unconsciously, are therefore difficult to measure, and require interpretation. Untraditional approaches can generate deeper insights (Aurelio, 1995, p. 349). Therefore, this book borrows a concept from psychology and the humanities, which has the power to uncover concealed psychological patterns and provides the language to openly talk about them: archetypes in the Jungian sense as defined in the introduction. The idea of archetypes looks back at a history of over 2000 years; but it was the Swiss psychiatrist Carl Gustav Jung who, as a part of his idea of the collective unconscious, developed it into a psychological concept (Marneros, 2018, p. 3), which is nowadays employed in many different fields. This chapter gives an overview of the Jungian understanding of archetypes and its modern forms of application.

V. Miller, J. U. Pätzmann, *Archetypical Roles in Startups*, Business Guides on the Go,
https://doi.org/10.1007/978-3-031-22253-5_3

3.1 C. G. Jung's Concept of the Collective Unconscious and Archetypes

Carl Gustav Jung developed his psychological model of the collective unconscious in conjunction with archetypes at the beginning of the twentieth century during his work in clinical psychology and tested his hypotheses in many different cultures (Redfearn, 1985, p. 89). He discovered that myths, fairytales, and dreams repeatedly display the same patterns in different appearances. In a refurbished fashion, myths are still omnipresent in modern culture. Repetitive patterns in dreams and storytelling help to make sense of crucial moments in life (Marneros, 2018, p. 1). Jung also noticed that these powerful psychological schemes guide set perceptions of human types (Kleine Wieskamp, 2019, p. 237). Jung's ideas were further developed by important thinkers like Joseph Campbell, Carol S. Pearson, Christopher Vogler, Maire-Louise von Franz, and many others, to make them useful for modern applications. Although Jung's operationalizations do not meet present-day scientific standards, modern science has confirmed that something like universal, innate, or at least (neuro-)physiologically anchored qualities are verifiable in the human psyche (Roesler, 2016, p. 99), which probably results from a combination of genetic predisposition and environmental influences (Roesler, 2016, p. 111).

3.1.1 The Collective Unconscious According to Jung

Critical for the understanding of archetypical roles is Jung's conception of the unconscious, which he saw as an influential shaper of human life (Wertime, 2002, p. 60). Jung's early work was greatly influenced by Sigmund Freud. In contrast to him, Jung placed more emphasis on collectively and timelessly recurring myths, symbols, and fantasies, not only on urges (Collin, 2012, p. 104; Moxnes & Moxnes, 2016, p. 1522). He promoted a positive attitude toward the unconscious as something natural and neutral which should not be repressed (Suter, 2016, p. 143). From the standpoint of evolution, Jung claimed that the unconscious preceded

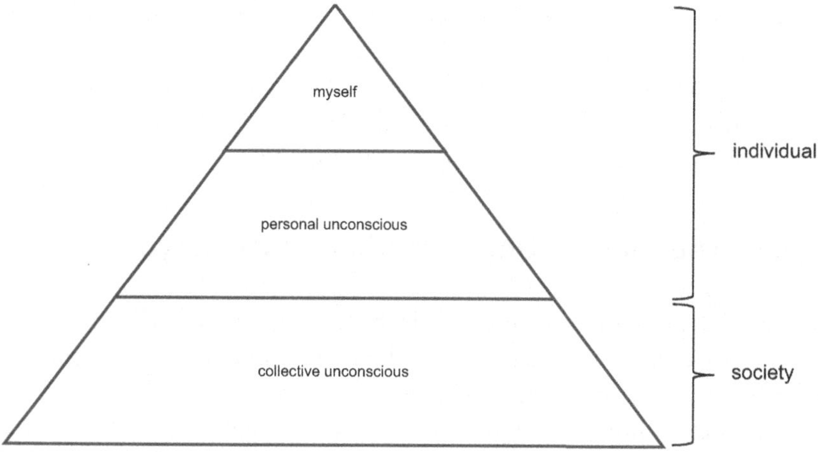

Fig. 3.1 Layers of the human psyche according to Jung. Source: Based on Pätzmann and Benzing (2017, p. 18)

the emergence of the conscious in nature, which is not yet fully mature (Suter, 2016, p. 141). Accordingly, the unconscious still powerfully influences human actions and erupts in behavior patterns, dreams, symptoms, personifications, games, storytelling, and culture (Savett, 2016, p. 164).

Jung conceptualized the human psyche as composed of three layers, which is visualized in Fig. 3.1: (1) the self, ego, or conscious is actively accessible; (2) underneath lies the personal unconscious which is unknowingly shaped by personal experiences and filled by personal complexes; (3) the collective unconscious is the deepest layer underneath the personal parts of the psyche. It is common to all human beings and contains universal psychological patterns (Carducci, 2009, p. 137; Carr, 2002, p. 478; Collin, 2012, p. 105; Marneros, 2018, p. 3; Ritter, 2008, p. 4; Wertime, 2002, p. 60; Wulff, 1997, p. 426).

The collective unconscious differs from the personal unconscious in that it is not based on individual experience (Collin, 2012, p. 104; Jung, 2018, p. 55). Its contents are passed on from generation to generation (Carducci, 2009; Collin, 2012, p. 104). Jung (2018) defended his ideas against criticism by comparing the collective unconscious to animal instincts (p. 57). The value of archetypes "is to *predispose* individuals to respond to certain external situations in a given manner" (Carducci, 2009, p. 137, original emphasis). They can be understood as humanity's collected wisdom, which steers individuals in navigating through essential challenges, moments, and stages of human life.

3.1.2 The Jungian Understanding of Archetypes

While the personal unconscious is filled with emotional complexes, unique to every individual, Jung called the contents of the collective unconscious *archetypes*: primal images or universal patterns which are common to all human beings and help them to make sense of the world (Collin, 2012, p. 104; Jung, 2018; Marneros, 2018, p. 3; Moxnes, 1999, p. 1432; Roesler, 2016, p. 29; Wertime, 2002, p. 60). Jung discovered them by noticing striking similarities in dreams, fantasies, myths, storylines, symbols, and artworks across cultures and over time, where they are most naturally expressed (Collin, 2012, p. 104; Jung, 2018, p. 63; Redfearn, 1985, p. 90; Ritter, 2008, p. 5; Wertime, 2002, p. 64). Archetypes are prerational and directly related to emotions (Carducci, 2009, p. 137; Collin, 2012, p. 107; Führer, 2005, p. 144; Kostera, 2012, p. 21). They fulfill a variety of functions for individuals and societies: they give direction, automate processes, and order social structures (Collin, 2012, p. 105; Kociatkiewicz & Kostera, 2012, p. 863; Moxnes, 1999, p. 1432; Moxnes & Moxnes, 2016, p. 1522; Ritter, 2008, p. 18 f). Archetypes are particularly impactful in crucial life situations, like birth and death, adolescence, conflicts, crises, or social change processes (Mark & Pearson, 2001, p. 32; Moxnes, 1999, p. 1432; Roesler, 2016, p. 69). As such, they are highly relevant and omnipresent until today (Kleine Wieskamp, 2019, p. 236).

At first, Jung undertook great efforts to prove the existence of recurring psychological images in persons who could not have been exposed to them in real-life experiences. In 1947, however, Jung adjusted his theory and split the actual archetype, which lies in the hidden, from its concrete manifestation, which undergoes cultural adjustments (Roesler, 2016,

p. 67). Even though he described a few central archetypes, Jung did not leave a conclusive archetypical model with a coherent definition and concrete manifestations (Wulff, 1997, p. 426). He referred to a wide variety of patterns as archetypes, including personifications, objects, social patterns, storylines, and others (Roesler, 2016, p. 68). The reasoning behind this is that the archetype, being rooted in the collective unconscious, by definition cannot be fully grasped by the conscious (Ritter, 2008, p. 4). When working with archetypes, it is indeed useful to distinguish the deep-level dimension as a predisposition within the human psyche from their concrete, consciously perceivable manifestations. Archetypes are like stencils which can encompass differing contents, and they are open to interpretation (Collin, 2012, p. 105; Kociatkiewicz & Kostera, 2012, p. 865; Marneros, 2018, p. 2; Ritter, 2008, p. 4; Wulff, 1997, p. 426).

Consequently, archetypical patterns can be observed in a variety of contexts. Jung described both situations as well as figures as archetypes (Redfearn, 1985, p. 90). Accordingly, archetypes also influence human interactions, including the perceptions of human types and roles (Kleine Wieskamp, 2019, p. 237; Kociatkiewicz & Kostera, 2012, p. 863), in the form of "fantasies projected upon people" (Moxnes, 1999, p. 1432). In this sense, deep-level archetypical roles can be understood as "*social constructions* on the basis of *biogenetical origin*" (Moxnes, 1999, p. 1437, original emphasis).

Archetypes are polarized into pairs of opposites (Ritter, 2008, p. 10; Roesler, 2016, p. 30; Wulff, 1997, p. 430). They are neutral in essence but contain positive and negative manifestations; this distinguishes archetypes from mere stereotypes (Kociatkiewicz & Kostera, 2012, p. 865). Jung (1951) wrote about the bipolarity of archetypes: "at all events they are bipolar and oscillate between their positive and negative meanings" (cited by Redfearn, 1985, p. 90). Yet, archetypes always carry a moral dimension (Kociatkiewicz & Kostera, 2012, p. 863), since human beings tend to "dichotomize the world into 'good' and 'bad' objects—idealizing the good and, through projection, demonizing the bad" (Carr, 2002, p. 477). This "mechanism of splitting-and-projection" is present throughout life (Moxnes, 1999, p. 1430). Accordingly, the *shadow* is one of the archetypes described in detail by Jung himself. It represents the repressed, unwanted sides of an individual's personality, which must not be denied but incorporated into the conscious identity (Carducci, 2009, p. 139; Jung, 2018, p. 28; Kostera, 2012, p. 64; Roesler, 2016, p. 34). Its repression leads to dangerous projection onto others (Roesler, 2016, p. 35).

3.1.3 Weaknesses and Usefulness of Jung's Archetype Theory

Already during his life, Jung's concepts were subject to criticism for being too mystic, incoherent, and not verifiable (Carducci, 2009, p. 134; Wulff, 1997, pp. 461, 466). Jung (2018) emphasized that the existence of archetypes is an empirical question (pp. 57, 63). He supported his theories by identifying recurring patterns in dreams of individuals who could not have been exposed to such material throughout their life, and by comparing myths and stories of unrelated cultures (Jung, 2018, p. 68). Yet, his understanding of empiricism does not hold up to modern standards and his ideas are not fully empirically verified (Carducci, 2009, p. 150; Ritter, 2008, p. 4; Roesler, 2016, p. 80). Later in his career, Jung neglected the empirical part of his work and his adjustments to the theory made the hypothesis unfalsifiable by splitting the archetype from its conscious manifestation: something that cannot be grasped consciously can neither be verified nor be disproven (Roesler, 2016, p. 80). Another shortcoming of Jung's work is that he applies the term archetype for the most varied phenomena and thus it remains unclear what essentially constitutes an archetype (Roesler, 2016, p. 28).

Notwithstanding, the existence of universal psychological patterns corresponds to the understanding of modern psychology and philosophy (Marneros, 2018, p. 4; Ritter, 2008, p. 13 f; Roesler, 2016, p. 99). Jung's ideas are accepted by many influential thinkers (Ritter, 2008, p. 4). They proved to be useful not only in (clinical) psychology, but also in many other fields like cultural studies, religious studies, or management studies, where they generate useful results despite their empirical shortcomings (Roesler, 2016, p. 203 f). For the fruitful work with archetypes, it is ultimately irrelevant whether they are completely universal and whether they are transmitted biologically or through socialization and enculturation (Roesler, 2016, p. 205). For this reason, Jung's theories maintain high practical relevance, which has, for example, made them again fashionable in marketing studies since the early 2000s (Pätzmann & Adamczyk, 2020, p. 7). The present work explores how far archetype theory can be usefully applied to social interactions in startup teams.

3.1.4 The Archetypical Model by Pätzmann and Hartwig

Subsequent thinkers modernized and translated Jung's theories into workable archetypical models. Archetypes can be helpful to understand group dynamics in the sense of the deep roles as described before. Moxnes created a model of 12 deep roles based on archetypes as they appear in fairytales and related it to psychological concepts like the Big Five Model of Personality and recognized personality disorders (Moxnes, 1999, p. 1441; Moxnes & Moxnes, 2016, p. 1533). He also traced Belbin's nine team roles back to archetypical deep roles, which are easier to understand compared to abstract terms because they directly relate to familiar patterns in the human psyche (Moxnes, 1999, p. 1441). Consequently, a number of archetypical personality tests have been developed, for example, the famous Pearson-Marr Archetype Indicator, which displays satisfactory validity criteria and is widely used in organization and management contexts (Pearson, n.d.; Roesler, 2016, p. 97).

However, many archetypical models have significant disadvantages like excluding feminine archetypes, using archaic language, or not being empirically sound (Pätzmann & Adamczyk, 2020, p. 8). For this reason, Pätzmann and Hartwig (2018) developed an archetypical model based on an empirical analysis of the 50 internationally most successful blockbuster movies from the preceding decade. Popular films are modern fairy tales that contain archetypes in their currently relevant appearance (Moxnes & Moxnes, 2016, p. 1520). Pätzmann and Hartwig's model is composed of 14 archetypes and 14 corresponding anti-archetypes, includes feminine figures and uses contemporary language (Pätzmann & Adamczyk, 2020, p. 8). The model combines archetype theory with the three basic human motivational needs safety, autonomy, and excitement. Hence, it is compatible with current motivational-, social-, and neuropsychological theories (Pätzmann & Adamczyk, 2020, p. 8).

Bischof (2001, n.d.) identified three motivational force fields that underlie the social behavior of animals and humans based on biological roots. His ideas are encompassed in the Zurich Model of Social Motivation. The three basic motivational systems have an ideal target value which is compared to reality. Deviations motivate appropriate behavior to restore the target value, depending on whether it is overachieved or underachieved. Thus, each motivational system contains motivational endorsers as well as barriers (Schönbrodt, 2006). The security system regulates proximity to familiar objects and persons, with the endorser being relationship (attachment) and the barrier being tedium. The excitement system responds to novel stimuli, with fear and curiosity. The autonomy system relates primarily to power and validity in the social structure, with self-assertion and subjugation (Pätzmann & Genrich, 2020, p. 12; Schönbrodt, 2006). Each of the 28 archetypes and anti-archetypes by Pätzmann and Hartwig (2018) is allocated a motivational endorser or barrier (p. 7). Figures 3.2 and 3.3 show the 28 (anti-)archetypes and their allocation to the three motif systems. Refer to Chap. 9 for a detailed profile of each (anti-)archetype.

3.1.5 The Archetypical Personality Test by Pätzmann and Genrich

Because archetypes are suitable for addressing hidden motifs and values, Pätzmann and Genrich (2020) further developed the model into an archetypical personality test, which overcomes the weaknesses of extant personality tests (p. 3). The test consists of a total of 84 items. Every archetype is assigned three motifs, each of which is tested by a statement.

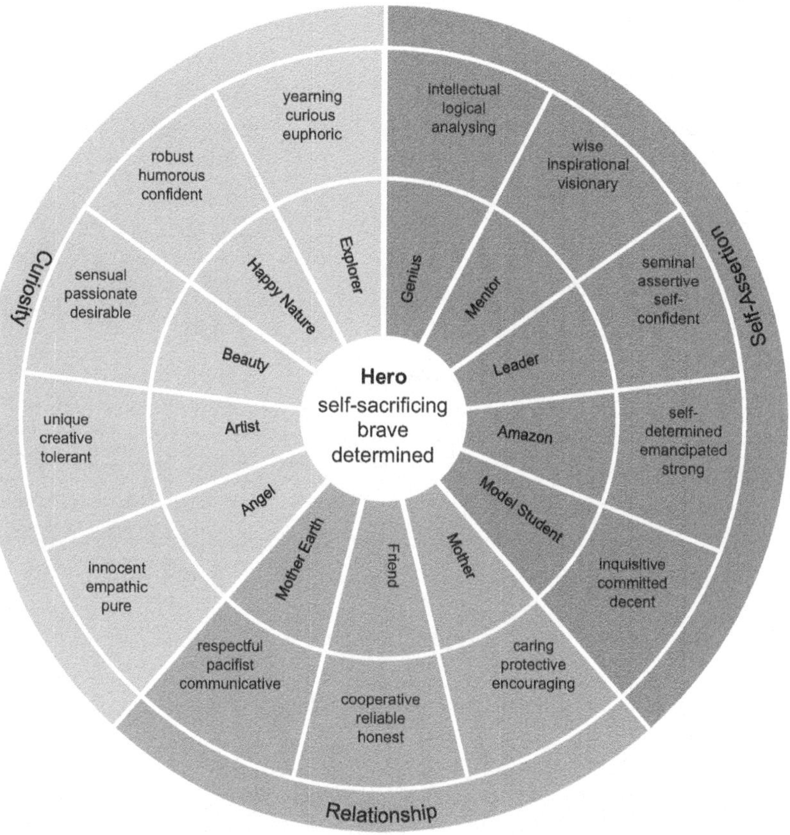

Fig. 3.2 Archetypes of the archetypical model by Pätzmann & Hartwig. Source: Pätzmann & Hartwig, 2018, p. 8

On a five-point Likert scale, the test takers rate how much this statement applies to them (Pätzmann & Genrich, 2020, p. 18 f). The archetypical personality test can be a useful tool for startups because thinking in archetypes corresponds to the structure of the human psyche, so that it is less abstract than other personality measurement instruments. Therefore, this book applies the archetypical personality test to startup teams.

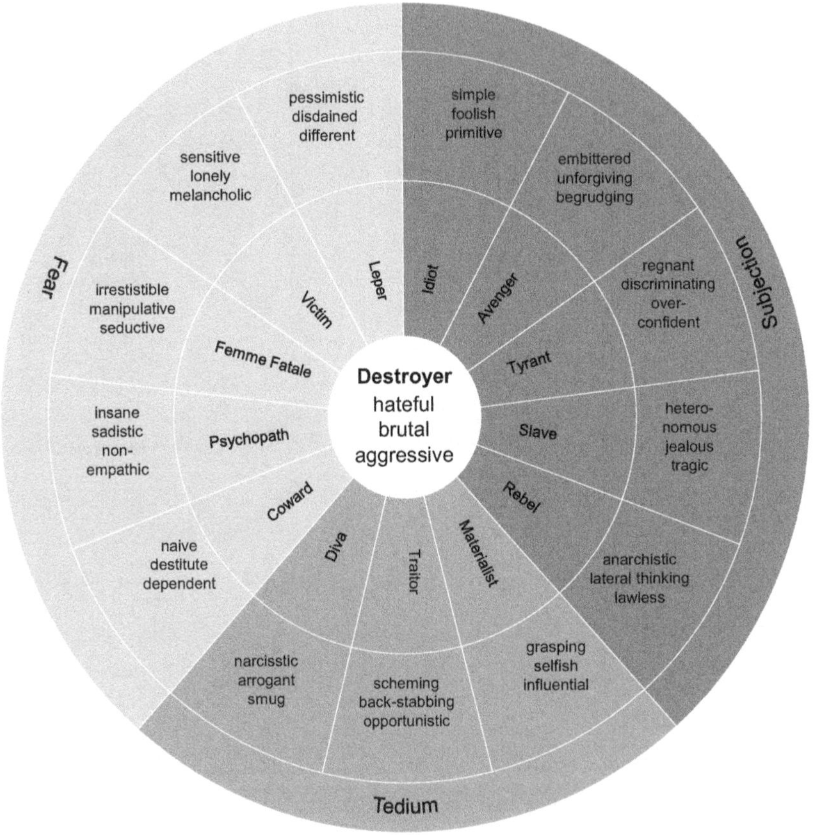

Fig. 3.3 Anti-archetypes of the archetypical model by Pätzmann & Hartwig. Source: Pätzmann & Hartwig, 2018, p. 27

3.1.6 Cross-Cultural Transferability of Archetype Theory

Since this book is written for an international audience, the question of intercultural transferability of the archetype concept is crucial. Jung postulated the universality of archetypes in all human beings (Roesler, 2016, p. 53). He was fascinated by the predictability of themes in stories and dreams from people of very distant cultures (Bacon, 2003, p. 89; Mark &

Pearson, 2001, p. 31). Jung undertook great efforts to prove his thesis by conducting research in various countries and cultural milieus. His ideas build on research trips to Kenya, Uganda, India, and the United States (Carducci, 2009, p. 134; Collin, 2012, p. 107; Vogel, 2016, p. 29). He also compared cultural artifacts across time periods and substantiated his theories with evidence from Western and Eastern religions (Carducci, 2009, p. 141; Wulff, 1997, p. 414). Already before Jung's research, ethnologists had noticed that the same narrative patterns appear in cultures far apart from each other, and the thesis that these similarities are exclusively caused by migration is considered disproved (Roesler, 2016, p. 88).

Their independence from culture is the essence of archetype theory. Their substance remains stable worldwide, even if their concrete content varies in different cultures (Führer, 2005, p. 144; Ritter, 2008, p. 6; Roesler, 2016, pp. 27, 84; Wertime, 2002, p. 62 f). Therefore, archetypes appear with different names and specific characteristics depending on culture and context, but the underlying patterns are always the same. The mentor, for example, also appears as counselor, father, teacher, professor, wizard, master, or guru (Pätzmann, 2020). Modern-day globalized culture even reinforces archetypes' worldwide recognizability. Brand managers are taking advantage of this fact, as archetypes can be used to spread globally consistent messages (Führer, 2005, p. 144; Ritter, 2008, p. 49). In human interactions, archetypical roles also have a certain degree of validity across cultures, whereas the preference for certain archetypes can be colored by culture (Moxnes & Moxnes, 2016, pp. 1520, 1531).

Archetypes' universality and cross-cultural relevance are not generally recognized; some findings point in the opposite direction or provide alternative explanations (Roesler, 2016, pp. 72, 89). The criticism refers mainly to the innateness and the radical universality of archetypes (Roesler, 2016, p. 103). It is therefore of no consequence for applying archetype theory to startup teams, since only the practicability of the model and not the origin of archetypes counts. The advantage of Pätzmann and Hartwig's (2018) archetypical model is that the archetypes were extracted from international blockbuster movies. Consequently, those figures are globally well-known, not least because of cultural imperialism.

3.2 Practical Application of Jungian Thinking

Today, archetype theory is still relevant in psychotherapy and brain research (Vogel, 2016). Besides, it also influences other disciplines, like sociology, religious studies, economics, political science, cultural studies, philosophy, art, personality coaching, and others (Carducci, 2009, p. 149; Fuchs, 2018, p. 175; Roesler, 2016, p. 130; Savett, 2016, p. 160; Wulff, 1997). Storytellers, marketers, and organizational researchers particularly like archetypes because they are intimately familiar and can easily access emotions (Kleine Wieskamp, 2019, p. 236; Kostera, 2012, p. 31 f; Mark & Pearson, 2001, p. 4; Moxnes, 1999, p. 1428; Moxnes & Moxnes, 2016, p. 1521; Wertime, 2002, p. 61). The following section demonstrates how archetypical thinking has been applied in management studies in order to gain a better understanding of how startups can benefit from the archetypical personality test.

3.2.1 Storytelling

The most powerful stories contain archetypical figures and plots. Recurring storylines have been identified in fairytales and myths (Roesler, 2016, p. 176). These enduring narrative patterns nowadays appear in movies, series, novels, or video games (Roesler, 2016, p. 192; Suter, 2016, p. 129). Aware of its power, some storytellers deliberately draw on Jung's theory and its adaptations (Roesler, 2016, p. 197). Joseph Campbell and Christopher Vogler developed standardized versions of the hero's journey (Suter, 2016, p. 136 f). *The Star Wars* series or Disney's *The Lion King*, for example, deliberately follow the hero's journey (Mark & Pearson, 2001, p. 4; Suter, 2016, p. 138). The advantage: even though the archetypical plot can take infinitely varying forms, it is intimately familiar to the audience (Suter, 2016, p. 137). For this reason, media studies also draw on Jung's concepts to analyze cultural expressions of the digital era (Brock Schafer, 2016, p. 128). The enactment of crucial archetypes in films and video games fulfills important psychological functions for the consumers, they are "a theatre for soul" (Savett, 2016, p. 158). Cultural studies using archetype theory can generate deep insights into processes of social transformations (Broodryk, 2016,

p. 197), and archetypical storytelling can purposefully be used to incite favorable social change (Hall, 2016, p. 227).

Because archetypes are so powerful in storytelling, marketing, and branding are one of the main application areas of archetypical thinking. Archetypes have always unknowingly been underlying marketing tools, but since the early 2000s their use has been systematized and scientifically substantiated (Kroll, 2001, p. xi). Archetypes are employed to convey emotions in advertisements and to make them globally comprehensible (Führer, 2005). Storytelling in (content) marketing is more compelling when it follows archetypical storylines like the hero saga (Führer, 2005, p. 142; Pätzmann & Busch, 2019), (Fuchs, 2018; Kleine Wieskamp, 2019). They are potent because they are simultaneously adaptable and enduring (Fuchs, 2018; Führer, 2005, p. 144; Ritter, 2008, p. 13; Wertime, 2002, p. 61). These qualities make them powerful to sustainably convey messages to customers and to build durable brand identities. The use of archetypes does not only start with the final advertisement but can help to better understand customers already during product development (Kleine Wieskamp, 2019, p. 236 f; Kroll, 2001, p. viii; Pätzmann & Adamczyk, 2020). For this reason, archetypical models and insights into their workings have primarily emerged in marketing studies.

3.2.2 Organizational and Management Studies

Although professional organizations are commonly approached in a dry, non-mythical mode, researchers increasingly appreciate that archetypical narratives and roles perfuse organizations (Kostera, 2012, p. 26). Archetype theory is used to better understand communication between players in organizations or to uncover hidden identities and unconscious themes within organizations (Aurelio, 1995; Carr, 2002, p. 477; Czarniawska-Joerges & Wolff, 1991; Kostera, 2012, p. 31 f; Moxnes, 1999; Moxnes & Moxnes, 2016; Zanetti, 2002). Studies using archetypes have produced robust results verified by triangulation (Aurelio, 1995). Working with archetypes can deliberately be employed to incite positive change (Kociatkiewicz & Kostera, 2012, p. 868). The book at hand connects to the literature on archetypes in management studies.

Some researchers have looked at archetypes embedded within an organization itself to classify organizational identities and intentions. Whole organizations or characteristic figures like managers or celebrities are sometimes mythologized and enact a certain archetype (Kostera, 2012, p. 26; Mark & Pearson, 2001, p. 6). Individuals need to fit into the organizational archetype (Henderson, 2005, p. 16). Archetypes have also successfully been employed on experience industry and pedagogy, like Kociatkiewicz and Kostera's (2010) ethnography of the shadow archetype in the experience economy or Bacon's (2003) recommendations on deliberately employing archetypes in the *Outward Bound* experience.

Ambos and Birkinshaw (2010) were the first to use archetypes in a startup context (p. 1229). They looked at the creation of new firms and classified significant phases into capability-, market-, and aspiration-driven archetypes depending on key identities and motivations in the founding process. In differing sequences, each venture underwent a transition of archetype as it evolved (Ambos & Birkinshaw, 2010, p. 1131). Their "findings demonstrate that ventures adopt coherent archetypes for specific periods of time; these archetypes are based on a shared understanding among the venture leaders and are skewed toward a specific driver of action" (Ambos & Birkinshaw, 2010, p. 1138). Archetype theory has been helpful to understand covert dynamics in organizations.

Archetypical roles and narratives also strongly influence the human interactions within what Czarniawska-Joerges and Wolff (1991) call the "organizational theater" (p. 530). Working with archetypes can be a powerful strategy to uncover unconscious and irrational emotions, motivations, and patterns in group interactions, and to understand behavior in critical periods of change (Carr, 2002, p. 488; Moxnes & Moxnes, 2016, p. 1522). Through the mechanisms of projection, archetypical roles strongly influence human relationships, especially to figures of authority (Moxnes, 1999, p. 1431; Moxnes & Moxnes, 2016, p. 1523). The unconscious collective projection of archetypical roles onto members of the organization structures the group and protects it against chaos and ambiguity (Moxnes, 1999, p. 1441). Moreover, Henderson (2005) employed an archetypical approach to draw lessons about successful project management.

Archetype theory has generated insightful research about leadership. Ylimaki (2006) looked at the visionary leader archetype in education, and Kociatkiewicz and Kostera (2012) investigated morally sustainable leadership through an archetypical lens, while Harvey et al. (2007) explored bullying as a form of archetypical destructive leadership. Dammann (2007) cites Moxnes' archetype model in his book about narcissistic, egoistic, and psychopathic leadership. Czarniawska-Joerges and Wolff (1991) took a macrolevel view of symbolical leadership archetypes in eras of societal change, embodied in managers, leaders, and entrepreneurs. The power of archetypical roles and narratives can purposefully be harnessed for positive change. Mack (1999) proposes an archetypical approach to positively influence leadership through coaching, workshops, and role plays, employing four key patterns of human behavior based on Jungian archetype theory. Similarly, Schedlitzki et al. (2015) propose a workshop concept using Greek mythology storytelling and re-storying for positive leadership development interventions.

The intentional use of archetypes has also been suggested to improve communication. In her book about negotiation strategies, Andjelkovic (2017) describes five fundamental archetypes of negotiation and how to purposefully manage those for desired outcomes. She intentionally chooses the term archetype instead of scheme or pattern to emphasize that these are a fundamental part of human history rather than individual experiences (Andjelkovic, 2017, p. 114). On an organizational level, Güldenberg (2001) proposes the use of archetypes as a cultural memory system to store organizational knowledge. This brief overview demonstrates that working with archetypes is useful both for better understanding hidden aspects of organizations and for positively influencing them. This capacity can be beneficial for startup teams, as we will explore in Part II of this book.

References

Ambos, T., & Birkinshaw, J. (2010). How do new ventures evolve? An inductive study of archetype changes in science-based ventures. *Organization Science, 21*(6), 1125–1140. https://doi.org/10.1287/orsc.1090.0504

Andjelkovic, S. (2017). *Verhandlungen intuitiv und ergebnisorientiert gestalten.* Schäffer-Poeschel Verlag.

Aurelio, J. M. (1995). Using Jungian archetypes to explore deeper levels of organizational culture: Facing your Organization's psyche. *Journal of Management Inquiry, 4*(4), 347–368.
Bacon, S. (2003). *Die Macht der Metaphern* (2nd ed.). ZIEL.
Bischof, N. (2001). *Das Rätsel Ödipus* (5th ed.). Piper.
Bischof, N. (n.d.). *Das Zürcher Modell der sozialen Motivation*. Retrieved Nov 23 2021 from https://www.bischof.com/norbert_forschung.html
Brock Schafer, S. (2016). *Exploring the collective unconscious in the age of digital media*. IGI Global.
Broodryk, C. (2016). Jungian reflections on south African cinema: An exploration of cinema and healing. In S. B. Schafer (Ed.), *Exploring the collective unconscious in the age of digital media* (pp. 197–213). IGI Global.
Carducci, B. J. (2009). *The psychology of personality* (2nd ed.). Wiley-Blackwell.
Carr, A. (2002). Jung, archetypes and mirroring in organizational change management: Lessons from a longitudinal case study. *Journal of Organizational Change Management, 15*(5), 477–489.
Collin, C. (2012). Das Psychologie-Buch.. Dorling Kindersley.
Czarniawska-Joerges, B., & Wolff, R. (1991). Leaders, managers, entrepreneurs on and off the organizational stage. *Organization Studies, 12*(4), 529–546.
Dammann, G. (2007). *Narzissten, Egomanen, Psychopathen in der Führungsetage* (1st ed.). Haupt Verlag.
Fuchs, W. T. (2018). *Crashkurs storytelling* (2nd ed.). Haufe Group.
Führer, B. (2005). *Werbung und Mythos* (1st ed.). VDM Verlag Dr. Müller.
Güldenberg, S. (2001). *Wissensmanagement und Wissenscontrolling in lernenden Organisationen* (3rd ed.). Deutscher Universitäts-Verlag.
Hall, C. (2016). The group hero: An archetype whose time has come. In S. B. Schafer (Ed.), *Exploring the collective unconscious in the age of digital media* (pp. 214–231). IGI Global.
Harvey, M. G., Buckley, M. R., Heames, J. T., Zinko, R., Brouer, R. L., & Ferris, G. R. (2007). A bully as an archetypal destructive leader. *Journal of Leadership & Organizatioanl Studies, 14*(2), 117–129.
Henderson, L. S. (2005). Reflecting on Athens 2004: What we can learn about modern project management from ancient Olympian archetypes. *Organization Development Journal, 23*(4), 10–19.
Jung, C. G. (1951). The psychological aspects of the Kore. *Coll. Wks* 9, Part I.
Jung, C. G. (2018). *Archetypen*. Patmos Verlag.
Kleine Wieskamp, P. (2019). *Visual storytelling im business*. Hanser.
Kociatkiewicz, J., & Kostera, M. (2010). Experiencing the shadow: Organizational exclusion and denial within experience economy. *Organization, 17*(2), 257–282.

Kociatkiewicz, J., & Kostera, M. (2012). The good manager: An archetypical quest for morally sustainable leadership. *Organization Studies, 33*(7), 861–878. https://doi.org/10.1177/0170840612445124

Kostera, M. (2012). *Organizations and archetypes*. Edward Elgar.

Kroll, A. (2001). Foreword. In M. Mark & C. S. Pearson (Eds.), *The hero and the outlaw* (pp. vii–ix). McGraw-Hill.

Mack, B. (1999). *Kontakt, Intuition und Kreativität*. Junfermann.

Mark, M., & Pearson, C. S. (2001). *The hero and the outlaw*. McGraw-Hill.

Marneros, A. (2018). *Mein Bruder Sisyphos, mein Freund der Minotauros*. Springer.

Moxnes, P. (1999). Deep roles: Twelve primordial roles of mind and organization. *Human Relations, 52*(11), 1427–1444.

Moxnes, P., & Moxnes, A. (2016). Are we sucked into fairy tale roles? Role archetypes in imagination and organization. *Organization Studies, 37*(10), 1519–1539. https://doi.org/10.1177/0170840616634135

Pätzmann, J. (2020). Of heroes & destroyers.. Hochschule Neu-Ulm.

Pätzmann, J., & Adamczyk, Y. (2020). *Customer insights mit Archetypen*. Springer Gabler.

Pätzmann, J., & Busch, A. (2019). *Storytelling mit Archetypen*. Springer Gabler.

Pätzmann, J., & Genrich, R. (2020). *Employer branding mit Archetypen*. Springer Gabler.

Pätzmann, J., & Hartwig, J. (2018). *Markenführung mit Archetypen*. Springer Gabler.

Pätzmann, J. U., & Benzing, T. (2017). Was wir von C.G. Jung lernen können– Ansätze für ien archetypisches Markenmanagement. *inside Marketing*, 18–19.

Pearson, C. S. (n.d.). *Assessments for discovering the archetypes active in your life and work*. Retrieved Jan 26 2022 from https://www.carolspearson.com/about/archetypal-assessment-pearson-marr-archetype-indicator-r

Redfearn, J. W. (1985). *My self, my many selves*. Academic Press.

Ritter, L. (2008). *Erfolgreich werben mit Archetypen–Helden und Narren in der Werbung*. VDM Verlag Dr. Müller.

Roesler, C. (2016). *Das Archetypenkonzept C.G. Jungs* (1st ed.). Verlag W. Kohlhammer.

Savett, S. M. (2016). Virtual psyche in play and tending the collective unconscious: An archetypal psychology perspective of digital games. In S. B. Schafer (Ed.), *Exploring the collective unconscious in the age of digital media* (pp. 156–179). IGI Global.

Schedlitzki, D., Jarvis, C., & MacInnes, J. (2015). Leadership development: A place for storytelling and Greek mythology? *Management Learning, 46*(4), 412–426.

Schönbrodt, F. (2006). *Das Zürcher Modell sozialer Motivation*. Retrieved Jan 19 2021 from http://www.nicebread.de/research/zm/

Suter, B. (2016). The collective unconscious as culprit: Archetypal projections from the unconscious in video games (and film). In S. B. Schafer (Ed.), *Exploring the collective unconscious in the age of digital media* (pp. 129–155). IGI Global.

Vogel, R. T. (2016). *C.G. Jung für die Praxis* (2nd ed.). Verlag W. Kohlhammer.

Wertime, K. (2002). *Building Brands & Believers*. Wiley.

Wulff, D. M. (1997). *Psychology of religion: Classic and contemporary* (2nd ed.). Wiley.

Ylimaki, R. M. (2006). Toward a new conceptualization of vision in the work of educational leaders: Cases of the visionary archetype. *Educational Administration Quarterly, 42*(4), 620–651.

Zanetti, L. A. (2002). Leaving our fathers' house: Micrologies, archetypes, and barriers to conscious femininity in organizational contexts. *Journal of Organizational Change Management, 15*(5), 523–537.

Part II

The Relevant Archetypes for Startup Teams

We propose to apply archetype theory, or specifically the archetypical model developed by Pätzmann and Hartwig (2018), to dynamic personality interactions in startup teams. Part II presents the findings of research conducted in three stages: (1) a study to confirm content validity for the archetypical personality test; (2) a quantitative study with entrepreneurship experts, using the archetypical personality test as a tool to identify the most relevant (anti-)archetypes for startup teams; (3) qualitative expert interviews to triangulate, elaborate, and evaluate the ideal archetypical setup of a startup team.

A detailed explanation of the research methodology can be found in Chap. 4. Those interested in how the archetypical personality test was developed and validated refer to Chap. 5, which also specifies the test's 84 statements. The ideal archetypical role setup for startups is presented in Chap. 6, which also elaborates on how those various characters can collaborate. Chapter 7 details the profiles of the eight most significant archetypical roles for startups. Chapter 8 looks at the different archetypical roles' interactions within the founding team and how they can and should change throughout the startup journey.

4

Studying Archetypical Team Roles

The insights about archetypical roles in startup teams presented in Part II of this book stem from a mixed methods study conducted by the authors. The study followed an explanatory subsequential design, as described by Bryman and Bell (2011) as well as Watkins and Gioia (2015), whereby the qualitative research was built on the quantitative part. Phase one served to confirm content validity of the archetypical personality test. In phase two, the seven relevant (anti-)archetypes were deductively selected in a quantitative survey. In phase three these results were explained, evaluated, confirmed, and complemented by qualitative expert interviews. The in-depth interviews draw on experience from German, Israeli, and Kenyan entrepreneurship experts, who take on a variety of functions in the entrepreneurship ecosystem and bring in experience from a wide range of industries. This broad expertise increases the robustness of the results. The research process is summarized in Table 4.1.

Phase one was a quantitative validation of the archetypical personality test developed by Pätzmann and Genrich (2020). Hitherto, face validity of the archetypical personality test had been confirmed by five experts (Pätzmann & Genrich, 2020, p. 18), which constitutes the minimum standard of validity (Bryman & Bell, 2011, p. 160). Therefore, the test's content validity needed to be validated by a large number of test takers.

V. Miller, J. U. Pätzmann, *Archetypical Roles in Startups*, Business Guides on the Go,
https://doi.org/10.1007/978-3-031-22253-5_4

Table 4.1 Overview of the research process. Source: Own representation

Phase	Procedure	Result
Phase 1: Test validation	Checking content validity Sample: $n_1 = 88$, $n_2 = 97$ Survey in Germany January to February 2021 Reformulating non-validated statements	Revised version of the archetypical personality test with content validity confirmed for all statements
Phase 2: Quantitative survey with entrepreneurship experts	Based on archetypical personality tests in third person In German and in English Sample: $n_{Eng} = 14$, $n_{Ger} = 72$ March to April 2021	Archetypical personality profile of ideal startup team. Identification of 7 most relevant (anti-) archetypes for startup teams
Phase 3: In-depth expert interviews	Fifteen semistructured interviews with investors, founders, academics, and mentors from Germany, Israel, Kenya June to December 2021	Roles and characteristics of the relevant (anti-) archetypes, interaction in teams, and relevancy over evolution of the startup

In this study, the items were tested by means of two online surveys with sample sizes of $n_1 = 88$ and $n_2 = 97$ participants in the German language. The test takers were asked to assess the match between an archetype and its three ascribed statements plus two cross-check statements. As a result, four statements were identified as not matching, reformulated, and confirmed in a further survey. The validated archetypical personality test is presented in Chap. 5.

Phase two was a quantitative online survey with 86 entrepreneurship experts, mainly from Germany with a few respondents from Israel and Kenya. The questionnaire was exclusively answered by experts able to evaluate startups based on their experience. The sample cannot be described as representative, but it constitutes a robust trend analysis. The test takers were confronted with the validated archetypical personality test in an online survey. The experts were asked to assess how relevant each statement is for a startup team. The results were clustered by corresponding archetypes and summarized in a spider web diagram, portraying the relevance of the 28 (anti-)archetypes for startup teams. The five most relevant archetypes and two most tolerable anti-archetypes were selected for research phase two, which are namely the mentor, leader, friend, artist, hero, rebel, and femme fatale.

The research questions answered were:

Sub-question 1: Which archetypes are most relevant for startup teams?

Sub-question 2: Which anti-archetypes are most tolerable in a startup team?

The online survey was conducted in March and April 2021 using the online survey tool *UmfrageOnline.com* (UmfrageOnline, n.d.). The survey provided a brief introduction to the research goals and an explanation of the archetypical personality test. The questionnaire started with the demographic data to confirm test takers' eligibility, and then presented the main question on one page with a short explanation: "Which personality traits must be present in a startup team?" Then, the respondents were presented with the statements of the archetypical personality test, rephrased in the third person with the subject "a team member." On a five-point Likert scale, respondents were asked to assess this statement's relevancy in a startup team. The statements were mixed and randomly arranged. A neutral response option was deliberately given to avoid forced misdeclarations as suggested by Gräf (2010, p. 78). A pretest was conducted with an expert from Neu-Ulm University of Applied Science's Competence Centre for Marketing and Branding. Completing the survey took approximately 15–20 min. Although longer questionnaires lead to a higher cancellation risk (Braunecker, 2021, p. 118; Gräf, 2010, p. 64), it was not possible to reduce the survey length by splitting it in half, as this would have rendered incomplete and incompatible results. Therefore, other strategies were applied to reduce the cancellation rate. Potential respondents were personally approached and followed up by the researchers, emphasizing the use of the research and building on personal rapport and the university's renown as suggested by Gräf (2010).

The German language survey was started by 86 and completed by 72 participants, leaving a cancellation rate of 16%. Male survey participants prevailed, but a wide range of age groups and experiences was represented, with the largest group being entrepreneurs and the smallest group being investors. All survey respondents had gathered their entrepreneurial expertise in Germany. Details about the test takers' expertise were inquired in a free text field. This indicated that many of the participants fall into more than one category, especially those who chose higher education as their current profession often look back at extended experience with founding own startups and coaching and mentoring other founders. Many entrepreneurs have experience with more than one startup, often as founder or early employee. Respondents of the category "Other" hold positions within the innovation ecosystem, e.g., at incubators or public support institutions. A variety of different industries was represented, ranging from medical, high-tech, education, not for profit, automotive, and consulting to nutrition, banking, and others. Thus, the survey pools a broad range of experience, and the results are not specific to any one industry or founding phase. The demographic information of the German survey is visualized in Figs. 4.1, 4.2, and 4.3.

The English language survey was started by 20 respondents, but only completed by 14, with a cancellation rate of 30%. The analysis only considered the completed questionnaires. Male participants as well as those

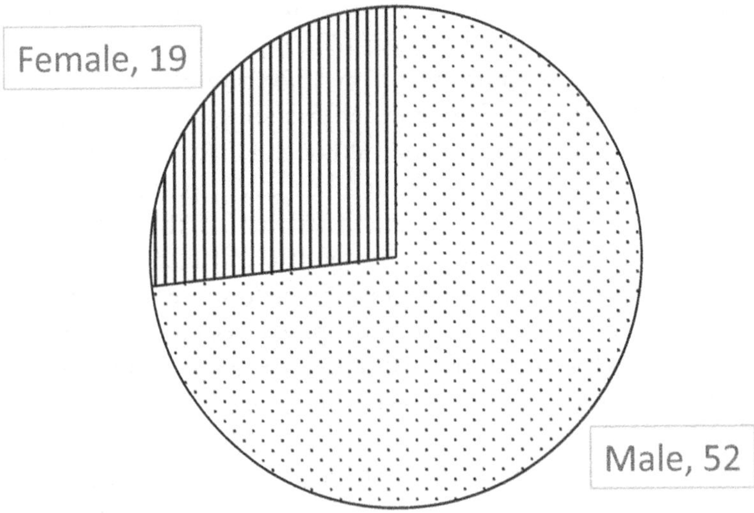

Fig. 4.1 Gender distribution of the German survey. Source: Own representation

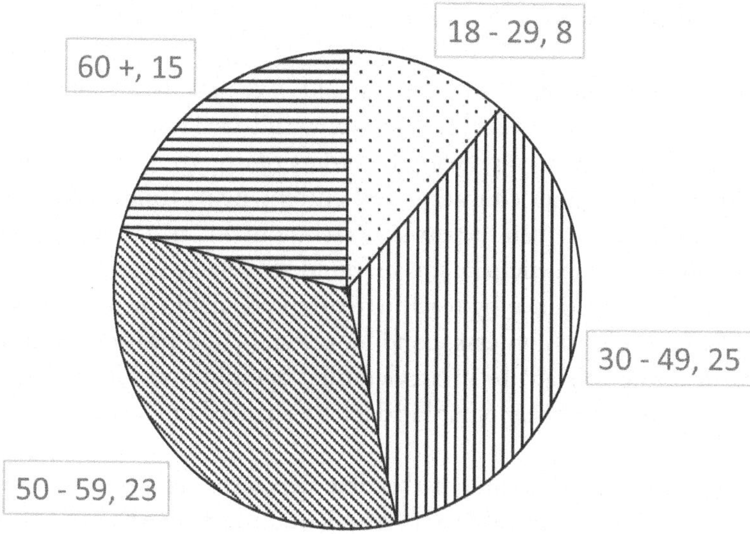

Fig. 4.2 Age distribution of the German survey. Source: Own representation

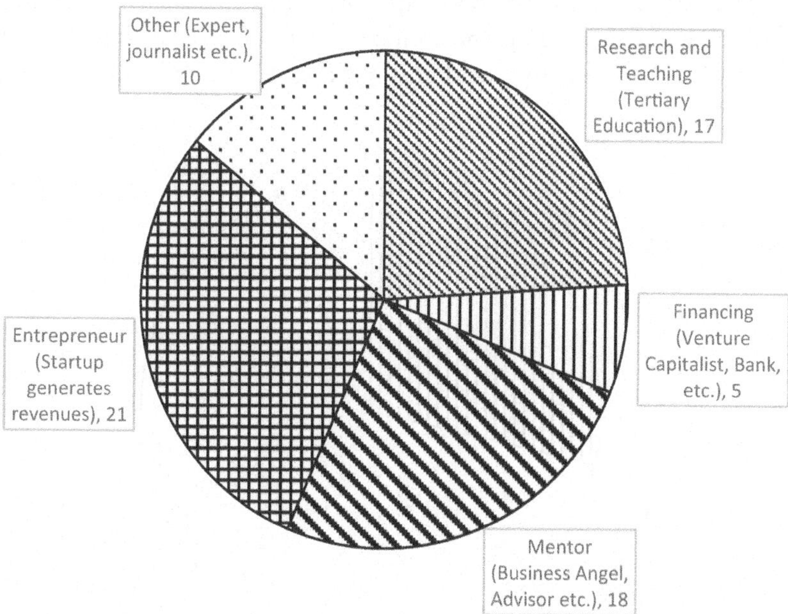

Fig. 4.3 Distribution of expertise in the German survey. Source: Own representation

from the age group of 30- to 49-year olds were overrepresented. Most participants came from Israel and Kenya, with Israeli respondents slightly prevailing. Participants represented a variety of expertise, with a majority of experts from higher education and entrepreneurs from mature startups. Details about their expertise were inquired in a free text field. According to this, participants have founded their own companies and/or share their experience by teaching entrepreneurship at universities or in other educational contexts, conduct research, and provide mentoring and consulting to startups in accelerators, open innovation projects, or other contexts. Their demographic data is visualized in Figs. 4.4, 4.5, 4.6, and 4.7.

In phase three, the results of the first step were applied by means of expert interviews. Four to six experts per country from the categories of mentor, founder, investor, and academic participated in a total of 15 semistructured interviews. This served to evaluate and to deepen the previous results, to systematize them, and to set them into context (see Flick, 2014, p. 228). The interviewees are considered specialists in the area of entrepreneurship in different contexts; thus, they were interviewed as experts speaking for their field and not about their individual cases (see

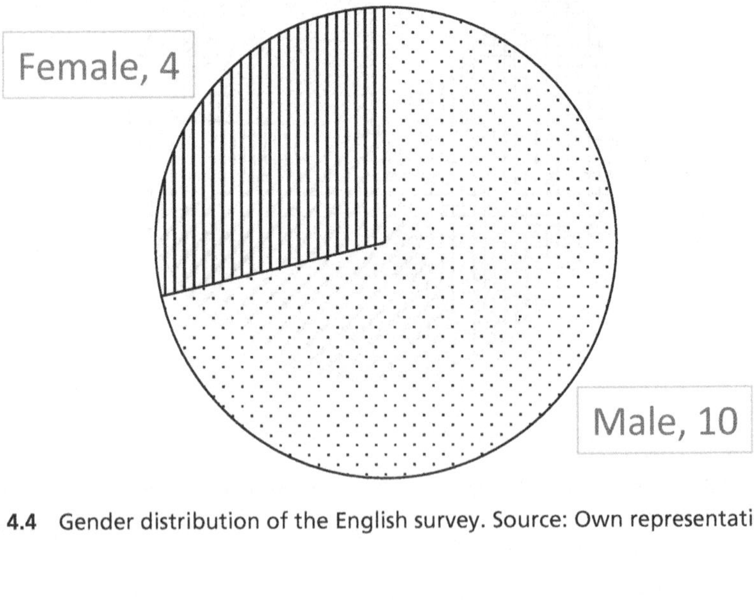

Fig. 4.4 Gender distribution of the English survey. Source: Own representation

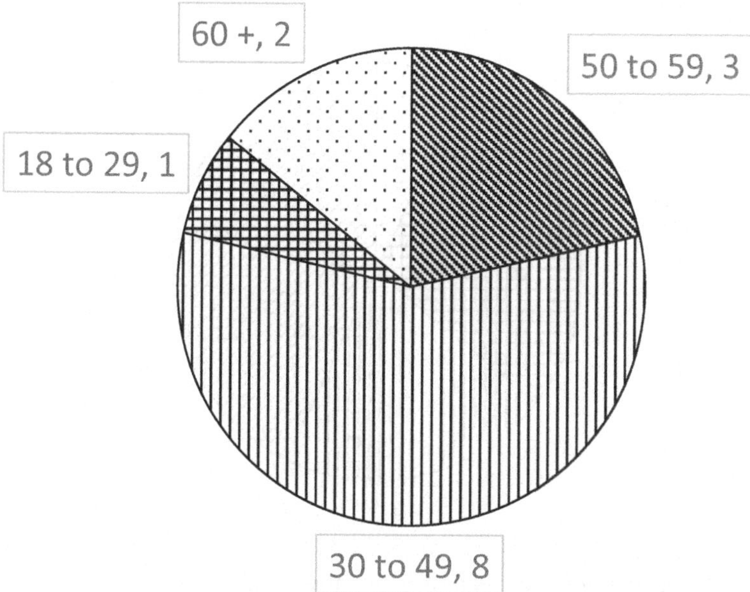

Fig. 4.5 Age distribution of the English survey. Source: Own representation

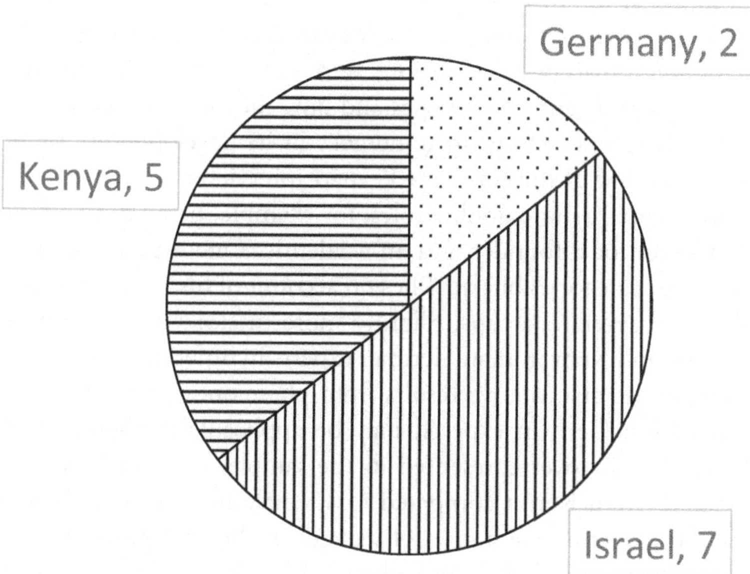

Fig. 4.6 Country of entrepreneurship expertise. Source: Own representation

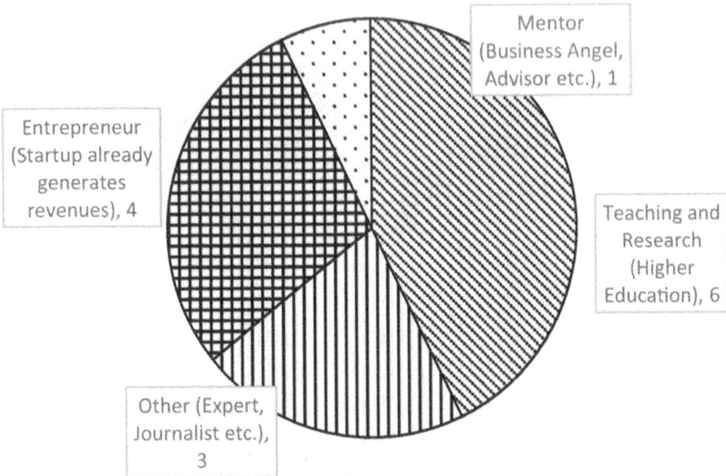

Fig. 4.7 Distribution of expertise in the English survey. Source: Own representation

Flick, 2014, p. 227; Mayring, 2010, p. 490). The interviews were subjected to a systematic coding process following the methodology of qualitative content analysis. Conclusions were drawn about the function of the most relevant (anti-)archetypes and how they interact within a team and over the phases a startup undergoes in its development. Table 4.2 gives an overview of the conducted expert interviews.

Some experts assume double roles, for example, being both a founder and a mentor, or a founder and an academic. One expert does not fall into the four categories but qualifies on account of his experience as a key employee in several startups. Slightly more interviews were conducted with Israeli and Kenyan than German experts in order to gather feedback on whether the quantitative results from phase one, which were mainly collected from German experts, may be applicable in these countries. Males are heavily overrepresented in the sample, with only two female respondents from Kenya compared to 13 male respondents. This likely reflects the underrepresentation of females in the entrepreneurship ecosystem at large, which was also observed by Brattström et al. (2020).

Table 4.2 Overview of in-depth interviews. Source: Own representation

	Germany 4 interviews	Israel 5 interviews	Kenya 6 interviews
Mentor	*A_Men_G:* Business startup advisor in commercial chamber	*E_Men_I:* Serial founder and startup mentor	*J_Men_K:* Female mentor at a university-based incubation center *K_Men_K:* Cofounder of grassroots startup incubator
Academic	*B_Aca_G:* Professor for entrepreneurship, organization and leadership	*F_Aca_I:* Founder, researcher of organizational psychology	*L_Aca_K:* Director of a university-based incubation center
Investor	*C_Inv_G:* Managing director at private equity company	*G_Inv_I:* Principal at venture capital and private equity firm	*M_Inv_K:* Program manager at incubator and startup financer
Founder	*D_Fou_G:* Cofounder of three companies in digitalization and consulting	*H_Fou_I:* Cofounder of high-tech company *I_TM_I:* Startup team member	*N_Fou_K:* Female startup founder in biochemicals *O_Fou_K:* Founder of biotech startup

After conducting the 15 interviews, a certain level of theoretical saturation was reached, meaning that new findings yielded by the later interviews were limited (see Mayring, 2007).

Interviews were conducted between June and December 2021 and lasted 45–60 min. They were carried out via videoconference which also allowed screen sharing for discussing the quantitative results. The interview language was German as the mother tongue of both researcher and interviewee, or English, which is commonly used as a business language in Kenya and Israel. The interviews were transcribed, which is necessary to enable meaningful interpretation of the data (Fox, 2009, p. 293). As the research interest only concentrated on *what* was said, not *how* it was said, transcription did not faithfully capture personal language coloring and skipped irrelevant passages (see Flick, 2014, p. 237; Mayring, 2016, p. 91). Resultant transcripts ranged from 2279 to 6599 words, the average being 4234.

The interviews followed a problem-centered approach with a semistructured questionnaire and open-ended questions, using the results of the quantitative survey to work out the essential aspects as suggested by Mayring (2016). Questions concerned the importance and role of the identified (anti-)archetypes, the team structure, and the relevance of the model in practice. Themes which came up in earlier interviews informed probing in later interviews, for example, the question of whether an archetype is more likely to be represented in an internal or external team member. In order to test whether the archetypes are naturally understood, the experts were not presented with the results for the individual statements and motifs, only with the aggregated version. This widened the way how some archetypes were interpreted. Some experts might also have contributed to the quantitative survey, though, and thus seen the individual statements. It was made clear to the interviewees that archetypes do not necessarily have to correspond to a single person, and a team member can incorporate more than one archetype or shift over time.

The data was interpreted using a rigorous qualitative content analysis (QCA) approach. QCA is a systematic, comprehensible, and replicable method to analyze qualitative data through a theoretical lens, it considers the context and has the ability to uncover latent meaning (Mayring, 2010, p. 50; Schreier, 2012, pp. 3, 16). Thus, QCA combines the advantages of a systematic, controlled process with a context-related deep understanding of the material (Mayring, 2016, p. 114). It is therefore very appropriate for theory-guided text analysis (Mayring, 2016, p. 121), which in this case is archetype theory based on the model of Pätzmann and Hartwig. The web-based tool QCAMap developed by Mayring and Fenzl (2020) was employed for coding.

The addressed research questions were:

Sub-question 3: What is the role of the identified (anti-)archetypes in a startup team?

Sub-question 4: How do archetypical team roles interact within a startup?

Sub-question 5: Which practical relevance does the archetypical model have for the entrepreneurship ecosystem?

In the first step, the data was segmented into thematic chunks of data on a macro-level (see Miles et al., 2020, p. 66; Schreier, 2012, p. 127). Segmentation employed exploratory coding with deductive categories loosely following the interview guide. Segmenting categories included the seven relevant (anti-)archetypes and major themes which appeared throughout the interviews, like the evolution of a startup over time, team balance, missing aspects in the model, and the practicability of the model. Afterward, the data segments were ascribed inductive codes and analytic memos were written in parallel as suggested by Miles et al. (2020). Heuristic coding served to arrive at a deep understanding of the data (see Saldaña, 2021, p. 23). Codes were subsequently grouped into overarching categories. This methodology constitutes an appropriate approach for the data at hand and justifies the findings' solid level of validity; as in qualitative research, generalizability cannot be inferred from a representative sample (Mayring, 2016, p. 23).

The interplay of personalities in startup teams is a complex research field. The subject of investigation does not lay overt as interpersonal processes and personalities are multifaceted topics with plenty happening unconsciously. Thus, the topic must be opened up through interpretation and a quantitative survey alone would be too one-dimensional to do justice to something so complex and intertwined. The need for interpretation applies particularly to subjects in human sciences and areas where verbal material needs to be analyzed (Mayring, 2016, p. 22). To ensure a comprehensible and adequate interpretation, qualitative content analysis was chosen as a systematic and reviewable analysis method. While this study did not work with representative samples, the combination of quantitative and qualitative methods increases the argumentative generalizability of the results (Mayring, 2007). The quantitative study sought for a high number of representatives (albeit only accomplished in Germany), whereas the qualitative interviews with experts from three different countries and a wide range of perspectives were conducted until a level of theoretical saturation was reached as envisaged by grounded theory (Mayring, 2007).

Chapters 5–8 present the findings from the three research phases. Overall, the 15 experts confirmed the validity of the seven identified (anti-)archetypes, with variations of whether an archetype should be external or internal and occasional emphasis on further archetypical team roles. The manager was identified as an additional role relevant to startup teams.

References

Brattström, A., Delmar, F., Johnson, A. R., & Wennberg, K. (2020). A longitudinal project of new venture teamwork and outcomes. In *Research handbook on entrepreneurial behavior, practice and process* (pp. 309–334). Edward Elgar Publishing. doi:https://doi.org/10.4337/9781788114523.00023.

Braunecker, C. (2021). *How to do empirische Sozialforschung*. UTB Facultas.

Bryman, A., & Bell, E. (2011). *Business research methods* (3rd ed.). Oxford Univ. Press.

Flick, U. (2014). *An introduction to qualitative research* (5th ed.).

Fox, N. (2009). Using interviews in a research project. *The NIHR research design service for the East Midlands*. https://bit.ly/3B9bKHv

Gräf, L. (2010). *Online-Befragung*. LIT.

Mayring, P. (2007). On generalization in qualitatively oriented research. *FQS Forum: Qualitative Social Research, 8*(3).

Mayring, P. (2010). *Qualitative Inhaltsanalyse* (11th ed.).

Mayring, P. (2016). *Einführung in die qualitative Sozialforschung* (6th ed.).

Mayring, P., & Fenzl, T. (2020). *QCAmap: A software for qualitative content analysis*. Retrieved Nov 23 2021 from https://www.qcamap.org/ui/home

Miles, M. B., Huberman, A. M., & Saldana, J. (2020). *Qualitative data analysis* (4th ed.). SAGE.

Pätzmann, J., & Genrich, R. (2020). *Employer branding mit Archetypen*. Springer Gabler.

Saldaña, J. (2021). *The coding manual for qualitative researchers* (4th ed.). SAGE Publications.

Schreier, M. (2012). *Qualitative content analysis in practice*. SAGE.

UmfrageOnline. (n.d.). *enuvo GmbH*. Retrieved Jan 05 2022 from https://www.umfrageonline.com/

Watkins, D. C., & Gioia, D. (2015). *Mixed methods research*. Oxford University Press.

5

The Validated Archetypical Personality Test

The archetypical personality test was developed in 2020 by Pätzmann and Genrich because a personality test based on the latest state of research on archetypes had not been available (p. 8). It is a multidimensional personality test with 84 unidimensional items, meaning that each item measures only one motif (Pätzmann & Genrich, 2020, p. 17). In the development process, face validity of the archetypical personality test had been confirmed by five experts (Pätzmann & Genrich, 2020, p. 18), which constitutes the minimum standard of validity (Bryman & Bell, 2011, p. 160). Therefore, the personality test needed validation by a large number of respondents in order to optimize, modify, and change items that do not match the right motifs and archetypes.

In research phase one, a quantitative trend analysis was conducted to confirm content validity of the test's items matching the respective archetype and its motifs. Content validity confirms whether the statements do in fact measure what is supposed to be measured (Schnell, 2013, p. 145). An adaptation of Lawshe's (1975) quantitative approach to confirming content validity was chosen as an appropriate research design. Lawshe (1975) proposes a panel of experts to evaluate the validity of test items. A particular item is maintained or rejected based on the panel's mean

V. Miller, J. U. Pätzmann, *Archetypical Roles in Startups*, Business Guides on the Go,
https://doi.org/10.1007/978-3-031-22253-5_5

assessment value. From a strong consensus of the experts' judgment, the validity of their accumulated ratings can be inferred, whereas a great variance in their responses indicates reason for concern about this item (Lawshe, 1975, p. 567).

For the purpose of this book, Lawshe's research design was adapted. The goal was to confirm content validity between the test items and the archetypes with their respective motifs in a general audience's understanding. Therefore, the surveyed public had to consist of an average population sample rather than a small group of experts. The survey asked the participants to evaluate how well a statement fits an archetype and its respective motifs. In accordance with Lawshe, content validity was operationalized as follows for the purpose of this study: the extent to which the survey participants perceive overlap between the test statement and the corresponding archetype with its motifs.

A larger number of survey participants was to enhance robustness of the results. The items were tested by means of two online surveys with sample sizes of $n_1 = 88$ and $n_2 = 100$ participants in the German language. The survey was conducted using the web-based survey software UmfrageOnline.com (UmfrageOnline, n.d.). Data was collected between January and February 2021. A convenience sampling approach was applied, and the survey was circulated among the professional and private circles of the involved researchers. To reduce the arbitrariness of the convenience sampling approach, the survey response was regulated to ensure a reasonably dispersed distribution of the demographic data. This procedure is recommended by Braunecker (2021, p. 74). In sample 1, female participants and people under the age of 30 years prevail. Sample 2 includes slightly more male than female participants and the age distribution is more evenly spread. The distribution is illustrated in Table 5.1.

The survey was designed as follows: After a brief introduction to the archetypical model according to Pätzmann and Genrich (2020), the respondents were presented with one of the archetypes or anti-archetypes and the three corresponding motifs. Then they were confronted with five statements from the archetypical personality test. These included the three statements presumed to match with the named archetype plus two statements from each of the other two motivational force fields. The respondents were asked to rate the five statements' matching to the

Table 5.1 Demographic information about the two validation surveys' samples. Source: Own representation

	Sample 1 $n_1 = 88$	Sample 2 $n_2 = 100$
Gender		
Female	60.3%	44.8%
Male	39.7%	55.2%
Other	0.0%	0.0%
Age		
18–29 years	65.4%	36.5%
30–49 years	21.8%	22.9%
50–65 years	10.3%	29.2%
66 or older	2.6%	11.5%

archetype on a five-point Likert scale ranging from "applies fully" to "does not apply at all." The statements were rephrased in the third person, naming the archetype being tested. In order to avoid results being distorted because of habitual answers (bias of the first questions) (Braunecker, 2021, p. 120), answer options were arranged randomly. Archetypes and anti-archetypes as well as the three different motivational force fields appeared in mixed order; but cross-check statements were chosen from the motivational endorsers for the archetypes and motivational barriers for the anti-archetypes. Because the hero and destroyer are overarching across all three motivation force fields, one cross-check statement was chosen per each force field. A pretest was conducted in January 2021 with one expert from Neu-Ulm University of Applied Science's Competence Centre for Marketing and Branding.

Surveys must not be too long to avoid fatigue and cancellation (Braunecker, 2021, p. 112; Gräf, 2010, p. 64). To shorten the survey and thus to reduce the cancelling rate, it was randomly split into two halves, both of which tested a mix of archetypes and anti-archetypes from all three motivational fields. Survey 1 was completed by $n_1 = 88$ out of $n_3 = 97$ started surveys, leaving a cancellation rate of 9.28%. Survey 2 was completed by $n_2 = 100$ out of $n_4 = 104$, leaving a cancellation rate of 3.85%.

The survey results were analyzed with the help of *UmfrageOnline.com* (UmfrageOnline, n.d.). The responses per statement were counted and percentages were calculated. From those results, the arithmetic middle as well as the standard deviation were calculated. A low arithmetic middle suggests that the statement was rated as applying to a great extent to the tested archetype. A low standard deviation suggests that the respondents were in agreement. A large standard deviation suggests that there was a great variation in the responses, that is, the respondents were divided about the matching between statement and archetype. The results were interpreted as follows: Statements with an arithmetic mean below 2.4 and a standard deviation below 1.2 were considered as confirmed. These thresholds suggest a solid validation.

In the first run, four of the envisaged statements were identified as not matching their respective archetype with its three motifs. They were reformulated and revalidated in a second survey. After this run, all statements were confirmed except for one, which was again reformulated and eventually confirmed in a third survey. The sample size for the second survey was $n_5 = 64$ (51.56% female, 48.44% male; 28.1% 18–29 years old, 39.1% 30–49; 28.1% 50–65; and 4.7% 66 and older). The sample size for the third survey was $n_6 = 65$ (55.4% female, 43.1% male, 1.5% other; 66.2% 18–29 years old; 16.9% 30–49; 13.8% 50–65; 3.1% 66 or older).

The unconfirmed statements concerned the anti-archetypes slave with two statements, as well as diva and coward with one statement each. For the slave, the two statements matching the motifs *jealous* ("The slave becomes angry when she cannot have people who are important to her all by herself.") and *tragic* ("The slave often has bad luck.") had to be reformulated. For the motif *jealous*, the new statement "The slave feels worthless and fears losing what she loves" emphasizes the lack of self-esteem and fear of loss. The new statement for the motif *tragic*, "The slave bears a heavy burden," accentuates the fate component instead of simple bad luck. Both statements were validated in the second survey run.

For the diva, the statement ascribed to the motif *smug* ("Her skills clearly set the diva apart from the average.") was not confirmed. In the original personality test conceptualization, all statements were phrased in the first person. To avoid confusion with self-tests, all the statements had been reformulated to the third person for the purpose of these validation surveys. With this particular statement, however, it can be assumed that it connotes a different meaning whether used in the first or third person. Therefore, a more direct phrasing was chosen to avoid misunderstandings: "The diva thinks that she is better than the rest." This statement clearly distinguishes between actual skills and self-perception and was confirmed in the second validation survey.

For the archetype coward, the statement matching the motif *naïve* ("The coward always trusts others without reservation.") was not confirmed. Two reformulations were necessary, as the first rephrased statement "The coward does not question problems" was not confirmed either. The original statement likely appealed too much to the emotional level and the second statement probably overemphasized the cognitive domain. Thus, the third statement was reformulated to capture both dimensions of the adjective naïve which implicates an element of guileless trustfulness as well as a lack of judgment (Dudenverlag, 2021). This was captured in the final statement "The coward is gullible and always follows others uncritically," which was validated in the third run.

This quantitative trend analysis confirmed content validity of all the (reformulated) statements and their corresponding archetypes in the German language. For an international application of the archetypical personality test, the validated statements were translated from German to English with the help of native English speakers. However, nuances of meaning might have been lost in translation, so the test would have to be validated again in the English language for a broader international application. Furthermore, caution must be applied as the subtleties of the English language vary worldwide and according to the context.

Research phase 2 underlying this book used the validated archetypical personality test as a tool to identify the archetypes relevant for startup teams. To help the reader follow the findings in Part II of this book, Table 5.2 contains the test items with an assignment to the respective motifs and archetypes in the third person. In this format, the test can be used as a research tool. A self-test version of the validated archetypical personality test as well as the 28 (anti-)archetypes' profiles can be found in the appendix of this book. In addition, we plan to develop an app and a website through which the test can be performed digitally.

Table 5.2 Validated test breakdown by motif and (anti-)archetypes reformulated in the third person. Source: Adapted from Pätzmann and Genrich (2020, p. 19ff)

Archetype	Motif	Statement
Genius	Intellectual	A team member would like to find answers to fundamental questions about the world, about humankind and its relationship to its environment
	Logical	In a team member's eyes, everything is subject to a certain logic, coincidence plays a subordinate role
	Analyzing	A team member gets to the bottom of things in every detail
Mentor	Wise	A team member thinks in terms of the grand scheme of things
	Inspirational	With his/her experience a team member helps others to become better
	Visionary	A team member thinks in terms of future scenarios and their long-term effects
Leader	Seminal	A team member understands how to reconcile people and their goals
	Assertive	A team member leads the way when things need to be done
	Self-confident	A team member reacts confidently and thoughtfully in all situations
Amazon	Self-determined	A team member always makes independent decisions
	Emancipated	A team member does not allow him/herself to be pushed into any role
	Strong	A certain pressure encourages a team member to perform at his/her best
Model student	Inquisitive	In order to understand the complexity of things, a team member obtains a sound overview through research
	Committed	A team member handles tasks that arise with great vigor and enthusiasm
	Decent	A team member likes when everything is in its proper place
Mother	Caring	A team member likes to take care of the needs of others
	Protective	A team member stands up for the weak
	Encouraging	In a team member's opinion, everyone deserves a second chance

(*continued*)

Table 5.2 (continued)

Archetype	Motif	Statement
Friend	Cooperative	A team member always has an open ear for problems
	Reliable	A team member keeps his/her promises
	Honest	A team member tells the truth
Mother Earth	Respectful	A team member considers every individual on Earth to be valuable
	Pacifist	A team member always looks for balanced solutions
	Communicative	A team member can mediate well between different people
Angel	Innocent	A team member has never done anything evil before
	Empathic	A team member can easily put him/herself in other people's position
	Pure	A team member leads an exemplary life
Artist	Unique	A team member is unconventional
	Creative	A team member enjoys trying out new approaches
	Tolerant	A team member is open-minded about unknown and different things
Beauty	Sensual	A team member senses emotions intensely
	Passionate	A team member devotes him/herself fully to one thing when he/she is convinced of it
	Desirable	Others turn to look at a team member when he/she enters a room
Happy Nature	Robust	A team member does not allow him/herself to be ruffled
	Humorous	A team member can make people laugh
	Confident	Even if unexpected problems arise, a team member never loses confidence
Explorer	Yearning	A team member longs to constantly try new things
	Curious	A team member wants to explore the world with his/her own eyes
	Euphoric	A team member can easily be won over by new ideas
Hero	Self-sacrificing	Additional tasks are no problem for a team member, if he/she can achieve an improvement for everyone

(*continued*)

Table 5.2 (continued)

Archetype	Motif	Statement
	Brave	A team member is convinced that far-reaching changes can only be achieved with the necessary readiness to take risks
	Determined	A team member has a strong inner drive to put into practice what he/she has said
Idiot	Simple	In some situations a team member feels clumsy
	Foolish	Banal things often amuse a team member
	Primitive	Often a team member simply acts without bothering to think
Avenger	Embittered	A team member holds the view that life is unjust
	Unforgiving	A team member has difficulties forgiving when he/she experiences injustice
	Begrudging	A team member has difficulty acknowledging the success of others
Tyrant	Regnant	A team member likes to be in command
	Discriminating	A team member often sets him/herself overambitious goals
	Over-confident	A team member excludes other people when they do not share his/her opinion
Slave	Heteronomous	A team member adopts values from his/her superiors without critically questioning them him/herself
	Jealous	A team member feels worthless and fears losing what he/she loves
	Tragic	A team member bears a heavy burden
Rebel	Anarchistic	A team member does not fit into any system
	Lateral thinking	The further a team member moves away from routines, the more new things emerge for him/her
	Lawless	A team member breaks existing rules according to his/her own discretion
Materialist (female)	Grasping	If others have more than a team member has, he/she wants to catch up with them
	Selfish	A team member always acts in such a way that no disadvantage arises for him/her
	Influential	A team member can steer people and processes to further his/her interests
Traitor	Scheming	To achieve his/her goals, a team member plays other people off against each other

(*continued*)

Table 5.2 (continued)

Archetype	Motif	Statement
	Back-stabbing	A team member disguises his/her true intentions
	Opportunistic	A team member adjusts his/her position on critical issues to achieve a general consensus
Diva	Narcissistic	A team member cannot pass a mirror without looking at him/herself
	Arrogant	A team member always remains in the memory of others
	Smug	A team member thinks that he/she is better than the rest
Coward	Naive	A team member is gullible and always follows others uncritically
	Destitute	A team member finds it difficult to cope with unexpected situations
	Dependent	A team member always makes decisions after consultation with a person close to him/her
Psychopath	Insane	A team member's thoughts disturb normal people
	Sadistic	A team member enjoys the misfortune of others
	Non-empathic	A team member feels little sympathy for the fate of others
Femme Fatale	Irresistible	Others would prefer to spend their time exclusively with a team member
	Manipulative	A team member is aware of his/her effect on others and uses it skillfully
	Seductive	A team member can get others to do things for him/her in a charming way
Victim	Sensitive	A team member thinks about past conversations often and for a long time
	Lonely	A team member finds it difficult to establish social contacts
	Melancholic	A team member thinks about the meaning of life and his/her individual place in society
Lazar	Pessimistic	A team member has fears about the future
	Disdained	A team member takes it upon him/herself not to be accepted by society
	Different	Others think a team member is strange
Destroyer	Hateful	A team member detests most people in his/her environment

(continued)

Table 5.2 (continued)

Archetype	Motif	Statement
	Brutal	A team member sanctions the misconduct of others ruthlessly
	Aggressive	A team member quickly becomes irritated when things do not go according to his/her plan

References

Braunecker, C. (2021). *How to do empirische Sozialforschung*. UTB Facultas.

Bryman, A., & Bell, E. (2011). *Business research methods* (3rd ed.). Oxford University Press.

Dudenverlag. (2021). *naiv. Bibliographisches Institut GmbH*. Retrieved Nov 23 2021 from https://www.duden.de/node/153773/revision/484851

Gräf, L. (2010). *Online-Befragung*. LIT.

Lawshe, C. H. (1975). A quantitative approach to content validity [article]. *Personnel Psychology, 28*(4), 563–575. https://doi.org/10.1111/j.1744-6570.1975.tb01393.x

Pätzmann, J., & Genrich, R. (2020). *Employer branding mit Archetypen*. Springer Gabler.

Schnell, R. (2013). *Methoden der empirischen Sozialforschung* (10th ed.). Oldenbourg.

UmfrageOnline. (n.d.). *enuvo GmbH*. Retrieved Jan 05 2022 from https://www.umfrageonline.com/

6

A Balanced Team

The second research phase consisted of a quantitative survey with entrepreneurship experts and resulted in a spider web profile of the ideal archetypical setup of startup teams. The results of the English and German questionnaires were combined. From all the answers, a mean value was calculated for each statement. The potential values ranged from 1 = "must be very strongly present" to 5 = "should not be present at all." This value conveys to which extent the respondents consider the characteristic to be relevant for an entrepreneurial team. The results ranged from 1.26 to 4.90. The standard deviation for this value ranged from 0.63 to 1.42, with a mean of 1.06. This indicates that the disagreement between experts was marginal, and the results can be considered quite solid.

The mean values per statement were then clustered according to the corresponding (anti-)archetype, so that a mean value for the entire (anti-)archetype could be calculated. The lowest value represented the most relevant archetype. To make visual representation easier, these values were then subtracted from 15, the maximum achievable value per (anti-)archetype, so that a higher value now signifies a higher relevancy. This yielded the following results for each of the (anti-)archetypes, values rounded to two decimals (Table 6.1).

The ideal archetypical setup of a startup team is graphically represented in a spiderweb diagram (Fig. 6.1).

V. Miller, J. U. Pätzmann, *Archetypical Roles in Startups*, Business Guides on the Go,
https://doi.org/10.1007/978-3-031-22253-5_6

Table 6.1 Relevancy of the (anti-)archetypes for startup teams. $n = 86$, values rounded to two decimals. Source: Own representation

Archetypes	Mean value	Anti-archetypes	Mean value
Genius	7.91	Idiot	4.74
Mentor	10.58	Avenger	2.34
Leader	10.15	Tyrant	3.84
Amazon	7.74	Slave	2.66
Model Student	9.06	**Rebel**	6.72
Mother	8,49	Materialist	5.40
Friend	10.18	Traitor	2.35
Mother Earth	8.99	Diva	4.52
Angel	6.82	Coward	3.41
Artist	10.36	Psychopath	2.47
Beauty	7.91	**Femme Fatale**	7.37
Happy Nature	9.49	Victim	4.64
Explorer	8.90	Lazar	4.44
Hero	9.94	Destroyer	2.07

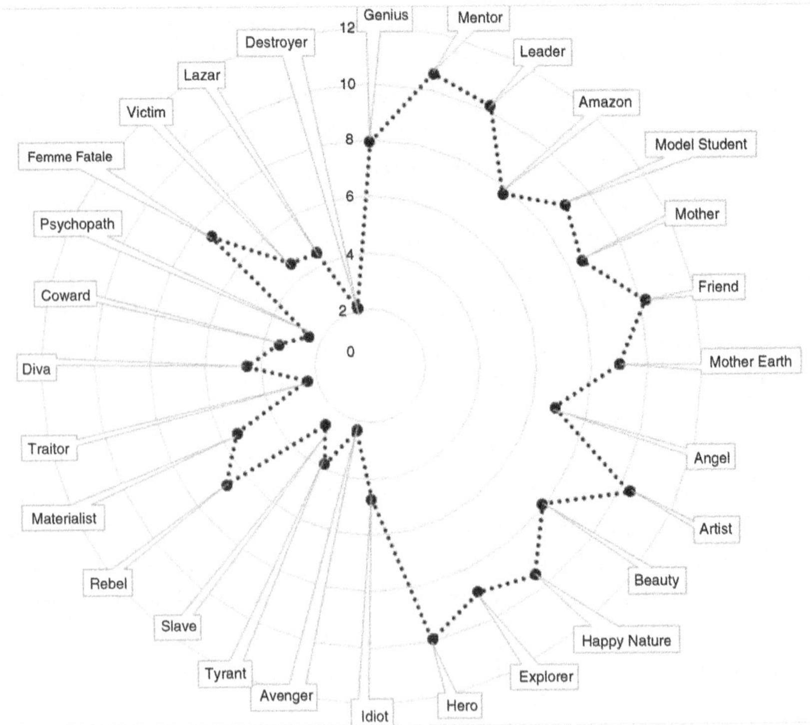

Fig. 6.1 Spiderweb diagram of the relevancy of archetypical roles in startup teams. $n = 86$. Source: Own representation

The five highest ranking archetypes with a rating of 9.49 and above were considered as the most relevant for startup teams, namely mentor, leader, friend, artist, and hero. Overall, archetypes were rated significantly more positively than anti-archetypes, with the highest score of the best rated anti-archetype, femme fatale, being 7.37 and the lowest score of the least rated archetype, angel, being 6.82. This can be explained by the negatively charged nature of anti-archetypes and a human inclination to favor traits with positive connotations. Therefore, it can be assumed that the significance of anti-archetypes was underrated. Hence, it was decided to consider anti-archetypes with a score of 6.00 or above as most tolerable for a startup team, namely the femme fatale and the rebel.

Box 6.1 The Shadow

The in-depth interviews strongly supported the decision to include the two most tolerable anti-archetypes by revealing that the anti-archetypes were generally underrated in the quantitative survey. Expert E_Men_I criticized that the archetypes received so much higher ratings than anti-archetypes: "entrepreneurship isn't a fairytale." His view is supported by six other experts. Respondent A_Men_G cites click-dummy online shops to test whether customers are ready to push the "buy" button as an example. He asserts:

> because you also have to become a bit, well, known on the market and bring up wind and must also at first come out with elbows, so it needs not only these nice and good ones, but also at times, I say, a bit of slyness is also needed at times (A_Men_G, translated from German)

Anti-archetypes contribute to the startup team's assertiveness and cunning. A likeable person is not always the best entrepreneur.

The shadow is one of Jung's core archetypes, representing the repressed, unwanted sides of personality. Well-adjusted persons learn to integrate those aspects into their self-identity (Carducci, 2009, p. 139; Jung, 2018, p. 28; Roesler, 2016, p. 34; Wulff, 1997, p. 427). Like Kociatkiewicz and Kostera (2012) maintain, archetypes as such are morally neutral and can take good or bad manifestations (p. 865). Similarly, startup teams must learn to deal with the negative sides of their archetypes. The leader, the artist, the friend, the hero—they all have their dark sides and shortcomings as well. If they are overrepresented, too much in the spotlight, or scattered, archetypes with positive connotations can do more harm than good, just as anti-archetypes can also work to the startup's advantage.

Data analysis To avoid inaccuracies, the results of English and German surveys were compared and found to be largely congruent, so the data from the two surveys were combined in the final results, see Fig. 6.2. A comparison was also drawn between the three countries, see Fig. 6.3. The datasets for Israel and Kenya were too small to yield robust results. However, the outcomes for these small datasets are principally congruent with the bigger dataset from Germany. This is an indication that a larger survey in Kenya or Israel would not deviate too much from the survey in Germany. In addition, the results were compared across the different categories of expertise, which did not yield relevant differences (see Fig. 6.4). This also makes sense since the free field text information indicates that many respondents fall into more than one category. These checks confirmed that the quantitative study had generated a robust trend analysis of relevant characteristics in startup teams according to experts'

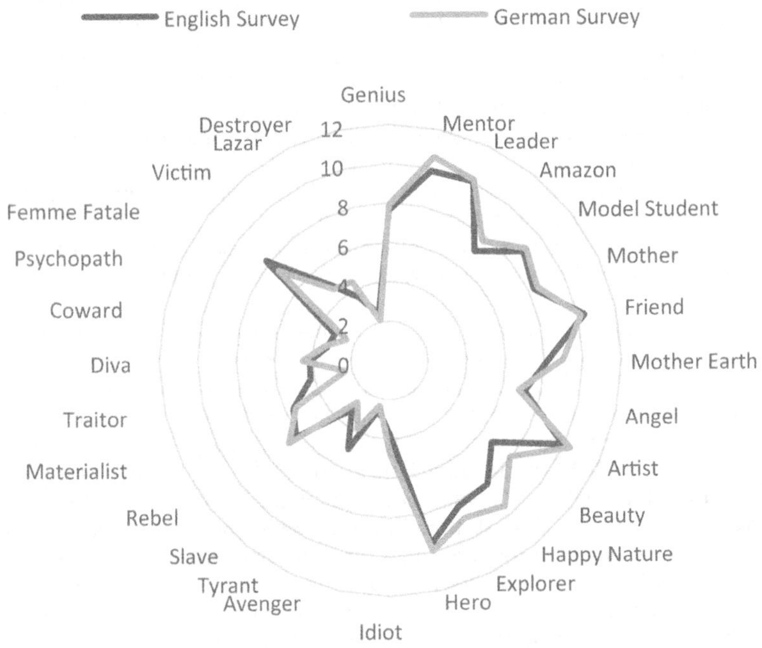

Fig. 6.2 Comparison English vs German survey results. Source: Own representation. $n_{German} = 72$; $n_{English} = 14$

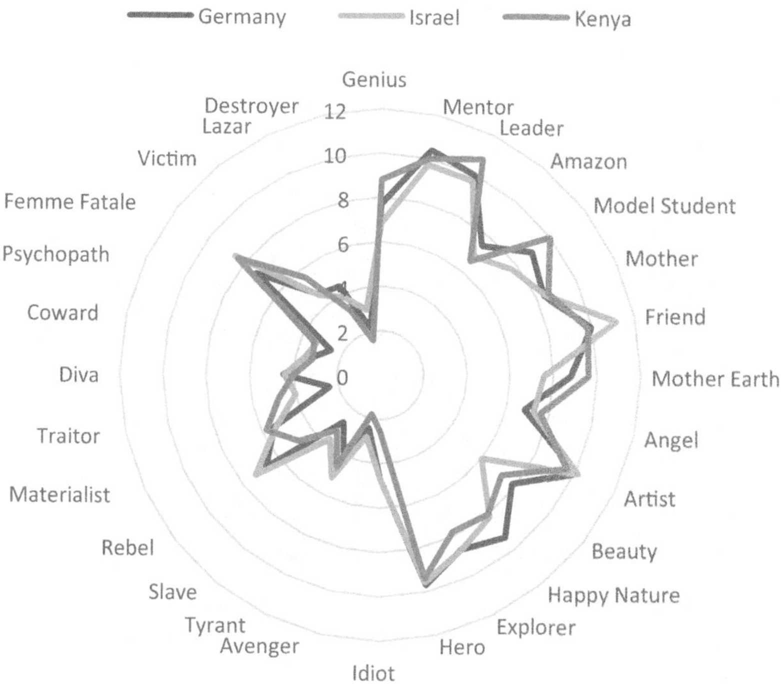

Fig. 6.3 Comparison across the three countries. Source: Own representation. $n_{Germany} = 72$; $n_{Israel} = 7$; $n_{Kenya} = 5$

experience. The spider web diagram in Fig. 6.1 was thus used as the basis for the in-depth expert interviews in research stage three. Focus was placed on the five most relevant archetypes mentor, leader, friend, artist, and hero, as well as the two most tolerable anti-archetypes femme fatale and rebel.

To allow a more accurate interpretation of the results, Table 6.2 presents an overview of the seven (anti-)archetypes in focus, their motifs, and the results for the corresponding statements. The values in this table are not reversed, so that a lower value represents a stronger relevancy. By considering the ratings of the individual statements, the interpretation of data from the in-depth interviews in research phase three becomes more accurate. In this way, it can be seen which characteristics of an (anti-)archetype are the decisive ones, despite the small deviations between the statements.

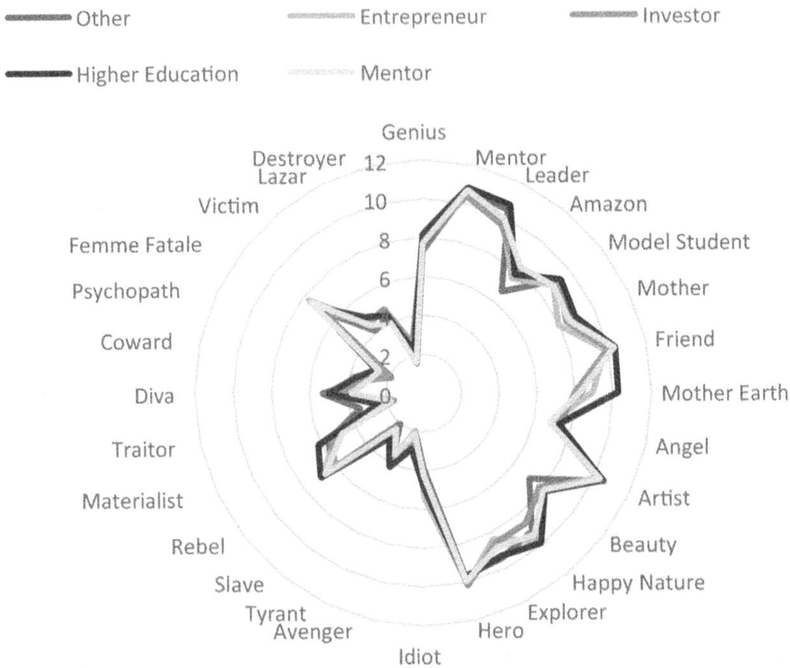

Fig. 6.4 Comparison of results across expertise. Source: own representation. $n_{Other} = 13$; $n_{Entrepreneur} = 25$; $n_{Investor} = 5$; $n_{Higher\ Education} = 24$; $n_{Mentor} = 19$

The expert interviews in research phase three revealed that the balance of the archetypical roles represented in a startup team is central for its success. Creativity and productivity (execution focus) must be weighed in the right proportions, and someone needs to moderate between these opposing ways of thinking, which both have their relevancy. One person can represent multiple archetypical roles, and also shift according to the current necessities. This ability to shift the enacted archetype according to the needs of the development phase the startup is currently undergoing, can be a key success factor. Contingent on personal inclinations, the archetypes can also be understood similarly to Edward de Bono's *Six Thinking Hats* (1999) which recommends to consciously switch between different styles of thinking. Depending on the requirements, an archetype embodying a certain way of thinking must be brought more to the fore.

Table 6.2 Results of the seven relevant (anti-)archetypes per statement, rounded to two decimals. Source: Own representation

Archetype	Motif	Statement	Mean value
Mentor Autonomy + Self-Assertion	Wise	A team member thinks in terms of the grand scheme of things.	1.85
	Inspirational	With his/her experience a team member helps others to become better.	1.85
	Visionary	A team member thinks in terms of future scenarios and their long-term effects.	2.06
Leader Autonomy + Self-Assertion	Seminal	A team member understands how to reconcile people and their goals.	1.73
	Assertive	A team member leads the way when things need to be done.	2.01
	Self-confident	A team member reacts confidently and thoughtfully in all situations.	1.99
Friend Safety + Relationship	Cooperative	A team member always has an open ear for problems.	2.49
	Reliable	A team member keeps his/her promises.	1.81
	Honest	A team member tells the truth.	1.55
Artist Excitement + Curiosity	Unique	A team member is unconventional.	2.04
	Creative	A team member enjoys trying out new approaches.	1.86
	Tolerant	A team member is open-minded about unknown and different things.	1.93
Hero + All three basic motivational systems Autonomy, Safety and Excitement	Self-sacrificing	Additional tasks are no problem for a team member, if he/she can achieve an improvement for everyone.	2.14
	Brave	A team member is convinced that far-reaching changes can only be achieved with the necessary readiness to take risks.	2.25
	Determined	A team member has a strong inner drive to put into practice what he/she has said.	1.92

(continued)

Table 6.2 (continued)

Archetype	Motif	Statement	Mean value
Femme Fatale Excitement – Fear	Irresistible	Others would prefer to spend their time exclusively with a team member.	3.32
	Manipulative	A team member is aware of his/her effect on others and uses it skillfully.	2.25
	Seductive	A team member can get others to do things for him/her in a charming way.	2.25
Rebel Autonomy – Subjection	Anarchistic	A team member does not fit into any system.	2.83
	Lateral thinking	The further a team member moves away from the routines he/she has followed so far, the more new things emerge for him/her.	2.24
	Lawless	A team member breaks existing rules according to his/her own discretion.	3.01

There are also some archetypical roles which only play out their value in conjunction with another role, like the friend or rebel. The leader role should not be present in more than one or few team members, whereas every team member should contain a share of the hero and friend archetypes. Entrepreneurial teams often accumulate "superstars." They may be the idea generators or magician-like developers. In order to go places, those must be counterbalanced by humbler but hardworking team members who are satisfied to do the operations and keep the startup going. Some archetypes, like the mentor or in some cases the femme fatale, are better represented by external team members.

As outlined in Chap. 2, research about team diversity already showed that knowing one's own personality as well as appreciating and accommodating others' is key for managing heterogeneous teams. Similarly, the interviews revealed that teams should deliberately foster their ability to manage heterogeneity. Respondent D_Fou_G emphasized that teams usually assemble "naturally" instead of approaching team member selection strategically. This makes awareness and careful management of the team role constellation, not only functional roles, even more important in order to harvest the benefits of the creativity bred by heterogeneous mindsets. This is in line with extant findings that self-reflection and mutual understanding are strategies to deal with the imminent risk of affective conflict, which is most likely to arise by individuals with vastly similar or completely opposite archetypical roles (Chowdhury, 2005, p. 742; Pearson et al., 2002, p. 366). The importance of self-awareness is even greater in unbalanced teams with an overrepresentation of a certain archetype, as Belbin's (2010) work about team roles suggests (p. 52). Careful attention to the team dynamics can overcome shortcomings in its composition.

Diversity of archetypical team roles helps to reach better levels of innovativeness, which matches existing findings that demographically homogeneous teams can benefit from heterogeneous thinking styles and opinions (Chowdhury, 2005, p. 730; West III, 2007, p. 95). Thus, there is space for both the friend and the rebel. As Kollmann et al. (2017) observed, well-balanced teams perform best: "teams composed of both creative and conformist members produce superior innovation performance" (p. 847). Teams can choose between egalitarian or hierarchical decision-making (Wasserman, 2012, p. 129); but in any case, this research confirms the benefits of having clear and distinct team roles. Moreover, these findings corroborate the importance of following a common direction. Besides, they are consistent with Belbin's (2010) observation that it reaps rewards for entrepreneurial teams to take the time to work out a shared vision for the company (p. 101).

References

Belbin, R. M. (2010). *Team roles at work* (2nd ed.). Routledge.

Carducci, B. J. (2009). *The psychology of personality* (2nd ed.). Wiley-Blackwell.

Chowdhury, S. (2005). Demographic diversity for building an effective entrepreneurial team: Is it important? *Journal of Business Venturing, 20*(6), 727–746.

De Bono, E. (1999). *Six thinking hats (rev. and updated ed.)*. Little, Brown and Company.

Jung, C. G. (2018). *Archetypen*. Patmos Verlag.

Kociatkiewicz, J., & Kostera, M. (2012). The good manager: An archetypical quest for morally sustainable leadership. *Organization Studies, 33*(7), 861–878. https://doi.org/10.1177/0170840612445124

Kollmann, T., Stöckmann, C., Meves, Y., & Kensbock, J. M. (2017). When members of entrepreneurial teams differ: Linking diversity in individual-level entrepreneurial orientation to team performance. *Small Business Economics, 48*, 843–859. https://doi.org/10.1007/s11187-016-9818-6

Pearson, A. W., Ensley, M. D., & Amason, A. C. (2002). Understanding the dynamics of new venture top management teams: Cohesion, conflict, and new venture performance. *Journal of Business Venturing, 17*(4), 365–386.

Roesler, C. (2016). *Das Archetypenkonzept C.G. Jungs* (1st ed.). Verlag W. Kohlhammer.

Wasserman, N. (2012). *The founder's dilemmas: Anticipating and avoiding the pitfalls that can sink a startup*. Princeton University Press.

West, G. P., III. (2007). Collective cognition: When entrepreneurial teams, not individuals, make decisions. *Entrepreneurship Theory and Practice, 31*(1), 77–102.

Wulff, D. M. (1997). *Psychology of religion: Classic and contemporary* (2nd ed.). Wiley.

7

The (Anti-)Archetypes You Need in a Startup Team

This chapter elaborates on the findings about the relevant archetypes and builds their individual profiles in a startup setting. In terms of gender, the pronoun appropriate to the archetypes' label will be used. However, it must be emphasized that the findings are gender-neutral in nature. Archetypical roles can be assumed by all genders and this research does not provide any findings about their gender distribution. It was a deliberate decision to write from the perspective of the archetype's gender, as identified in Pätzmann and Hartwig's (2018) study of blockbuster movies, instead of using gender-neutral language because the profiles refer to the archetypes themselves instead of individuals who may at times embody them.

7.1 Leader

The 15 experts are unanimous that the leader archetype must not be absent in a startup team. Respondent O_Fou_K fittingly summarized it: "a team without a leader is like a plane without a pilot." Strong leadership

V. Miller, J. U. Pätzmann, *Archetypical Roles in Startups*, Business Guides on the Go,
https://doi.org/10.1007/978-3-031-22253-5_7

is especially important in the chaotic early phase of ideation. It remains important throughout the startup journey, but with the maturing of the company the needs gradually shift toward more management. This goes in line with Belbin's (2010) findings about teamwork in general: "But while managers are essential and plentiful, leaders are needed only in special circumstances and are generally in short supply" (p. 119). The turbulent time of newly founding a business can be interpreted as a constant state of crisis. The scarcity of true leadership personalities has also been highlighted by experts C_Inv_G and G_Inv_I, interestingly both of them are investors.

Nine experts insisted that the leadership archetype should only be represented by one team member, which goes along with extant research (Foo et al., 2006, p. 389; Franke et al., 2008, p. 475), while four experts allowed for the possibility of having more than one leader, potentially according to their area of expertise. The key here is to follow one common strategy, otherwise having multiple leaders can cause devastating confusion and competition within the team, which is confirmed by extant literature (Pearson et al., 2002, p. 370; Wasserman, 2012, p. 117). Respondent I_TM_I took a broader view of the leader archetype, expressing that the "Do it" mentality must also be present in lower-ranking team members such as employees. They are the "initiators and implementors, they are the guys getting the things done" (I_TM_I) in every department. In line with extant literature, the complete absence of the leadership archetype is destructive for a startup (Foo et al., 2006, p. 391; Francis & Sandberg, 2000, p. 11; Lechler, 2001, p. 266; Wright & Vanaelst, 2009, p. xiv).

The leader archetypes' three chief characteristics are execution-focused, visionary, and assertive; see Fig. 7.1 for an overview. The leader persistently follows the business idea and ensures that consistent action is taken instead of getting stuck in cloud castles or lost in an endless maze of

Fig. 7.1 Characteristics of the leader archetype. Source: Own representation

opportunities. He has the necessary willpower and energy to implement the strategy. A leader often evolves naturally:

> no one nominates the person to be the leader, but the person feels 'hey we can't just be quiet like this, we need to have direction, we have five minutes, we have a goal, we have to achieve this in the next five minutes; guys let's do this' and then the rest just follows, you know (K_Men_K)

Table 7.1 Functions of the leader archetype. Source: Own representation

External role	Internal tasks
Face to the world • Being visible • Generating trust in the team	Bird's eye view • Providing direction • Making decisions • Structuring and monitoring
Selling the vision • Giving identity to the startup • Leading the strategy	People management • Building the team • Delegating tasks • Conveying confidence

On the one hand, the leader inspires and convinces external as well as internal stakeholders: "he's the vision-bearer" (N_Fou_K). He serves as the startup's symbolic focal figure, the chief function of leadership according to Czarniawska-Joerges and Wolff (1991). On the other hand, he is good at people management, knows how to delegate tasks, and to integrate a team. He has a bird's eye view of the startup, filters business opportunities, makes decisions, and monitors the progress. It is the leader's task to unite a team composed of capable and independent-minded individuals around a common goal. As expert C_Inv_G said: "[the team members] need someone to lead the way in these untraveled paths" (translated from German). Table 7.1 indicates the leader's external as well as internal roles.

Often, the leader is not a very likeable person and appears in combination with anti-archetypes such as the rebel, femme fatale, diva, avenger, or tyrant, from which he derives his assertiveness in the first place: "it's not a business that you can be modest and it's acceptable, you really need to be bold and sometimes show some negative characteristics, or bolder than folks that are less confident" (E_Men_I). The dark sides of the leader (often named king) have been emphasized by archetype literature (Kociatkiewicz & Kostera, 2012, p. 861; Kostera, 2012, p. 138). But agreeableness is not what it takes to push a startup: "[the leader] is the role whose popularity is in reverse proportion to its importance" (C_Inv_G, translated from German). Five interviewees mentioned Elon Musk as a prominent example of the leader archetype.

The experts are discordant about the leader's relationship to the mentor archetype. In some constellations, both archetypes occur in one person, especially when mentoring is executed as a leadership style. The leader shares the mentor's vision and capability to inspire but may be younger and less experienced. The leader is the execution-focused and operational implementor, whereas the mentor is the strategic thinker. Whether the leader occurs in conjunction with the mentor or rather the tyrant also depends on the organizational style and level of hierarchy in the young company. Especially if talent is short, the mentor or potentially femme fatale is the more suitable complement to the leader. Table 7.2 provides a detailed overview of the leader archetype's role in startup teams (Fig. 7.2).

Table 7.2 Archetypical profile for startups—leader. Source: Own representation

Leader Autonomy + Self-assertion	*Seminal*	The leader understands how to reconcile people and their goals
	Assertive	The leader leads the way when things need to be done
	Self-confident	The leader reacts confidently and thoughtfully in all situations
Characteristics	Execution-focused, assertive, visionary, outspoken, consistent, difficult	
Role in a startup	Toward the external world: Gives a face to the startup, sells the vision Inside the team: Takes on a bird's eye view (provides direction, makes decisions, structures, and monitors), manages people (builds the team, delegates tasks, conveys confidence)	
Moment to shine	In the ideation stage, the leader counterbalances the artist. He makes sure that ideas do not remain ideas but are actually implemented	
Light side	The leader gives a clear direction and implements it	
Shadow side	The leader is narrow-minded and not accommodating of alternative views	

Fig. 7.2 Symbolical representation of the leader. Source: Pätzmann (2020)

7.2 Mentor

The mentor is characterized by being visionary, inspirational, and wise. The 15 experts were in almost complete agreement that the mentor archetype is vital for a startup team. However, there were different views about whether the mentor should be an internal or an external team member. Five respondents decidedly argued that the mentor archetype should only be represented by someone from the outside assistance network. Four interviewees emphasized the mentor archetype's relevancy inside the core founding team. Six respondents adopted a mixed position. Table 7.3 gives an overview of the mentor's chief functions.

An external mentor can be provided by the startup ecosystem. Incubators frequently assign mentors to startup teams to help them navigate through the rocky journey of building a company, and many investors or business angels do a great deal of mentoring work. Mentors are also found in more informal settings, like the founders' social networks or professional circles. An external mentor can be a source of subject matter expertise and management know-how missing in the core founders' own human capital. He helps the passionate founders to mold their innovative ideas into a business structure. As a respected figure of authority and experience, he is in a position to challenge the founders from a sound distance and to open up their eyes to what they otherwise would not (be willing to) see. Respondent C_Inv_G, investor from Germany, summarized the mentor's role as an external sounding board:

Table 7.3 Functions of the mentor archetype. Source: Own representation

Functions of external mentoring	Functions of internal mentoring
• Subject matter expertise • Sharing life experience • Networking • Management know-how • For inexperienced founders	• Strategic vision • Confidence • Mentoring as a leadership style • Giving something back • For mature startup phase

> the role of a team, they are now setting out and have to change the world somehow and have to enter new paths on their own and of course they always need someone who mirrors what they are doing and helps them to find their way, so to speak, so a good mentor is a help for self-help, so in the sense of I now help people to assess themselves correctly (C_Inv_G, translated from German to English)

Being a well-networked professional, the mentor can open up doors to valuable contacts. Getting help from an external mentor is also suggested as a way to make up for missing resources (Brattström, 2019, p. 7).

In addition to these professional contributions, an external mentor can also fulfill valuable interpersonal functions. A mentor is usually someone with considerable business and life experience who probably has founded a successful startup already (Ruef, 2010, pp. 89–91), sometimes more than once, and has himself overcome more than one challenge. As such, he cannot only share professional knowledge, but also help the founders persevere through the dismal and devastating moments of the startup journey. Some mentors accompany the founding team very closely and almost become an integral part of it, even though they are not formally a cofounder. Vanaelst et al. (2006) call them "a surrogate entrepreneur" (p. 251). Like the cofounders themselves, such valuable mentors are usually driven by their entrepreneurial passion for the idea. External mentors are especially relevant for young and inexperienced founders who are on a comparable level in terms of power within the startup as well as experience and know-how. If an external mentor is very close to the startup's decision-making, cohesion and a shared vision between the internal members and the mentor are critical to avoid dilution of the strategy and conflicts (Klotz et al., 2013, p. 244). Strive Masiyiwa was named as a prominent example of a founder with strong mentor traits. He is a successful telecommunications businessman from Zimbabwe who strongly supports young entrepreneurs.

The mentor's visionary and inspirational traits, however, also have significance for internal team members, which was highlighted by four experts, three of which from Israel. The mentor is the key person to give the startup a common strategic direction. He does not get lost in the day-to-day business or plethora of business opportunities but maintains a strategic bird's eye view. He is also able to narrate a convincing story to sell this vision both outside and inside. This aspect of the mentor archetype does not necessarily go hand in hand with experience. Even a young and inexperienced mentor can take on this visionary function. This aspect of the mentor overlaps with the leader archetype. The mentor represents the vision whereas the leader is more execution-focused.

Another internal function of the mentor archetype is his interpersonal competency. He can moderate between the other different roles and intervene when conflicts start to become relational. As such, the mentor keeps the team together and makes sure each team member has the role it is best suited for. This is especially important because newly founded startups are chronically short of cash and therefore usually hire young and inexperienced employees to reduce expenses (Gopalkrishnan, 2017, p. 10). For these, mentoring works very well as a leadership style, as two respondents from Israel and one from Germany strongly highlighted (H_Fou_I, I_TM_I, A_Men_G). A company culture of mentors works best in a structure with low hierarchies. Startups attract free-spirited characters, so mentoring is often a more effective leadership style than authority: "in a startup, you have to get employees to work for you through idealism" (A_Men_G). Mentoring can be a great motivator and source of confidence for employees and external stakeholders alike because at the beginning, the founding team is a startup's sole asset. Respondent H_Fou_I, founder from Israel, described this confidence giving aspect of the mentor as follows:

> And one of the ways to overcome [uncertainty] and create some level of confidence within the team is to create assumptions and to clarify the unknown in a way that at the end of the day every individual is understand what he's doing and why he's doing it. Okay, because the why is not less important than the what (H_Fou_I).

In this capacity, the mentor goes hand in hand with the leader archetype. The internal aspect of the mentor archetype becomes more relevant when the startup is already expanding and potentially hiring employees. At this stage, successful founders often have the wish to contribute their experience by mentoring younger startups. Incubators often recruit mentors from former incubatees, as highlighted by respondent K_Men_K from Kenya. Thus, the mentor archetype maintains relevance throughout the startup's journey, but its concrete manifestation shifts from external to internal. See Table 7.4 for a complete overview of the mentor archetype's role in startup teams (Fig. 7.3).

Table 7.4 Archetypical profile for startups—mentor. Source: Own representation

Mentor Autonomy + Self-assertion	*Wise*	A team member thinks in terms of the grand scheme of things
	Inspirational	With his/her experience a team member helps others to become better
	Visionary	A team member thinks in terms of future scenarios and their long-term effects
Characteristics	Visionary, inspirational, wise, experienced, knowledgeable, a good teacher, authoritative, has the overview, well networked, reconciling	
Role in a startup	Functions of external mentors: Subject matter expertise, sharing life experience, networking, management know-how Functions of internal mentoring: Strategic vision, confidence, mentoring as a leadership style, giving something back	
Moment to shine	In the early stages, inexperienced founders benefit greatly from an external mentor. Once the business is established, internal mentoring becomes a useful leadership style to attract and maintain young employees	
Light side	Mentoring helps inexperienced talents realize their potential	
Shadow side	Overbearing mentoring can prevent young talents from flourishing	

Fig. 7.3 Symbolical representation of the mentor. Source: Pätzmann (2020)

7.3 Artist

Creative destruction is at the heart of entrepreneurship. This requires people who can leave well-trodden paths of thought. Pearson et al. (2002) claim:

> the task of the new venture [top management team (TMT)] is largely one of creativity and learning, where the ability to produce novel and integrated solutions is an important attribute that can distinguish high performing TMTs from others. (p. 367)

Therefore, the 15 experts are unanimous that the artist archetype is critical for a startup. He is inventive, thinks out of the box, and finds unconventional solutions. Kostera (2012) links this trait to Edward De Bono's concept of lateral thinking:

> Edward De Bono ([1967] 2007) uses the term 'lateral thinking' to refer to the kind of creative thinking that is free of the bonds of logic and criticism. Lateral thinking is not directly goal-oriented; instead, it follows unknown paths. It is especially helpful when we are faced with a problem that seems impossible to solve or when we want to discover something new or see something familiar in a new light (Kostera, 2012, p. 185)

A team can come up with unprecedented solutions if the artist archetype is strongly represented.

The artist can most likely be found in product development and business model innovation. Yet, the artist is quite the opposite of a typical engineer who thinks more in line with the conventions of the discipline. On the contrary, the artist approaches the subject from a completely different angle and finds solutions that no one had thought of before. In this capacity, this archetype is also very useful when it comes to understanding customers, testing the idea, and finding creative solutions to resource shortages. The artist unfolds his power best if he appears in conjunction

Table 7.5 Characteristics and functions of the artist archetype. Source: Own representation

Characteristics	Functions
• Creativity • Innovativeness • Thinking differently • Not a good manager	• Solving problems • Finding resources • Product development • Business model innovation

with another archetype or a particular technical skill. His characteristics and functions are illustrated in Table 7.5.

According to six experts, the artist archetype is most essential at the beginning, during the ideation stage. However, he retains relevancy in established companies that do not wish to be substituted by more innovative competitors or need to react to crises or changes in their business environment. The artist is wanted whenever a company is in need of innovating its business model or products. Interviewees J_Men_K and K_Men_K quoted the COVID-19 crisis as an instance when the artist's ability to adapt could really make the difference between a company surviving or dying:

> we are in an era where every business plan needs innovation, for example creativity, the more straight what is your value proposition, the more straight what is your how, you know, the innovation, how the creativity, and of course this doesn't mean literally creating a new stuff in the space but, yes, how do you fit the solutions to the users and I think this is now where creativity is needed; and look at now like the issue of the Covid-19, when a pandemic just hits no one is thinking about, what will you do, I mean how could we survive even if you people[???] Some businesses went down while others remained afloat. Why? The reason is how creative the founders are, the teams, how they are able to, you know, to be inventive like changing up things, getting away from the normal, you know, bringing out some unique solutions within the space and I think that's now why the artist also now comes in as a valuable archetype (K_Men_K)

Key: [???]=inaudible;

Lateral thinking allows the startup team to innovate its whole business model, not only a single product. The artist does not have to be a technical genius, but he can create true innovation: "change that adds value," as Tonny Omwansa, the CEO of the Kenya National Innovation Agency, boiled it down (Kenya National Innovation Agency, n.d.).

The artist's strengths, however, are also his weaknesses. Thrilled by the quest for ideas, the artist can get lost in spiritual spheres. He cannot decide on one idea and follow it through. The artist is difficult to manage. Team members with a high proportion of the artist archetype do not always get along well with those who are focused on business success or are very meticulous. In his team research, Belbin (2010) found out: "The more brilliant the Plant in a team [...], the greater is the need to master the arts of project team building and team management" (p. 104). Belbin's team role plant is comparable to the artist: creative and difficult to manage. So, while the artist is vital for a startup's innovative strength, he needs to be contained and carefully directed.

Rarely are the artist and leader archetypes combined in one person, but if they are, this can produce the most successful entrepreneurs. Accordingly, Steve Jobs and Elon Musk were frequently named as representatives of both the leader and the artist archetypes. They combine the traits of creative solution-finding with a strong focus on execution. The artist and leader archetypes must balance each other, as shown in Fig. 7.4. If the artist is not counterbalanced by the leader archetype, the startup will get stuck in endless innovation loops. Table 7.6 provides an overview of the artist's contributions to an entrepreneurial team (Fig. 7.5).

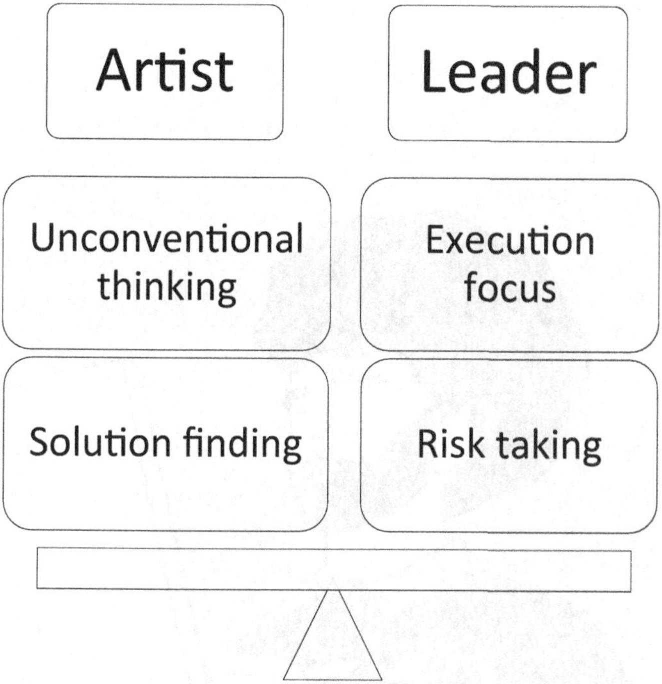

Fig. 7.4 Balance between artist and leader. Source: Own representation

Table 7.6 Archetypical profile for startups—artist. Source: Own representation

Artist	*Unique*	A team member is unconventional
Excitement	*Creative*	A team member enjoys trying out new approaches
+ Curiosity	*Tolerant*	A team member is open-minded about unknown and different things
Characteristics	Creative, innovative, think differently, not a good manager	
Role in a startup	Finding unconventional solutions to any problem, including the creative handling of resource shortages; creative product development and business model innovation	
Moment to shine	The artist has unconventional ideas to create value-added change during ideation and whenever innovation is needed	
Light side	The artist thinks freely and finds solutions no one has ever thought about	
Shadow side	The artist gets lost in ideas and cannot implement them	

Fig. 7.5 Symbolical representation of the artist. Source: Pätzmann (2020)

7.4 Friend

The experts were discordant about the friend archetype's significance for a startup team. Six experts count it among the very crucial archetypes, whereas seven challenge why it ranked so highly in the quantitative survey. Perhaps the insights of Chap. 2 provide an explanation: startup teams are held together by *emotions*. While the friend archetype does not necessarily have to be embodied in a specific individual, the findings suggest that it definitely must be present in the team as a whole. Recalling the details of the quantitative study results shows that honesty and reliability are the key factors that lead to the friend's high ranking. It all boils down to what has been explored in Chap. 2: trust is essential for fruitful teamwork. Among the seven (anti-)archetypes relevant to startups, the friend is the only one related to the safety system.

The friend archetype helps to build a cohesive team, motivate each other, attract people to join the startup in the first place, and to foster trust within the team as well as with customers and suppliers. Caring and kindness make the rocky startup journey bearable and keep motivation levels up even in the darkest moments. Expert H_Fou_I illustrated a scenario where the friend archetype is powerfully represented by an individual employee:

> friendships in a lot of the situations are based on someone that is, like an, if you want a creator, a motivator, and the engine of the friendship engine within the team, and in a lot of the cases you will find that this is not the same person that is the mentor or the leader; so I do agree that friendship is like key and when you look for a team you need to find the person that this is his role on a personal level, I can tell you that in a [???] of colleagues when we were three or four, we interviewed a very very young guy with zero experience, zero, we understood that he is extremely talented, and we saw that he is like a magnet to people, that he can bring energies that nobody can and that he can be like the seed of a type of the DNA that we are looking after, and till today even when the company is 80, 90 people he is still extremely significant in his role (H_Fou_I)

As stated by Chowdhury (2005), the loyalty of friendship increases commitment to the startup company (p. 728). The friend archetype brings in the people orientation in an otherwise goal oriented and ambitious setting. It amplifies the team members' motivation to give it all, which in turn enhances productivity: "people who think they are part of a team will perform better than when they don't; and one of the ways to do it is to create friendship" (H_Fou_I). An overrepresentation of the friend archetype, however, can kill the necessary drive and assertiveness, especially in the very early phases when strong leadership and execution focus are needed. Otherwise, the startup can get lost in a bubble of peace and joy, as West III (2007) already found. The friend archetype, however, can be very helpful in making sure that conflicts stay on a task level and do not affect interpersonal relationships.

Chapter 2 showed that real-life friendships play a significant but problematic role within startups. Friendships often already exist between team members before they embark on the journey of founding a startup together. This entails the benefits of trust and familiarity, but often hinders open and honest communication. Expert L_Aca_K as well as A_Men_G strongly highlighted the danger of socially expected positive feedback to the business idea instead of honest and constructive criticism. If founders cannot distinguish between friendship and business, they risk the "playing-with-fire-gap" of circumventing critical issues (Wasserman, 2012). Therefore, many experts expressed hesitation regarding the friend archetype: Expert E_Men_I quoted a saying popular in Israel: "you don't wanna start a startup with your friends," and experts N_Fou_K and J_Men_K underlined the importance of focusing on the business side in the startup and satisfying the need for friendship elsewhere. The risks of cofounding with friends have been stressed in Chap. 2. See Table 7.7 for a detailed profile of the friend archetype's role in founding teams (Fig. 7.6).

Table 7.7 Archetypical profile for startups—friend. Source: Own representation

Friend	*Cooperative*	A team member always has an open ear for problems
Safety	*Reliable*	A team member keeps his/her promises
+ Relationship	*Honest*	A team member tells the truth
Characteristics	Reconciling, people-centered, compromising, caring, loyal	
Role in a startup	The friend creates team cohesion and bonding between the team members so that they can effectively work toward a common goal; the friend may appear in individuals who are like "people-magnets," but it is most powerful if it appears on a group level—every team member has a share of it	
Moment to shine	The friend motivates the team to continue working together through the rocky startup journey and to settle their task-related disagreements in a respectful manner	
Light side	Friendship glues the team together	
Shadow side	The friend hesitates to address unpleasant issues	

Fig. 7.6 Symbolical representation of the friend. Source: Pätzmann (2020)

7.5 Hero

The hero is the most controversial archetype among the 15 experts. Five experts deem it relevant, whereas five question its significance within a startup team. The hero is brave and determined. He dedicates himself to a greater purpose, cares about others, and is ready to self-sacrifice, like having sleepless nights or relinquishing the salary for a period. The hero is characterized by self-confidence, exceptional competency and problem-solving skills, the readiness to take risks, and extraordinary resilience. According to expert K_Men_K, the hero is "this person who is not ready to see the organization die." Expert C_Inv_G sees it as a mix of the friend and leader archetype:

> that would be now from my point of view be a bit of a middle thing between friend and leader. Why? Because on the one hand he has, so to speak, courageously decided to go ahead, but it's not just someone who doesn't care about the others at all, that's black and white, who, so to speak, mainly tries to push through his ideas, but rather a person who just, who also cares about how the others are doing, about how the world is doing. (C_Inv_G, translated from German)

This balance of determination and care for others makes the hero archetype a strong asset for any startup and is particularly relevant in startups with a social or environmental mission.

Due to his resilience, the hero archetype plays out his strength in times of crisis. It becomes most relevant after ideation, when the startup needs funding and must win over customers because this is when frustrations start hitting. Interviewee K_Men_K illustrated it like this:

> Frustrations never come at, ah, ideation, they always come when you are now ready to meet the customer because the customer is the boss and this time you need to be very resilient and this time we have the hero mindset, the hero character comes in a lot because this is the person now who needs to be sacrificing a lot to save the situation (K_Men_K)

Or in respondent M_Inv_K's words: "so when things are as bad as they could be, who is there to be rising up to the occasion, who is there to be ready to take a bullet for the team?" The hero shines in crisis. Similarly,

Pätzmann and Hartwig (2018) emphasize that the hero is made by the circumstances. In narratives, it is often a figure representing another archetype at first and undergoing a transformation by altruistic and brave deeds throughout the hero's journey (p. 26).

In a crisis, a team member who is set apart by extraordinary commitment becomes a role model to others to dedicate their best and never give up. According to expert H_Fou_I, this can greatly enhance team cohesion:

> the heroness contributes to two things: (a) to the friendship and to this teaming need of doing things together because you feel that you're not on your own, and second it creates confidence, you create confidence that is a key thing for overcoming the challenges of a startup because there is so much unknown that everyone is looking for confidence and the confidence is coming from believing in the leadership team but also from not feeling alone, and feeling that *we* will overcome everything and not *I* will overcome everything, and I think that having a hero around, someone on that you can count, someone that will be there for you no matter what, this is how I understand this archetype, is something that brings confidence to everyone just to know that we have this guy there that no matter what he will be there for us. (H_Fou_I)

The hero helps so that nobody feels alone, he gives a sense of security and of being able to rely on the team as a safety net. The hero archetype can create greater confidence in the startup's top management team, but it is also useful in lower-ranking team members, regardless of their formal function.

In its exaggerated form, the hero archetype can also be quite destructive to the startup. If the hero does not appear on a group level, but is personified in a single individual who is portrayed like the company's star, it can lead to a quite ego-centric manifestation. A hero works until burnout without proper self-care and fails to accommodate others' ideas. Expert J_Men_K cautioned:

> R: these heroes sometimes tend to destroy when they think they're helping
>
> I: okay, can you give me an example?
>
> R: I've seen startups form and we have one person who really believes in his idea or feels that they're really important in that company and they don't want to take ideas from others, they are so determined, yes, and they are brave, yes and they are selfless, yes, but are they accommodating? Yes. Because you know for a startup to be well grounded and solid, they need

to accommodate each other's ideas and [degoose???] You know, they don't have to agree but they have to accommodate each other and consider and discuss together and agree and disagree so that they can come up with a you know a result that's their all, that they all accept is important for their startup to move forward

I: so, the hero mentality can make them blind? They don't look at others' ideas or listen to advice?

R: yes, they believe they are, you know, they are the warriors, like its put here, they are the warriors, they are the saviors, they, for me, that hero thing does not apply, run well with startups

I: so, you have seen this role in startups, but you have experienced that its more detrimental and not helpful?

R: yes, it has broken them! Some of the teams just disappeared because they can't accommodate each other's views! They break and they go back to incubation again.

I: so, in the end the hero is someone who wants to do it all alone but you can't found a startup alone?

R: no, you can't. you have to work with a team, they need to bring down their ego a bit

Key: I=Interviewer; R=Respondent; [???]=inaudible;

Thus, according to four experts, an overrepresentation of the hero archetype in a single individual can turn out to be quite damaging. Expert I_TM_I struggled with identifying a distinct hero archetype because in Israel, "there is a whole culture of it," "you're almost expected to do such," "so: it's not considered as a hero: that's what we do" (I_TM_). This goes in line with expert G_Inv_I's opinion, who sees determination as critical but not the willingness to self-sacrifice. These concerns point to the dark side of the hero, who can appear as the king in conjunction with the leader in archetype literature: "But the king also has a human side and is subject to weakness and failure. Danger lies in forgetting this side: if s/he does and starts to believe that s/he is superhuman or divine, the dark side takes over and the king falls into tyranny and madness"(Kociatkiewicz & Kostera, 2012, p. 866). The same happens to superstar entrepreneurs who want to do it all by themselves.

To overcome these shortcomings, three experts suggest that the hero archetype needs to be present in every single team member. Expert B_Aca_G explained why the hero archetype is more powerful if present in every team member:

> I think in principle it takes a certain courage, a certain revolutionary willingness to sacrifice, and determination to get the startup, a startup project, moving forward, so you need this hero type, or at least this determination, this willingness to get involved, this having the courage, being just or selfless, that's what you need for sure, you almost need it, I think, from all team members, I would almost find it more of a hindrance if there was only one, to come back to people, so to have only one hero in the team, I would find it rather dangerous, because then he works himself into burnout for the team, for the startup team, but in principle it needs this heroic character, everyone needs it to a certain extent (B_Aca_G, translated from German)

The hero archetype reveals his true strength if looked at from a team-level perspective instead of individual team members.

At this point it is helpful to borrow a concept from media studies: the group hero archetype. Hall (2016) introduced the concept of the group hero archetype in a study of the mass movies *The Avengers* and *Guardians of the Galaxy*. It presents an alternative to the classical hero's journey, where a lone hero is the focal point of everything. In a group hero story, a team composed of unique characters with individual strengths and weaknesses is united by their dedication to a larger cause. Everyone contributes their special abilities, leadership is situationally skill-based, and the members overcome their internal quarrels for the greater good. While each member gets their moment to shine, in the end the group is the hero and no one individual could have accomplished the task on their own (ibid, p. 219).

Hall (2016) observes that this group hero plotline is increasingly overtaking the lone hero tale in Western mass media like movies or online role-playing games and has been present in other cultures for a long time (p. 215). She explains its emergence with the growing complexity and interdependence of the modern world: "As a psychosocial archetype, the group hero reflects psychosocial processes occurring within humanity, in this case the emerging awareness of interconnectedness and the need for groups to unite to overcome current social problems" (Hall, 2016, p. 227).

This mirrors the evolution of entrepreneurship research, which initially fell for the myth of the entrepreneur as a lone hero and only turned to the startup team once it realized that entrepreneurship is a social undertaking (Vanaelst et al., 2006, p. 430).

Hall (2016) suggests to deliberately employ the group hero archetype in storytelling for good purposes, citing school bullying as a potential application area. With the present book we suggest that the group hero archetype is also a very powerful narrative for startup teams: determination, commitment, and skill are needed from every team member. But in the volatile and complex entrepreneurship world, a single team member could not raise the startup alone. The idea of "the team as hero" has already been taken up in the entrepreneurship literature (Francis & Sandberg, 2000, p. 5). Like *The Avengers*, the members of a startup team need to take their ego down a bit, overcome their quarrels, and work together for their common cause. Refer to Table 7.8 for a detailed profile of the hero archetype's role in startup teams (Fig. 7.7).

Table 7.8 Archetypical profile for startups—hero. Source: Own representation

Hero + All three basic motivational systems Autonomy, safety, and excitement	*Self-sacrificing*	Additional tasks are no problem for a team member, if he/she can achieve an improvement for everyone
	Brave	A team member is convinced that far-reaching changes can only be achieved with the necessary readiness to take risks
	Determined	A team member has a strong inner drive to put into practice what he/she has said
Characteristics	Dedicated to a greater purpose, caring, ready to self-sacrifice, determined, risk-taking, resilient, optimistic	
Role in a startup	In individuals: This person will solve any problem, overcome any crisis, and give their all to the cause, they will inspire others to keep believing in the idea and in the team Group hero archetype: The hero archetype is most powerful on the group level—like *The Avengers*, the startup team members overcome their quarrels and contribute their specific talents to the common goal; the team is the hero, not the individuals	
Moment to shine	The hero is needed in times of crisis: When he went down, he gets up and tries again. He inspires the team to persevere	
Light side	The hero makes sacrifices to keep the vision alive	
Shadow side	The hero thinks he can do everything alone and excludes others. He works until exhaustion and pushes others to the fringes	

Fig. 7.7 Symbolical representation of the hero. Source: Pätzmann (2020)

7.6 Rebel

The rebel archetype is very common in the startup world. Nine experts emphasized its importance, while six interviewees stressed its shortcomings. In his best sense, the rebel constitutes an execution-oriented version of the artist. He is lateral thinking and determined to execute his idea against all odds. Like the artist, he leaves established trails, thinks outside of the box to find workarounds, and dares to challenge the status quo of an industry. It takes a good deal of rebelliousness to continue persisting on an innovative idea, which is generally not easily recognized by the outside world. A rebel is an independent thinker, not a blind follower. In an act of creative destruction, a rebellious entrepreneur turns an industry's rules on the table: "of course, when you get into an industry with a startup, you have to break the rules, not by law, but by saying how can I navigate established, entrenched patterns?" (D_Fou_G, translated from German). This innovativeness attracts other bright team members. The rebel's traits of persistence and self-confidence are success factors for startups (Brattström, 2019, p. 9). Still, the rebel archetype must be kept in check to avoid crossing boundaries that would spell the demise of the startup: breaking laws or evading taxes are taboo.

Three experts pointed out that the rebel is dangerous if his recalcitrance constantly turns against his own team. Challenging leadership decisions with constructive criticism can at times be to the benefit of the startup and help to avoid the trap of groupthink, as stated by experts N_Fou_K, J_Men_K, and H_Fou_I. Constantly undermining decisions, however, wrecks group cohesion, destroys processes, creates chaos, and dilutes the vision. The rebel undertakes a balancing act between constructive critique and destructive criticizing. Expert N_Fou_K put it as follows:

> in most cases it would be now a rebel is not agreeing to the vision of the startup and if somebody becomes rebellious in an honest manner because they honestly believe maybe the way the leader is taking the vision and the mission is not right (…) in a positive manner to now correct the leader and now give them a better opinion or perspective, I think that can be something to build the startup, but if they are not even providing an alternative to what they are rebelling, that definitely means they are just maybe malicious or just disobedient. (N_Fou_K)

Expert H_Fou_I expressed a similar view, stressing the importance of challenging from within:

> but if you have someone that is also rebel, okay, then he's taking the role of the challenging guy, he will challenge everything, and this is a good thing, because you need someone that will help the managing team and the founding team to challenge themselves, and why is that? In the end, the managing team and the founding team is looking for clarity in a space where there is almost zero clarity, so they build theories, okay, based on assumptions, because this is what you have, the actual business clarity and the actual technical clarity is still not there, but this is the job, to find it and it takes time, so usually the managing team and the founding team they will create assumptions and they will base a lot of theories and a lot of decisions on those assumptions, and because they are looking for their own confidence and they need it for their confidence to be able to be mentors and leaders and all the things we discussed before they usually they do not challenge themselves enough, so having someone that they trust on the one hand and is part of the team, but on the other hand is all the time challenging, is extremely important; but this is a very tricky one because he, if he's not part of the team, and he's only challenging all the time then it's a catastrophe because there is no productivity in the process, so it's a very very sensitive one, but some level of rebelness within the team you need to have, but it's impossible in my opinion if you have someone that is only a rebel, it needs to be a rebel and something else
>
> I: rebel and friend, rebel and mentor?
>
> R: rebel and friend, rebel and mentor, rebel and a technical expert, rebel and a team member. (H_Fou_I)

In sum, the rebel archetype is most helpful if it either appears on a group level to turn over the rules of an existing industry, or in an individual team member in conjunction with another team role. As long as the rebel is following the team's vision, challenging from within can protect the startup against many perils from outside. Kostera (2012) observed a similarly thin line for organizational troublemakers: deviating behavior creates value, but overdoing it creates desolation (p. 166). This warns founders to choose their cofounders based on their passion and commitment to the same vision. A team member with the most brilliant technical abilities can turn out to be a mismatch if he or she does not commit to the strategy. Table 7.9 summarizes the rebel's strengths and weaknesses and Table 7.10 shows the rebel anti-archetype's complete profile for startup teams (Fig. 7.8).

Table 7.9 Strengths and weaknesses of the rebel anti-archetype

Idea generation	External	Internal
+ Lateral thinking + Creative destruction	– Breaks laws + Questions the status quo of an industry	+ Challenges groupthink – Destroys cohesion – Undermines decisions and vision

Key: + strength, - weakness
Source: Own representation

Table 7.10 Archetypical profile for startups—rebel. Source: Own representation

Rebel autonomy – Subjection	Anarchistic	A team member does not fit into any system
	Lateral thinking	The further a team member moves away from the routines, the more new things emerge for him/her
	Lawless	A team member breaks existing rules according to his/her own discretion
Characteristics	Lateral thinking, execution-focused, determined, self-confident, disobedient, daring	
Role in a startup	Idea generation: + lateral thinking, + creative destruction External effects: – breaks laws, + questions the status quo of an industry Internal effects: + challenges groupthink, - destroys cohesion, - undermines decisions	
Moment to shine	Like the artist, the rebel leaves well-trodden paths of thought and comes up with daring new ideas during ideation. Unlike the artist, the rebel has the courage and energy to execute them and to follow through against the common opinion or authorities	
Light side	The rebel has the courage to do things differently	
Shadow side	The rebel can kill the startup by crossing the line of laws or taboos or working against the team's common vision	

Fig. 7.8 Symbolical representation of the rebel. Source: Pätzmann (2020)

7.7 Femme Fatale

The femme fatale anti-archetype undertakes a similar balancing act. The experts are split about her significance for a startup. Three experts find her insignificant, three find her harmful, and four acknowledge that this type commonly exists. Five experts do see the femme fatale's importance for a startup's success, and one distinguishes whether the femme fatale archetype has an internal (destructive) or external (helpful) effect. The femme fatale is seductive, attractive to others, ambitious, and goal oriented. At the same time, she can be manipulative, self-confident up to the point of arrogance, narcissistic, and wants to be seen as the best at any price. Her advantages can be understood by recalling the ratings of her three statements in the quantitative expert survey: the two traits manipulative and seductive received an equally good ranking, with irresistible falling behind.

Some percentage of the femme fatale archetype is unavoidable in a startup because the founders must convince others to contribute resources to their idea when it is just that: an idea. A talent to attract and charm others helps to sell the idea to fellow cofounders, investors, and customers. The femme fatale is a champion of "storytelling, making something attractive and creating a fear of missing out" (G_Inv_I). Lean startup techniques which call for early customer feedback require a certain boldness to present unfinished and imperfect products to the market. Similarly, the femme fatale excels in recruiting resources like human or financial capital. She is "the hustler, the one who always can get us everything that we want" (E_Men_I). Even in the startup's leadership the femme fatale archetype is necessary. A young firm usually does not have much to offer to cofounders and employees in terms of salary and benefits. In alliance with the mentor, friend, and hero archetypes, the femme fatale helps to win people over without authority. Convincing others instead of ordering is a must in organizations with flat hierarchies. As long as the femme fatale's goals are in line with the startup's vision, "by the time that person reaches their goal the whole startup will have succeeded" (O_Fou_K). However, the line between motivating and manipulating is thin.

The ugly side of the femme fatale comes to light if this thin line is crossed. Manipulation and dishonesty destroy trust within the team. The femme fatale encourages her team members to overwork up to the point of burnout and does not care for others' wellbeing. Damaging behaviors like free riding, stealing others' accomplishments, or prioritizing personal interests over the startup will backfire. She will not manage to deceive people forever, at some point the fake role will be uncovered. Therefore, persons with a high femme fatale percentage cannot sustain a strong team in the long run. Once the mask falls, others will keep their distance and only weak personalities fail to escape. As demonstrated in Chap. 2, entrepreneurial team research has repeatedly substantiated the importance of trust and loyalty to a shared vision. This applies also to customers and business partners. Depending on the nature of the industry, loss of trust can be fatal. Especially in B2B sales, longevity of relationships is key. In B2C, false promises destroy the brand's reputation. Figure 7.9 visualizes the femme fatale's balancing act. The two mechanisms work both inside the team and toward external stakeholders. The femme fatale archetype only becomes valuable if her exceptional attraction skills are paired with moral integrity.

The femme fatale archetype can be understood as a personification of Machiavellianism. This concept describes a person's willingness to employ even unethical means to reach their goals. Besides a tendency to amoral manipulation, it also includes the desire for status and control, as well as distrust of others (Schippers et al., 2019, p. 2 f). Schippers et al. (2019) explored whether Machiavellians are more attracted to entrepreneurship than others. In a study with early-stage entrepreneurial teams, they found support for their hypothesis that an inclination toward Machiavellianism's

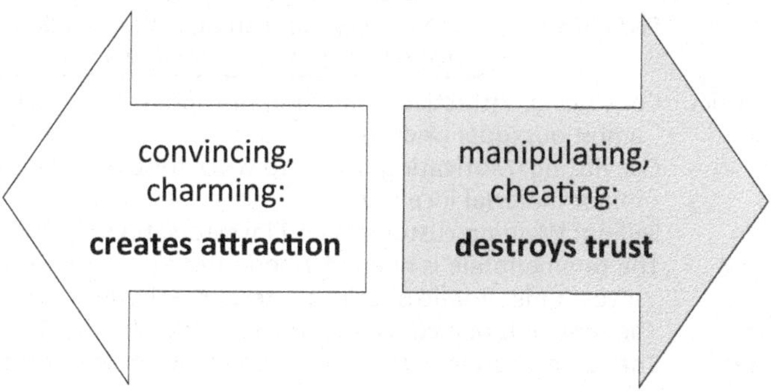

Fig. 7.9 The two sides of the femme fatale. Source: Own representation

sub-dimensions "amoral manipulation" and "desire for control" increase entrepreneurial intentions. Its downsides can be moderated by team resilience.

Respondent O_Fou_K brought in yet another perspective on the femme fatale archetype. He maintained that the femme fatale can also be a great motivator if embodied in an external authority. He gave an example from a university-based incubator setting:

> for example, if I have a group of young people and one professor, so to me that professor can be the femme fatale, you need to impress your professor that you know we have a nice idea you are part of the team and we will deliver by a certain date and then you can give us your input on our outcome (O_Fou_K)

The femme fatale can be embodied in any figure of authority who is critical for the next milestone, for example, an external mentor, an investor, a regulative body, or a significant B2B client. The desire to impress such a figure is a powerful motivating force that brings the startup forward, but it can also lead to overworking and exhaustion. Table 7.11 expounds on the femme fatale's profile for startup teams in detail (Fig. 7.10).

Table 7.11 Archetypical profile for startups—femme fatale. Source: Own representation

Femme fatale Excitement – Fear	*Irresistible*	Others would prefer to spend their time exclusively with a team member
	Manipulative	A team member is aware of his/her effect on others and uses it skillfully
	Seductive	A team member can get others to do things for him/her in a charming way
Characteristics	Convincing, attractive, charming, manipulating, cheating, ambitious, goal oriented	
Role in a startup	Convincing: Motivating others to work for the startup with minor material incentives Selling: Winning customers and investors, finding resources	
Moment to shine	The femme fatale is needed when others must be won to invest time, finances, or other resources in the startup	
Light side	The femme fatale convinces others to invest in her idea	
Shadow side	The femme fatale destroys trust and favors self-interest over the startup	

Fig. 7.10 Symbolical representation of the rebel. Source: Pätzmann (2020)

7.8 Manager

In addition, the experts highlighted some personality traits which they did not directly relate to the archetypical model. Some of those traits can be found in the model student and coward: subject matter expertise, analytic and systematic thinking, carefulness, and risk aversion. These roles are often unpopular in the bold and flashy world of entrepreneurship. A critical voice and cool, calculating head are, however, a necessary counterweight to the enthusiastic and risk-taking startup spirit. This helps to filter opportunities and to discriminate those worth pursuing from dead-ends. Expert C_Inv_G formulated it as follows:

> who makes sure that you don't overstretch yourself, that you are careful with your resources, that you always have enough air, that you are on the road on time, that you don't take any unacceptable risks, that you slow down a bit? So, where is the person who practically limits the hero and the mentor or the leader, who provides security and stability, where is that person? (C_Inv_G, translated from German)

This aspect might be embedded in the coward archetype but should not be so negatively connotated. The analytic and calculating dimension is not fully represented in the model student either. It is not about learning; it is about thinking things through in a systematic way. Expert C_Inv_G explained: "if someone says we want to do it this way and that way, then the first thing she says is: 'where is the budget?' secondly: 'where is the investment calculation?'" (C_Inv_G, translated from German). In other words: "someone who negotiates with reality" (F_Aca_I). Although entrepreneurship builds a new reality, it can only succeed if it does not stretch the present reality too much. Similar traits were mentioned by eight experts in total. The archetypical model was developed based on visible figures and thus overlooks those who work quietly in the background.

An overarching theme of these traits is: business administration; cool calculating, systematic management. Therefore, it makes sense to introduce an additional role: *the manager*. In contrast to the entrepreneur, the manager is understood as an unglamorous, operational resource guard (Czarniawska-Joerges & Wolff, 1991, p. 532), who "is focused upon the mundane performance of the organization, administrates and coordinates people and resources" (Kociatkiewicz & Kostera, 2010, p. 863). Besides, Kostera (2012) imparts: "The manager's domain is everyday work, ordering, looking after the organization. The role is less spectacular but very useful" (p. 140). This emotionless roll-out of the business side of things, however, is critical even in the shiny world of entrepreneurship.

While business administration skills and carefulness are important from the beginning, they gain significance with growth, when the firm leaves the startup phase and becomes an established company. Investor C_Inv_G talked about the necessity of adding experienced managers to a company's top management team when it reaches a certain growth level: someone "who has taught them some structures, processes, meetings, and whatnot, and also budgeting processes, a technocrat who also has no content-related aspirations, but who just rolls it out" (C_Inv_G, translated from German). Wasserman (2012) describes a similar dilemma for entrepreneurs: Their heart and soul goes into their business, but once it reaches a certain level of maturity, it outgrows the startup phase. Entrepreneurs often do not have the right personality for running a large enterprise. At this point, many investors, therefore, demand to replace the founder and idea generator with an experienced manager (Wasserman, 2012, p. 207). Table 7.12 details the manager's role in a startup team (Fig. 7.11).

Table 7.12 Archetypical profile for startups—manager. Source: Own representation

Characteristics	Coordinating, cautious, analytic, systematic, sensible, reliable
Role in a startup	Carefulness: Cautions against taking too many or too risky opportunities, voice of reason Rationality: He has an analytic way of working, coordinates, administers, manages, thinks systematically, and takes decisions based on data and evidence Subject matter expertise: The manager has know-how in business administration or other regulative areas
Moment to shine	This archetype is specific to startups. Throughout the startup journey, it should be present to mold a bold idea into a viable business model. It becomes crucial when the startup is expanding into an established business and finally needs systematic processes and organization
Light side	The manager administers the business and gives structure to the company
Shadow side	At heart, the manager is the antithesis to entrepreneurship: He manages resources instead of seizing opportunities

Fig. 7.11 Symbolical representation of the manager. Source: Own representation

7.9 Who Else Is Needed

In addition to the seven most significant (anti-)archetypes plus the manager, others also stood out as pertinent in the expert interviews, namely the amazon, the explorer, the genius, the happy nature, the model student, and the angel. The mother was mentioned in alliance with the friend. Among the anti-archetypes, the diva, tyrant, materialist, psychopath, avenger, traitor, idiot, slave, and coward were mentioned. These results overlap but are not fully congruent with the quantitative survey.

The amazon is a personification of emancipation, growth, and self-confidence. Outgoing communication and social networking are a must in a startup. Founders need to have negotiation and pitching skills. They must show their own initiative, confidence, assertiveness, decisiveness, and adaptability to new circumstances. They must be willing to fail and have the energy to restart all over. Extroversion is important in a startup but expert K_Men_K mentioned the job-sharing within the team: some team members are happy to do the work in the background, while others enjoy the spotlight. They must understand entrepreneurship as a journey of learning and personal development. Expert E_Men_I called it "the rockstar"—someone who is extroverted and confident enough to present their business idea in front of an audience. He cited an example of an entrepreneur who started out very shy and timid and after a few years presented like a rockstar—the amazon archetype has become stronger. Interviewee N_Fou_K narrated a similar learning journey. In order to move a startup from ideation to market validation, an entrepreneur needs to learn to switch from the creative artist who works in the closet to the outspoken, extroverted amazon.

The explorer is an even more pronounced representation of this willingness to learn. He is a close companion to the artist but has a more outgoing quality. Instead of quietly working in the closet on the details of the prototype, the explorer goes out into the world to better understand customers and competition and to fully comprehend the solution-independent customer problem. Being curious and inquisitive, the explorer is the personification of lean startup and design thinking principles. His strengths are in product development, but also sales and marketing.

The genius was identified as highly relevant for product development, even though it ranked surprisingly low in the quantitative survey. All Israeli respondents plus two Germans and three Kenyans granted the genius higher relevancy than its ranking in the quantitative survey. Exceptional technical skill is especially relevant in the high-tech sector. Geniuses are often highly talented beyond formal education; they can implement stunning ideas and solve even the most difficult technical challenge. They are "these guys who will actually make it work" (E_Men_I). The genius can be very powerful in conjunction with the hero archetype. Having such a talented and committed individual on board will provide the team with the good feeling that they can overcome any challenge.

The happy nature is very useful to keep up a team's morale, as highlighted by six interviewees. He is resilient in the face of uncertainty and failure, believes in the idea, and optimistically takes action. Expert E_Men_I maintained that optimism is at the core of entrepreneurship—founders dedicate themselves to their idea even though the failure rates are so high. If personified in an individual, the happy nature's good-hearted humor can relieve tension and cheer up the team's morale even in the darkest moments. Expert M_Inv_K cited a personal experience with a happy nature personality:

> in my team I have one such person and I find it interesting working with them because I think even at the hardest or difficult times they're still able to just make out of it going even to the extent of giving the team morale; probably things might not be working but they'll still be able to have the team, the team members in high spirits, might be also just in conversations, jokes coming out here and there, that he has been able to break sometimes that tension that is there (M_Inv_K)

A happy nature is needed to face frustrations when bringing the product to the market, and it is very useful in sales. This confirms the happy nature's comparatively high ranking in the survey.

The model student, next in line, also received great attention from nine experts. The model student is reliable, exact, systematic, analytical, careful, and diligent. He thoroughly thinks things through and thus counterbalances the rebellious assertiveness otherwise characterizing entrepreneurship. Such a person is also needed to avoid pitfalls of imperfect products or getting lost in the enthusiasm for an apparently great idea that is not backed by sufficient market potential. He may conflict with the artist, rebel, leader, or other execution-focused personalities, but for the best of the startup. The model student also represents solid subject matter expertise and continued learning. An overrepresentation of the model student archetype can, however, also be harmful, because he cannot move fast enough for a startup. The desire to keep learning and looking out for details is hindering to fast decision-making based on limited information. The model student's cautioning can be more helpful once the first bold steps have successfully been taken.

A number of anti-archetypes were also mentioned. The diva and materialist are figures which often can be found in an entrepreneurship context. Like the femme fatale, they contribute an aspect of execution focus and high levels of motivation. On the downside, they lead to too much drama, do not want to dirty their hands, and purely monetary motivations are not sufficient to survive the inevitable crises. Avenger and traitor are not per se useful anti-archetypes, but they are often present as strong motivators with an external focus, whereby founders try to compete with former employers out of hurt pride. Similarly, the psychopath personifies narcissism which is not helpful but often represented. The tyrant encompasses the negative aspects of the leader which are at times also necessary to get things going but need to be carefully contained. Idiot, slave, angel, or coward signify those modest team members who do the actual work without taking center stage.

References

Belbin, R. M. (2010). *Team roles at work* (2nd ed.). Routledge.

Brattström, A. (2019). Working with startups? These are the three things you ought to know about startup teams. *Technology Innovation Management Review, 9*(11), 5–14. https://doi.org/10.22215/timreview/1279

Chowdhury, S. (2005). Demographic diversity for building an effective entrepreneurial team: Is it important? *Journal of Business Venturing, 20*(6), 727–746.

Czarniawska-Joerges, B., & Wolff, R. (1991). Leaders, managers, entrepreneurs on and off the organizational stage. *Organization Studies, 12*(4), 529–546.

Kenya National Innovation Agency. (n.d.). *Enabling innovation for socio-economic development.* Retrieved Jan 29 2022 from https://www.innovationagency.go.ke/

Foo, M.-D., Sin, H.-P., & Yiong, L.-P. (2006). Effects of team inputs and intrateam processes on perceptions of team viability and member satisfaction in nascent ventures. *Strategic Management Journal, 27*(4), 389–399.

Francis, D. H., & Sandberg, W. R. (2000). Friendship within entrepreneurial teams and its association with team and venture performance. *Entrepreneurship Theory and Practice, 25*(2), 5–26.

Franke, N., Gruber, M., Harhoff, D., & Henkel, J. (2008). Venture Capitalists' evaluations of start-up teams: Trade-offs, Knock-out criteria, and the impact of VC experience. *Entrepreneurship Theory and Practice, 32*(3), 459–483.

Gopalkrishnan, S. (2017). The role of humor in startup success: The mediating role of team performance. *Journal of Organizational Psychology, 17*(3), 9–23.

Hall, C. (2016). The group hero: An archetype whose time has come. In S. B. Schafer (Ed.), *Exploring the collective unconscious in the age of digital media* (pp. 214–231). IGI Global.

Klotz, A. C., Hmieleski, K. M., Bradley, B. H., & Busenitz, L. W. (2013). New venture teams: A review of the literature and roadmap for future research. *Journal of Management, 40*(1), 226–255. https://doi.org/10.1177/0149206313493325

Kociatkiewicz, J., & Kostera, M. (2010). Experiencing the shadow: Organizational exclusion and denial within experience economy. *Organization, 17*(2), 257–282.

Kociatkiewicz, J., & Kostera, M. (2012). The good manager: An archetypical quest for morally sustainable leadership. *Organization Studies, 33*(7), 861–878. https://doi.org/10.1177/0170840612445124

Kostera, M. (2012). *Organizations and archetypes*. Edward Elgar.

Lechler, T. (2001). Social interaction: A determinant of entrepreneurial team venture success. *Small Business Economics, 16*(4), 263–278.

Pätzmann, J. (2020). Of heroes & Destroyers.. Hochschule Neu-Ulm.

Pätzmann, J., & Hartwig, J. (2018). *Markenführung mit Archetypen*. Springer Gabler.

Pearson, A. W., Ensley, M. D., & Amason, A. C. (2002). Understanding the dynamics of new venture top management teams: Cohesion, conflict, and new venture performance. *Journal of Business Venturing, 17*(4), 365–386.

Ruef, M. (2010). *The entrepreneurial group: Social identities, relations, and collective action*. Princeton University Press.

Schippers, M. C., Rauch, A., Belschak, F. D., & Hulsink, W. (2019). Entrepreneurial intentions of teams: Sub-dimensions of Machiavellianism interact with team resilience. *Frontiers in Psychology, 10*. https://doi.org/10.3389/fpsyg.2019.02607

Vanaelst, I., Clarysse, B., Wright, M., Lockett, A., Moray, N., & S'Jergers, R. (2006). Entrepreneurial team development in academic spinouts: An examination of team heterogeneity. *Entrepreneurship Theory and Practice, 30*(2), 249–271.

Wasserman, N. (2012). *The founder's dilemmas: Anticipating and avoiding the pitfalls that can sink a startup*. Princeton University Press.

West, G. P., III. (2007). Collective cognition: When entrepreneurial teams, not individuals, make decisions. *Entrepreneurship Theory and Practice, 31*(1), 77–102.

Wright, M., & Vanaelst, I. (2009). *Entrepreneurial teams and new business creation*. Edward Elgar.

8

How (Anti-)Archetypes Interact in Startup Teams

In successful startup teams, the eight different (anti-)archetypes interact in a balanced way. They can be understood as dynamics that are enacted by individual team members or appear on a group level. One person can incorporate more than one archetype and shift by situation and over time. Depending on the founding phase, the significance of individual (anti-)archetypes shifts, and conflicting archetypes must balance each other out. Section 8.1 explains how the significant (anti-)archetypes interact within a startup and Sect. 8.2 looks at their shifting significance throughout a startup's journey. Section 8.3 analyzes the interaction of (anti-)archetypes by means of fictitious, close-to-reality case studies.

8.1 Relationships Between (Anti-)Archetypes

The eight archetypical roles interact in a balanced way to create a powerful startup team. Their relationship is visualized in Fig. 8.1. It is important to emphasize that archetypes do not correspond to individual team members. They are dynamics that can be enacted by individual team members or appear on a group level. One person can incorporate more than one archetype and shift by situation and over time.

V. Miller, J. U. Pätzmann, *Archetypical Roles in Startups*, Business Guides on the Go,
https://doi.org/10.1007/978-3-031-22253-5_8

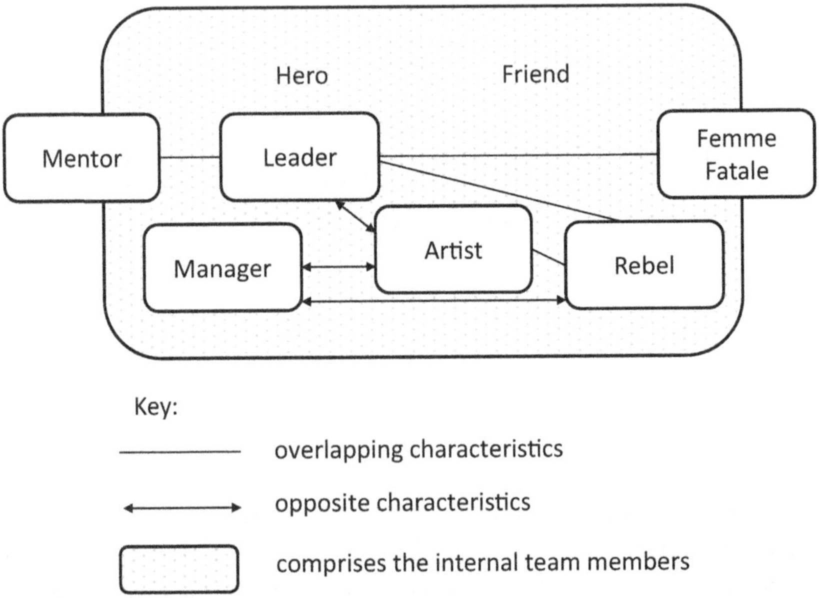

Fig. 8.1 Relationship between the eight archetypes in startups. Source: Own representation

As the key player, the leader archetype is in the center. He may overlap with the mentor, but the mentor may also be represented by an external person from the assistance network. The leader may also appear in conjunction with the femme fatale or the rebel.

The rebel and artist fulfill similar roles in the startup, whereby the artist is more concentrated on internal idea development and the rebel has a stronger execution focus on the external world. The rebel should appear in conjunction with another archetype to contain its dangerous sides. Similarly, the femme fatale is only helpful if aligned with the startup's goals. She can also be present in an external authority. The manager is the counterweight to the artist and rebel, who checks the feasibility of brilliant ideas with expertise and sound caution.

The friend and hero archetypes are overarching. They may be represented by individual team members, but in many cases, they are more powerful on a group level. In a nutshell, there must be enough similarity to allow for trust and understanding between the team members, but sufficient difference to allow for separate roles and diversity of ideas. The presence of the friend archetype helps to foster mutual understanding even across different thinking styles.

8.2 (Anti-)Archetypes Throughout the Startup Journey

Startup teams are dynamic entities which evolve over time and experience team member turnover (Brattström, 2019, p. 9; Brattström et al., 2020, p. 16; Foo et al., 2006; Quigley et al., 2018, p. 2; Vanaelst et al., 2006, p. 249; Wright & Vanaelst, 2009, p. xvii). Taking together the findings from the expert interviews, a shift in the archetypes' relevancy over the evolution of the startup stages can be observed. In simplified terms, the development of a startup can be divided into three phases: ideation phase, startup phase, and mature phase. This is an adapted version of Wasserman's (2012) conceptualization. He emphasizes that not all departments of the company go through the phases at the same time (p. 207). Figure 8.2 contains a graphic visualization of the archetypes relevant to the three critical phases.

During ideation, the business idea is developed. The startup does not yet have significant resources or a formalized structure. During this stage, the artist archetype is highly relevant. He contributes creativity and lateral thinking. To eventually go places, he must be counterbalanced by the leader archetype, who brings a focus on execution and action.

In the subsequent startup phase, the product is taken to the market, the company is formalized, and external funding may be sought. This is when setbacks and frustrations start to hit. To survive those, the (group) hero archetype is needed. The femme fatale archetype helps to attract customers and investors. Following design thinking principles, ideation is an iterative process. Therefore, phases one and two often overlap. The rebel archetype is relevant in both phases. He brings in the courage to go forward with an imperfect prototype.

In the mature stage, the company is well funded and has revenue streams from its own products and services. It develops a structure with different departments and formalized processes. In short, it has matured

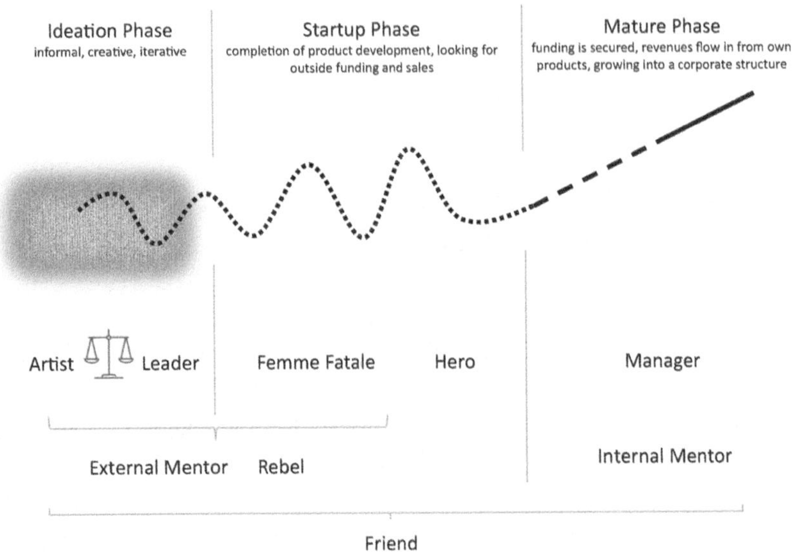

Fig. 8.2 Shift between archetypes over development phases. Source: Own representation

into an established organization. The transition between phases two and three is critical and not all entrepreneurs succeed to grow with their companies. This is where the story of entrepreneurship ends, and the manager comes in. The mentor is always relevant but shifts from external to internal with increasing company maturity. The overarching friend archetype is needed throughout the journey.

8.3 Exemplary Startup Journeys

The following three examples are fictitious cases of startups' founding journeys. They shed light on the collaboration between the cofounders. These fictional cases can be used to analyze how the different archetypes occur in individuals and at the group level and how they contribute to the success or failure of the startup. This shows how the results of the previous chapters can be used to purposefully manage the group dynamics in founding teams.

Example 1. Super-Software Ltd

Imagine Benny M., a brilliant software engineer. For some time now, he has been tinkering with an ingenious software solution for his own use, and he keeps refining it. He entrusts his project to his former colleague Fred, who immediately recognizes the business value in it. The two decide to bring the software to market together in a software-as-a-service business model. Benny continues to perfect the software while Fred considers where the revenues can come from, solicits feedback from potential customers, and looks for funding opportunities. They seek advice from an incubator that supports founders. This gives rise to the idea of trying out a business model that is unusual in the industry. Fred and Benny get along well, as they are both passionate about the idea and want to make their baby a success together. But there is always friction between the two, as Fred already wants to close the first deals, while Benny is still not satisfied with the prototype.

With the help of their mentor from the incubator, they nevertheless dare to take the next step and approach their first customers and investors. Fred is a good speaker who knows how to capture the attention of prospects with his enthusiasm. Setbacks always drag him down, but Benny, with his rock-solid belief in the idea and his sense of humor, manages to motivate them time and again and to overcome problems with unconventional solutions. Soon the first revenues are flowing in, and two more cofounders join in. The raw startup idea has become a small company that continues to grow. They have now reached a critical point where the informal and quick ad hoc completion of tasks repeatedly leads to chaos, problems, and extra work. Ultimately, the main investor insists on bringing in a CEO with a lot of business experience. In spite of the frictions, Benny and Fred remain important figures in the company, who inspire and guide inexperienced employees.

The interaction of the archetypes can be exemplified by this fictitious ideal case. Benny has a strong artist component in his personality, who lovingly refines his idea and always finds unconventional solutions to challenges. Fred, on the other hand, has a strong leader component. He pushes things forward and pragmatically moves on to the next milestone. In the initial phase, the external mentor from the incubator is also very important, without whom a clear roadmap would be missing. Both founders also embody the rebel, as they deliberately leave well-trodden paths by challenging common practices in the industry. The startup phase with its many setbacks is critical, but the two founders complement each other perfectly: Fred embodies the femme fatale and manages to get customers and investors excited about the business idea. Benny is a happy nature and has a very resilient personality. He can deal well with setbacks, and succeeds to activate the hero archetype at the group level. Another critical transition happens when the company starts to scale and outgrows its startup shoes. The investor's decision to bring in an experienced manager is painful but necessary. In this ideal case, the original founders find a new role and take on internal mentoring functions.

Example 2. Sustainable-Clothes Ltd

Very few startups proceed relatively harmoniously, as in the fictitious case of Super-Software Ltd. The failure of brilliant startup ideas can also be interpreted using the archetype model. Sustainable-Clothes Ltd. is an example of an archetypical imbalance in the founding team. Larissa, Conny, Melanie, and Anna studied together and became friends. During their time at university, they shared their love for fashion, but also developed ever greater concerns about the downsides of fast fashion.

Larissa is the one who has the idea to start a sustainable fashion company together. She also already has very concrete plans: Fairly and sustainably produced evening wear can be rented by customers for a fee. She is on fire for the idea and with her charm she convinces the others to give up their original career plans and start a company with her after graduation. She also convinces her partner Lewis, who already has a business background, to join the company. Thanks to his experience, they manage to achieve their first successes very early on.

After graduation, Larissa and Melanie dedicate themselves full-time to the startup. Lewis reduces his previous job to 75% and puts in countless hours of overtime at the startup. Conny and Anna also pursue other small side jobs in addition to their work at the startup to keep their heads above water. Initially, they finance the company through small loans and bootstrapping, as they want to be independent of large investors.

Once the company is officially founded, the question of how to divide the company shares arises. Larissa manages to get her own way and secures the largest shares for herself and for Lewis. Melanie, Conny, and Anna each receive equal shares. This decision soon stirs up resentment—Melanie feels disadvantaged because she invests more time than Conny and Anna, who only work part-time for the startup. The latter, in turn, argue that it is their additional earnings that make it possible for the startup to survive in the first place.

By reaching milestones thanks to Larissa's rousing pitches, the mood is lifted again. However, measurable financial successes remain a long time coming. The founding team keeps investing in the website, clothing selection, and adjustments to the business model, but they lack the financial resources to scale everything and change direction repeatedly. Melanie, in particular, becomes more and more dissatisfied and even goes so far as to override a mutual decision and launch a marketing campaign with a slogan the others disapproved. After 2 years, the team is severely disrupted, and the expected company growth fails to materialize. Melanie leaves the company, taking with her important business contacts and insider knowledge. Her exit also leads to heated discussions about how to deal with her company shares. Conny also increasingly turns to other jobs without officially quitting. Only Anna and Lewis remain loyal to the company. Particularly Larissa continues to push the business idea with all her might.

In this example, you can see a clear overemphasis on a single team member: Larissa is charismatic and very persuasive, which allows her to win others over to her and her cause. The weak side of this strong femme fatale profile is that she recruits and manipulates team members who are strongly under her influence but are not really willing to sacrifice their own dreams for the company's foundation. Also, due to this strong focus on one person, the hero archetype is not pronounced enough on the group level, but only on Larissa. She rocks everything but does not motivate her teammates sustainably as these recognize her selfishness. Due to this unfortunate constellation, Melanie increasingly embodies an internal rebel who ultimately takes disruptive decisions against the team. Even though the cofounders started out as a group of friends, the friend archetype on the group level was weakened over time by the numerous conflicts.

Example 3. Health-Robotics Ltd

Health-Robotics Ltd. is another fictional case of archetypical imbalance within a founding team. Frank is a professor at a technical university of applied sciences. He is a specialist in robotics applications in the health-care sector. Together with a group of researchers, he has been working on an innovation for complicated surgical operations for years. As the innovation matures, he and his two closest colleagues Mandy and Marc decide to bring the technology to market by founding their own startup.

They participate in an accelerator program and successfully complete the first financing phase. Against the advice of the investors, however, they decide not to add an experienced manager to their team. It is particularly important to Frank to successfully market this innovation on his own, as he worked for a company in the same industry before his appointment as a professor and still has hard feelings against his former boss. Having a successful company of his own would be his biggest triumph.

The cofounders focus on completing the prototype ready for the market and attracting their first customers. However, they neglect to observe the market and realize too late that there are now already powerful competing products out there. Because they are so fixated on their current product, which is the outcome of many years of research, they fail to make it attractive for the customers. In addition, there are always disagreements between Marc and Frank about the next step, so that they do not follow a coherent strategy, but half-heartedly chase after different opportunities. This lack of strategy and ability to adapt to changing market conditions prevents them from reaching important milestones and forces them to shut down the venture after 4 years of hard work.

In this example, you can observe that the artist archetype is abandoned too quickly. Frank and his colleagues assume that the product development phase is completed at the moment the startup is officially founded. They neglect gathering customer feedback (explorer) and adapting to changing market conditions through creative solutions (artist). Particularly Frank is deeply motivated by the avenger anti-archetype and therefore fiercely activates the leader in himself, which clashes with Marc's likewise strongly pronounced leader archetype. They do not pull together and do not manage to consistently implement a coherent business strategy. A stronger manager archetype is also missing here, which would have provided the critical view and the bridge to reality. A more present femme fatale archetype would have helped make the entire business model more attractive to customers.

References

Brattström, A. (2019). Working with startups? These are the three things you ought to know about startup teams. *Technology Innovation Management Review, 9*(11), 5–14. https://doi.org/10.22215/timreview/1279

Brattström, A., Delmar, F., Johnson, A. R., & Wennberg, K. (2020). A longitudinal project of new venture teamwork and outcomes. In *Research handbook on entrepreneurial behavior, practice and process* (pp. 309–334). Edward Elgar Publishing. https://doi.org/10.4337/9781788114523.00023.

Foo, M.-D., Sin, H.-P., & Yiong, L.-P. (2006). Effects of team inputs and intrateam processes on perceptions of team viability and member satisfaction in nascent ventures. *Strategic Management Journal, 27*(4), 389–399.

Quigley, N. R., Collins, C. G., Gibson, C. B., & Parker, S. K. (2018). Team performance archetypes: Toward a new conceptualization of team performance over time. *Group & Organization Management, 43*(5), 787–824.

Vanaelst, I., Clarysse, B., Wright, M., Lockett, A., Moray, N., & S'Jergers, R. (2006). Entrepreneurial team development in academic spinouts: An examination of team heterogeneity. *Entrepreneurship Theory and Practice, 30*(2), 249–271.

Wasserman, N. (2012). *The founder's dilemmas: Anticipating and avoiding the pitfalls that can sink a startup*. Princeton University Press.

Wright, M., & Vanaelst, I. (2009). *Entrepreneurial teams and new business creation*. Edward Elgar.

Part III

How to Work with Archetypical Team Roles

The preceding chapters have shown that archetype theory can be a useful instrument for startup teams. The research presented in this book revealed that there is an ideal setup of archetypical roles for startup teams. The (anti-)archetypes mentor, leader, friend, hero, artist, rebel, and femme fatale plus the manager have the greatest significance. Each (anti-)archetype has its distinct contribution to the startup team and throughout the development process. They need to counterbalance each other to avoid harmful predominance of any single one.

The archetypical model can be of great value for the entrepreneurship ecosystem if it is used wisely. Users must understand that archetypes, even though they are stylized in a personified fashion, are not personality types but themes which can act in individuals as well as on the team level. They can be represented by internal or external parties, and their effect can also be internal or external.

Chapter 9 presents a toolbox for working with archetypes: the whole set of 28 (anti-)archetypes according to Pätzmann and Hartwig (2018) and the validated archetypical personality test in a fillable version. Chapter 10 suggests methods on how to work with these in the entrepreneurship ecosystem. Chapter 11 explores further application fields for the archetypical personality test. Chapter 12 eventually sets the findings in context and highlights further interesting areas for research.

9

Archetypical Toolbox

9.1 Profiles of the 28 (Anti-)Archetypes

This section presents the 14 archetypes and 14 anti-archetypes according to the model by Pätzmann and Hartwig (2018). It was developed based on an empirical analysis of the 50 most successful blockbusters of the preceding decades, which were released in cinemas on all five continents (Pätzmann & Hartwig, 2018, p. 6). In the following, a visual representation and a profile based on their appearance in the movies are presented for each (anti-)archetype. In this form, the profiles are useful for brand building, for developing customer personas, for storytelling in marketing, and for emotionalizing business models.

When working with team dynamics in startups, the profiles presented in Chap. 7 should be used instead. The category scales old /young, female/ male, and good/evil are useful for storytelling, but when working with real human personalities, they are irrelevant and perpetuate stereotypes. Pätzmann and Hartwig's (2018) model is neatly ordered into 14

V. Miller, J. U. Pätzmann, *Archetypical Roles in Startups*, Business Guides on the Go,
https://doi.org/10.1007/978-3-031-22253-5_9

positively connotated archetypes and 14 negatively connotated anti-archetypes. Each anti-archetype corresponds to an archetype, which is either its antithesis or exaggeration. This dichotomization corresponds to humans' natural inclinations and its simplicity is very useful in storytelling. When applied to real personalities, however, it can reinforce prejudice and conflict. Therefore, the 8 profiles for startup teams as presented in Chap. 7 integrate the light and shadow sides of each (anti-)archetype (Figs. 9.1, 9.2, 9.3, 9.4, 9.5, 9.6, 9.7, 9.8, 9.9, 9.10, 9.11, 9.12, 9.13, 9.14, 9.15, 9.16, 9.17, 9.18, 9.19, 9.20, 9.21, 9.22, 9.23, 9.24, 9.25, 9.26, 9.27, 9.28, 9.29, 9.30, 9.31, 9.32, 9.33, 9.34, 9.35, 9.36, 9.37, 9.38, 9.39, 9.40, 9.41, 9.42, 9.43, 9.44, 9.45, 9.46, 9.47, 9.48, 9.49, 9.50, 9.51, 9.52, 9.53, 9.54, 9.55, 9.56, and 9.57).

Archetypical Motive Force Field

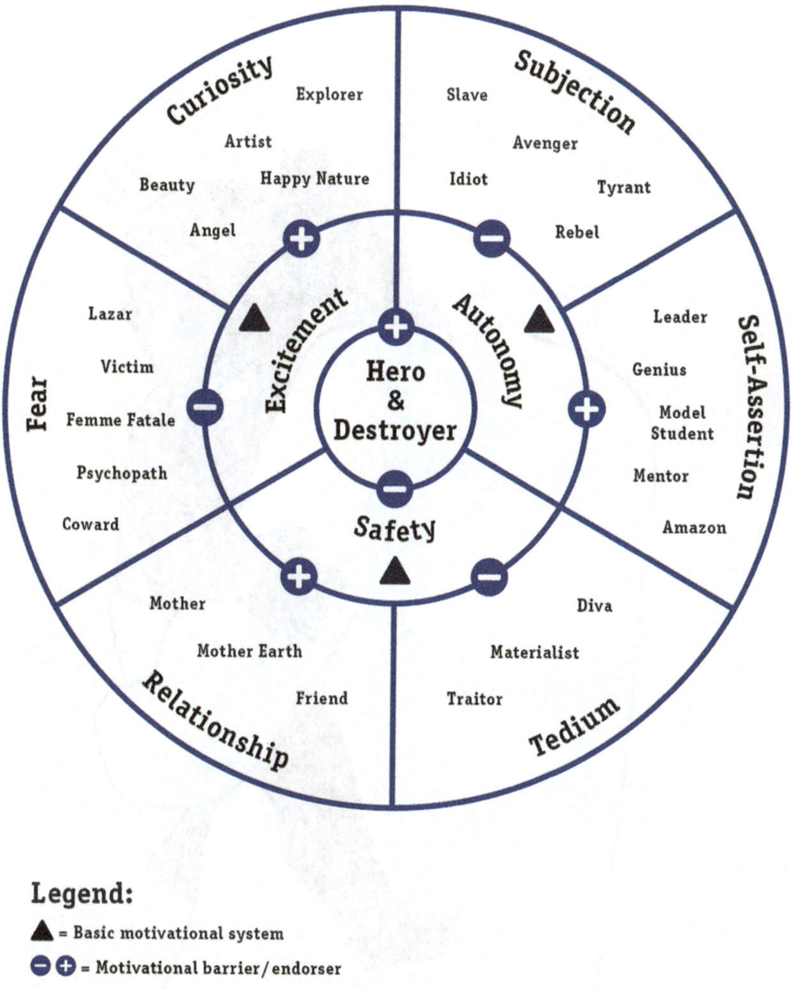

Fig. 9.1 Archetypical motive force field. Source: Pätzmann (2020)

Fig. 9.2 Symbolical representation of the archetype mother. Source: Pätzmann (2020)

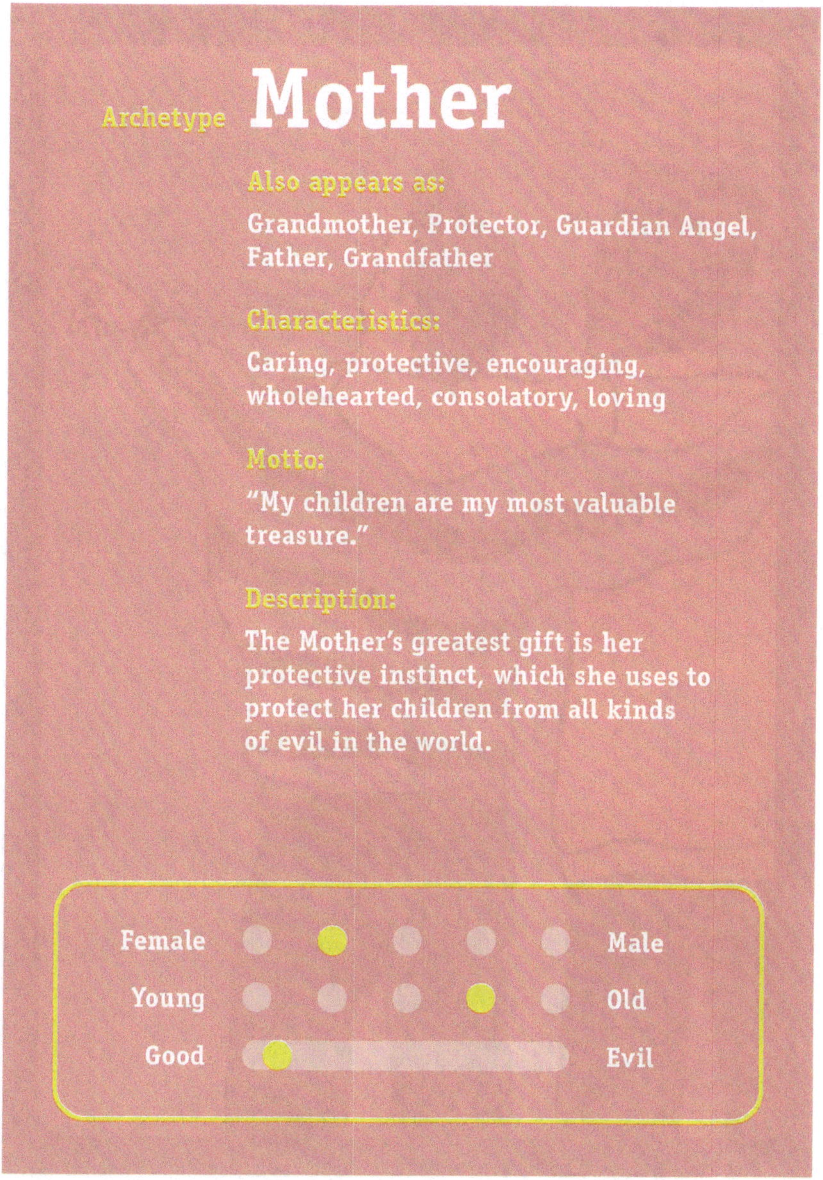

Fig. 9.3 Profile of the archetype mother. Source: Pätzmann (2020)

Fig. 9.4 Symbolical representation of the archetype friend. Source: Pätzmann (2020)

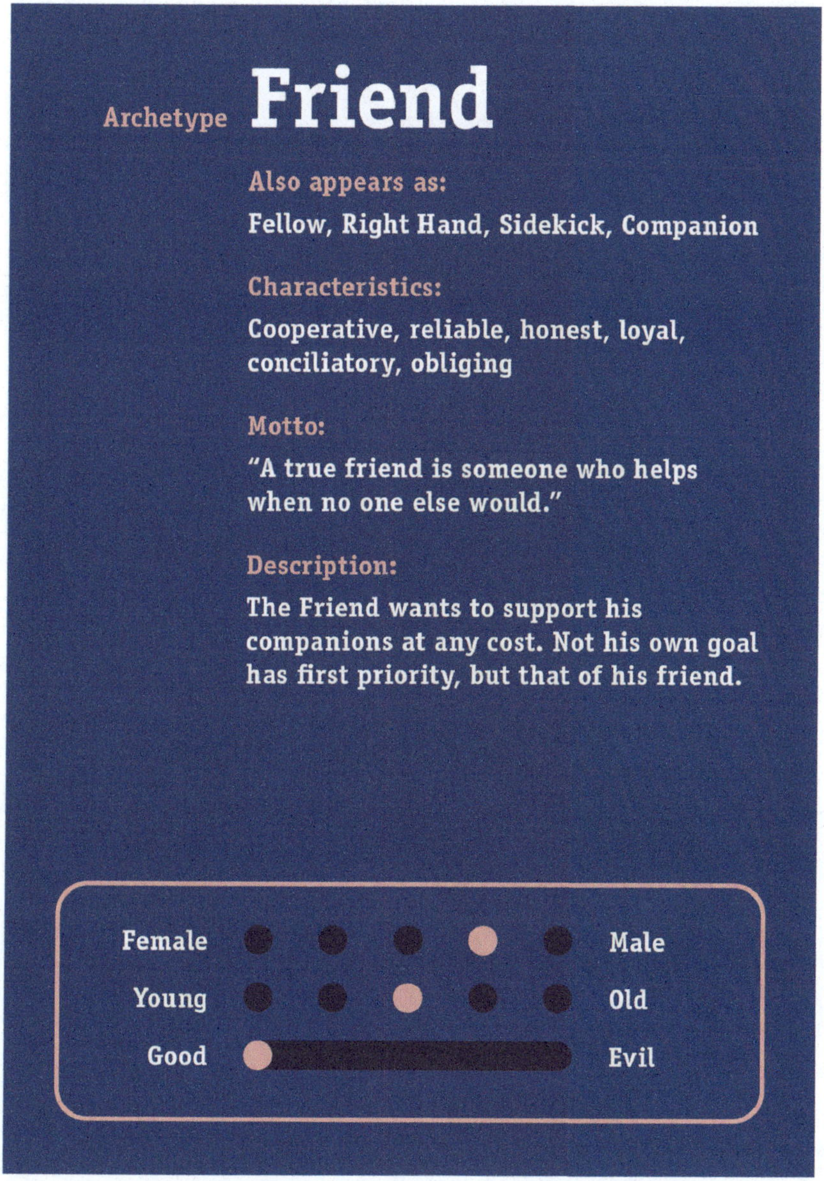

Fig. 9.5 Profile of the archetype friend. Source: Pätzmann (2020)

Fig. 9.6 Symbolical representation of the archetype mother earth. Source: Pätzmann (2020)

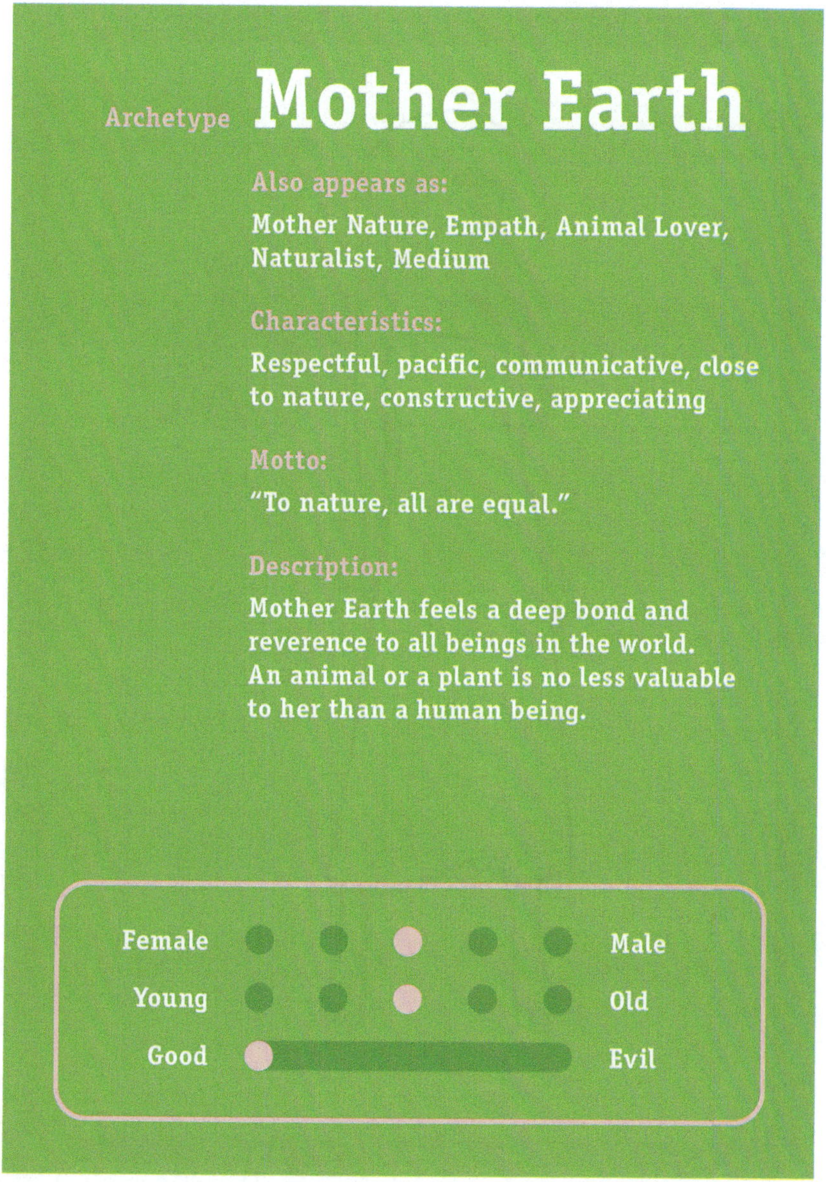

Fig. 9.7 Profile of the archetype mother earth. Source: Pätzmann (2020)

Fig. 9.8 Symbolical representation of the archetype angel. Source: Pätzmann (2020)

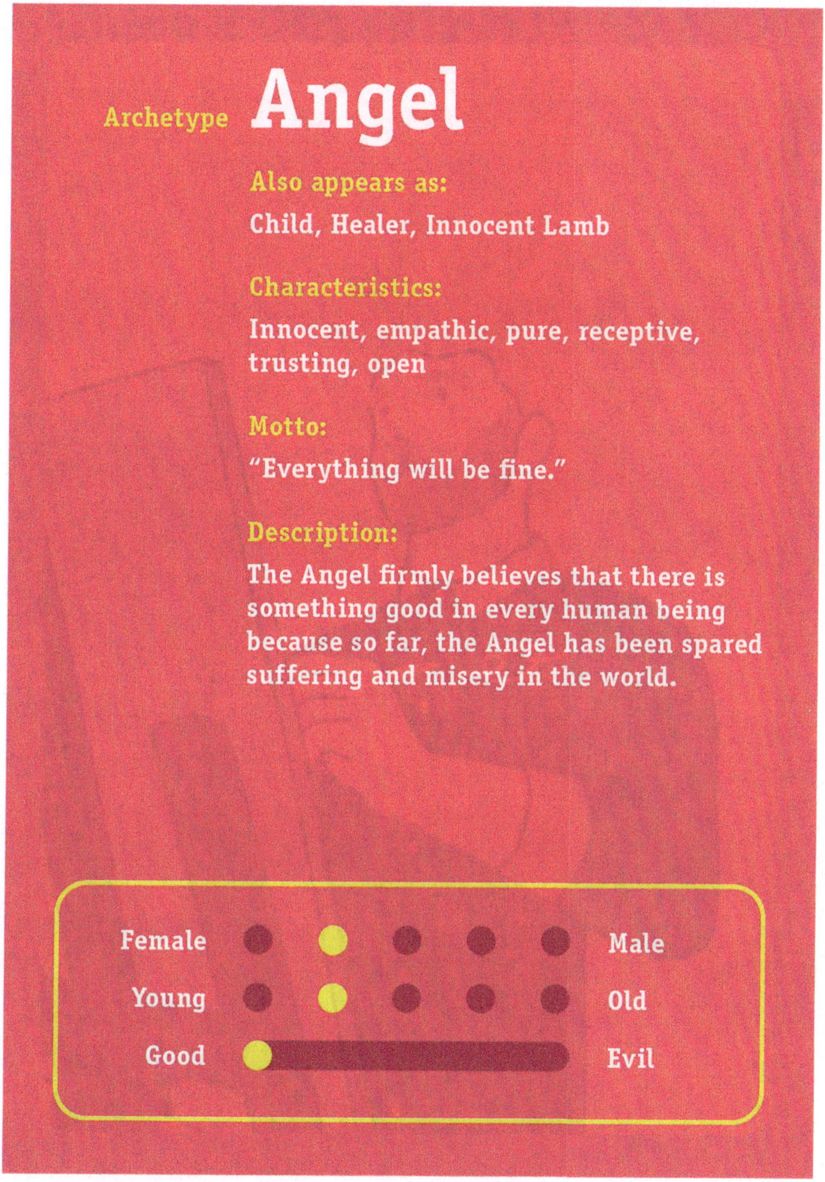

Fig. 9.9 Profile of the archetype angel. Source: Pätzmann (2020)

Fig. 9.10 Symbolical representation of the archetype artist. Source: Pätzmann (2020)

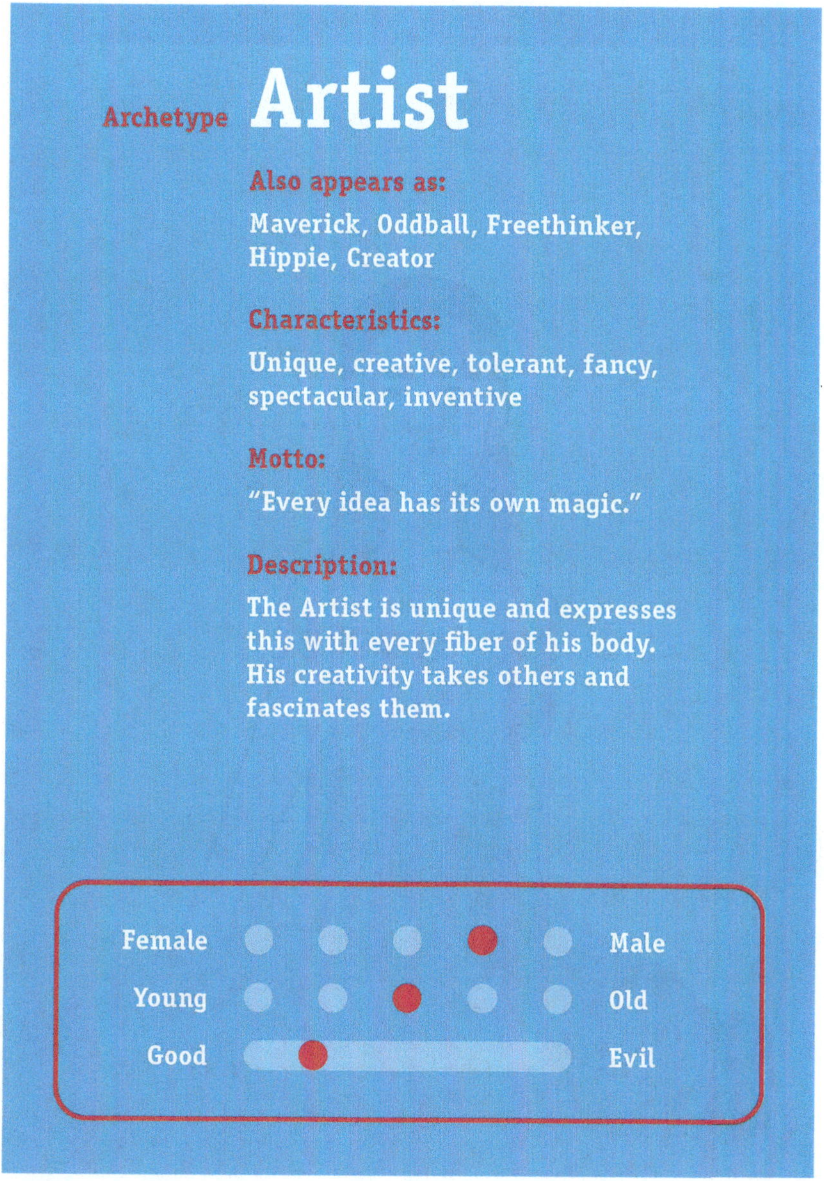

Fig. 9.11 Profile of the archetype artist. Source: Pätzmann (2020)

Fig. 9.12 Symbolical representation of the archetype beauty. Source: Pätzmann (2020)

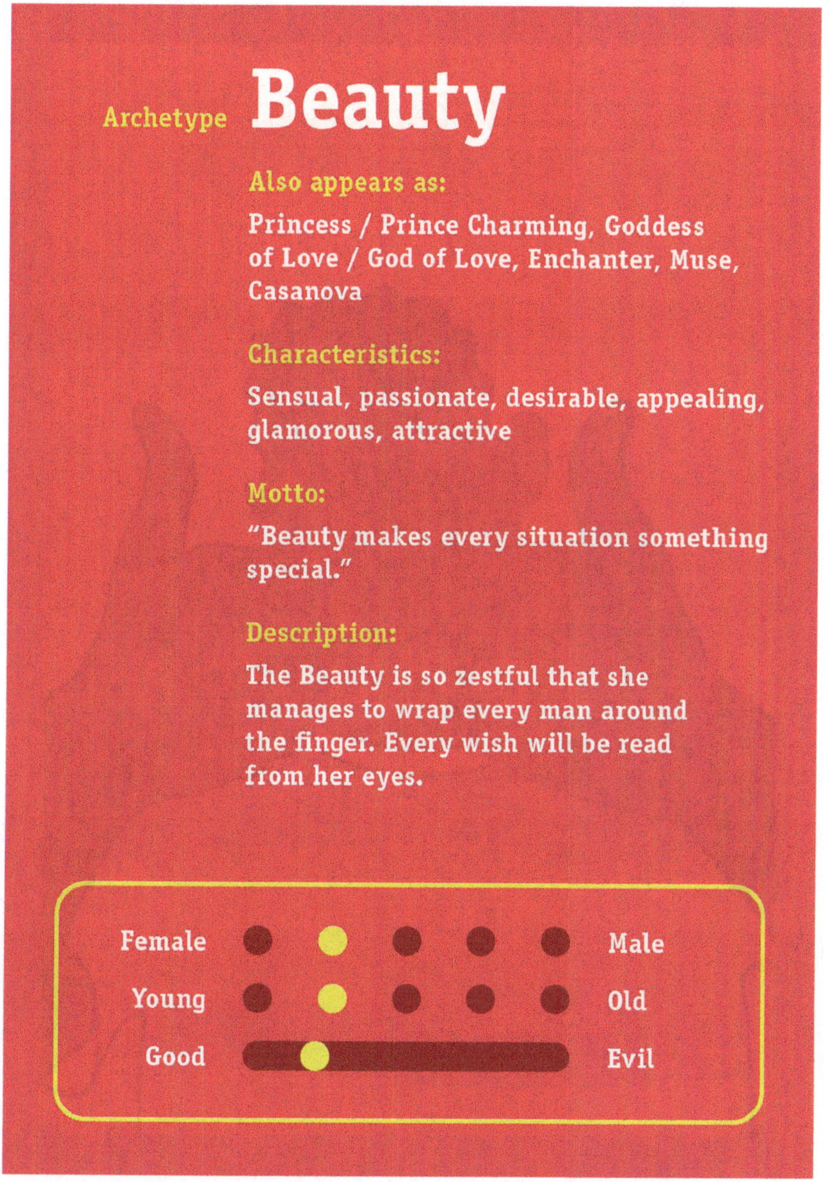

Fig. 9.13 Profile of the archetype beauty. Source: Pätzmann (2020)

Fig. 9.14 Symbolical representation of the archetype happy nature. Source: Pätzmann (2020)

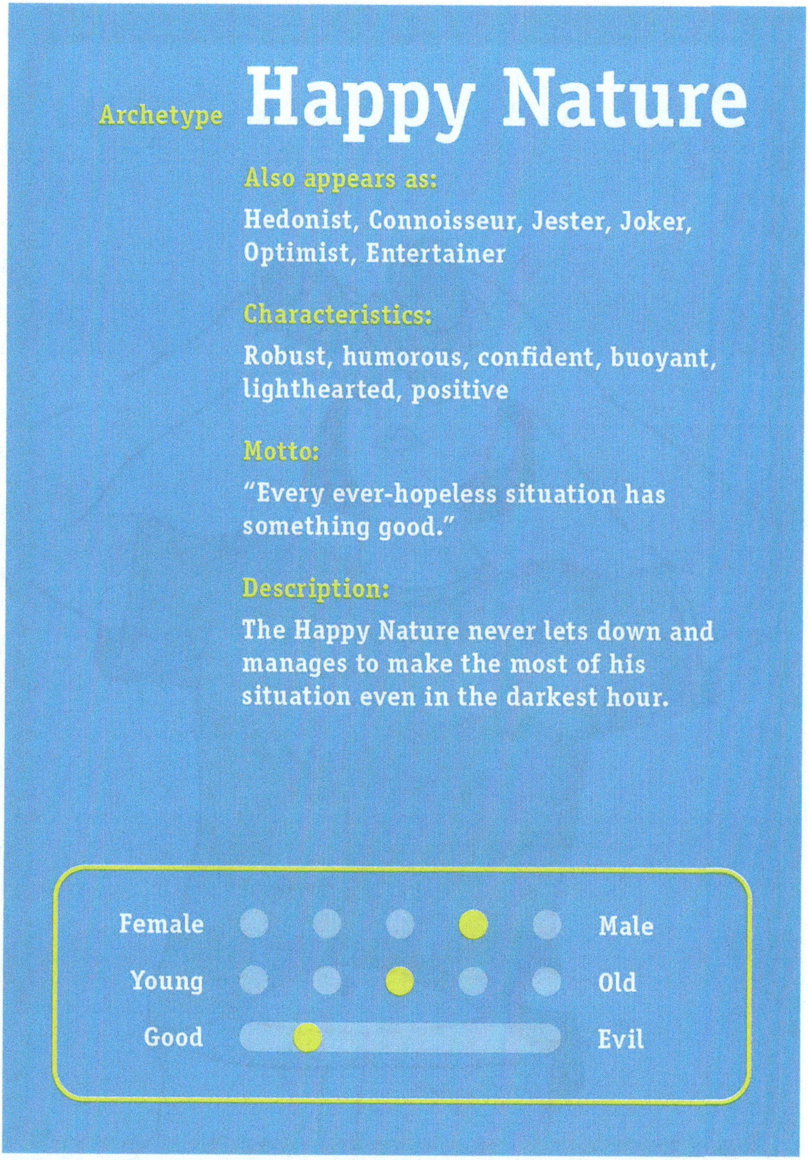

Fig. 9.15 Profile of the archetype happy nature. Source: Pätzmann (2020)

Fig. 9.16 Symbolical representation of the archetype explorer. Source: Pätzmann (2020)

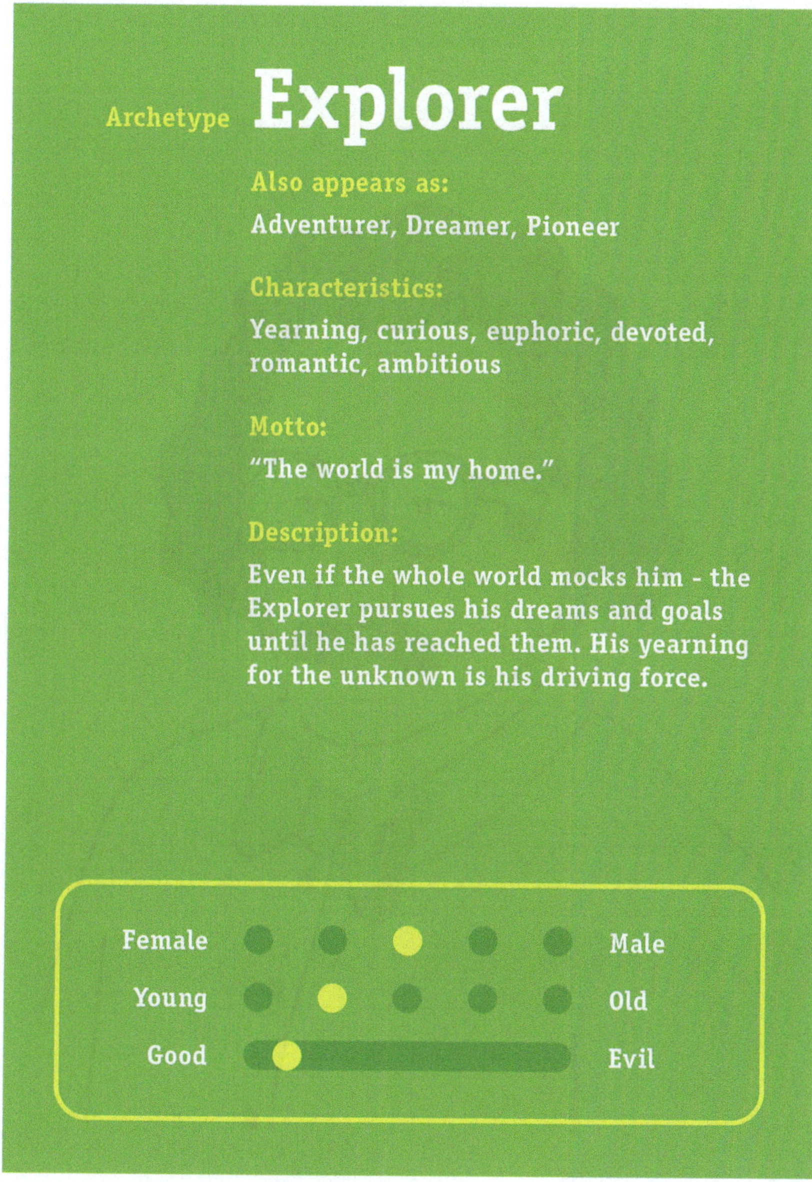

Fig. 9.17 Profile of the archetype explorer. Source: Pätzmann (2020)

Fig. 9.18 Symbolical representation of the archetype genius. Source: Pätzmann (2020)

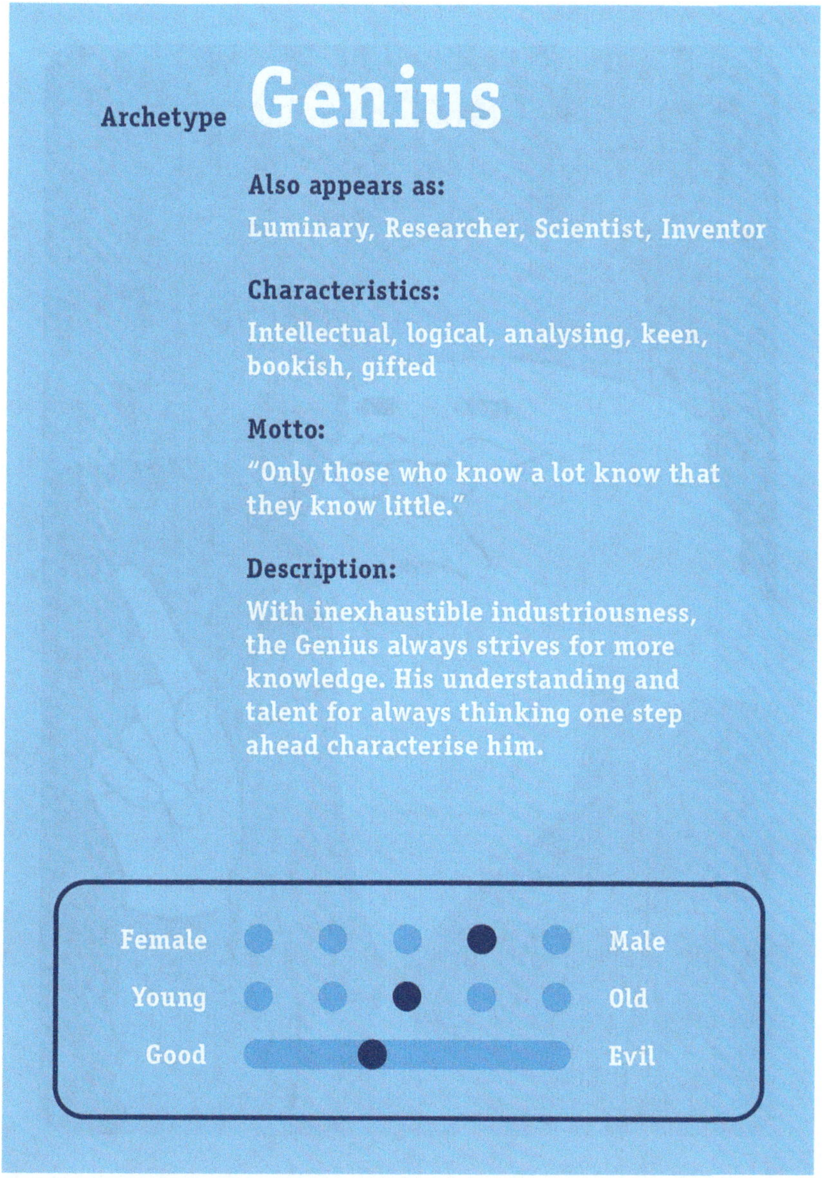

Fig. 9.19 Profile of the archetype genius. Source: Pätzmann (2020)

Fig. 9.20 Symbolical representation of the archetype mentor. Source: Pätzmann (2020)

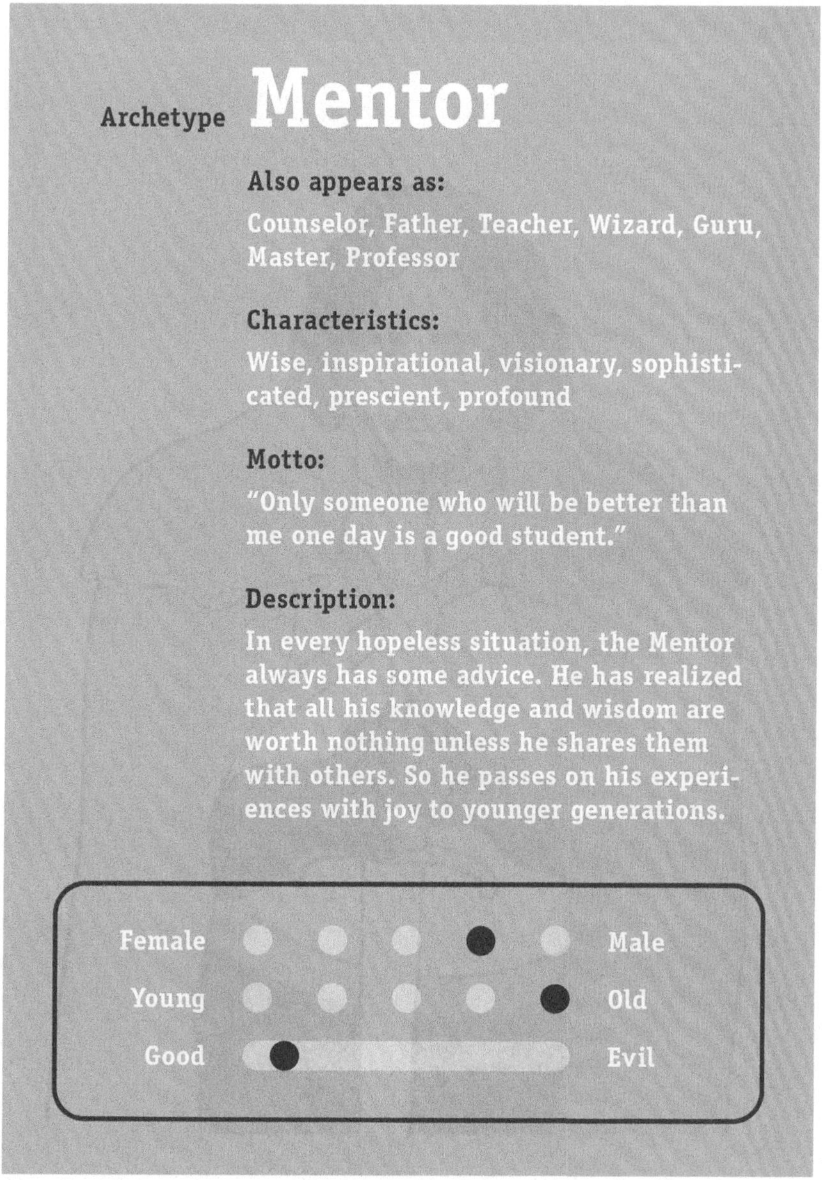

Fig. 9.21 Profile of the archetype mentor. Source: Pätzmann (2020)

Fig. 9.22 Symbolical representation of the archetype leader. Source: Pätzmann (2020)

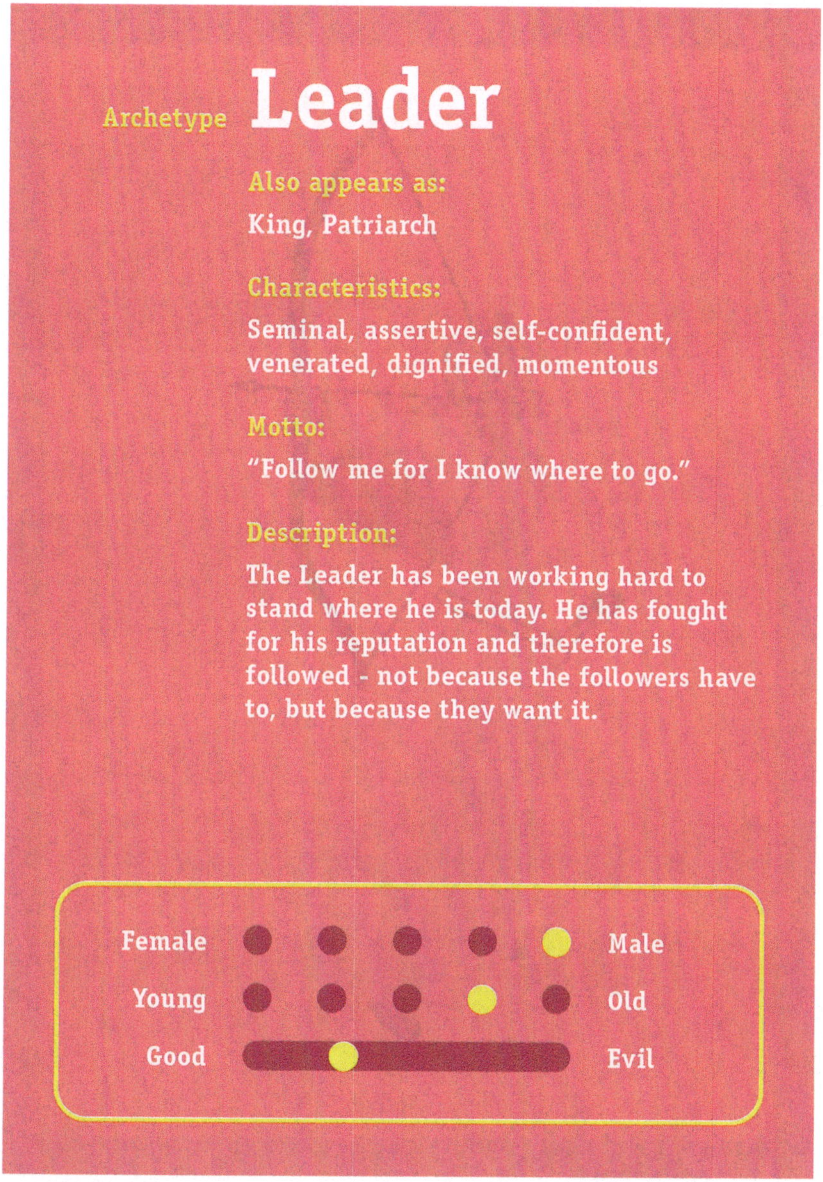

Fig. 9.23 Profile of the archetype leader. Source: Pätzmann (2020)

Fig. 9.24 Symbolical representation of the archetype amazon. Source: Pätzmann (2020)

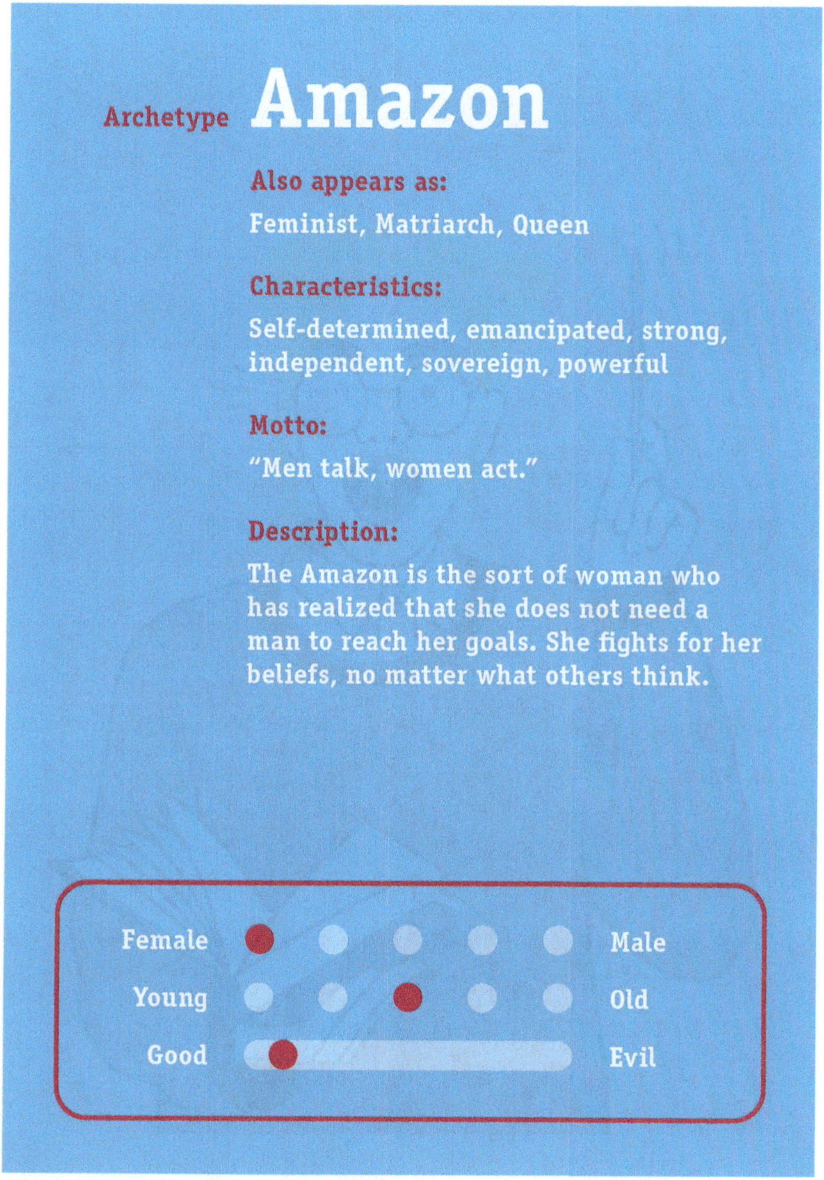

Fig. 9.25 Profile of the archetype amazon. Source: Pätzmann (2020)

Fig. 9.26 Symbolical representation of the archetype model student. Source: Pätzmann (2020)

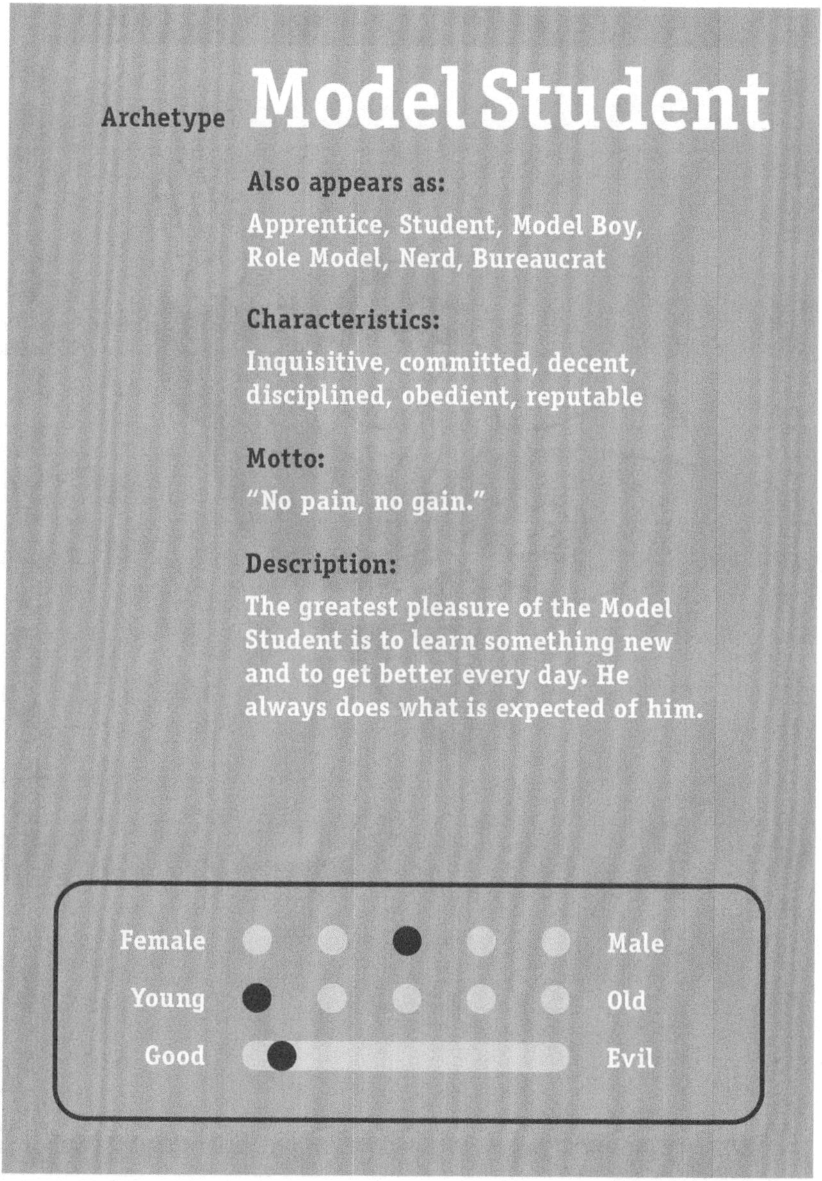

Fig. 9.27 Profile of the archetype model student. Source: Pätzmann (2020)

Fig. 9.28 Symbolical representation of the archetype hero. Source: Pätzmann (2020)

Archetype **Hero**

Also appears as:

Saviour, Liberator, Fighter, Warrior, Revolutionary, Altruist, Idealist

Characteristics:

Self-sacrificing, brave, determined, resilient, equitable, selfless

Motto:

"The world belongs to the brave, even if that makes them go west."

Description:

The Hero is fighting evil in the world. Not for himself, but for the big picture. To ban injustice and suffering in the world, he puts his own life on the line.

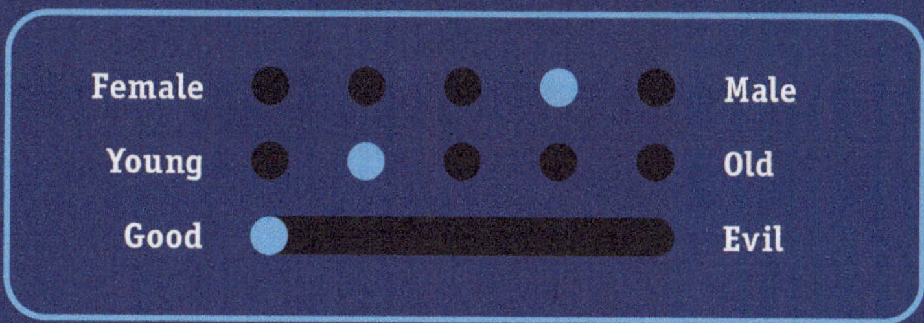

Fig. 9.29 Profile of the archetype hero. Source: Pätzmann (2020)

Fig. 9.30 Symbolical representation of the anti-archetype materialist. Source: Pätzmann (2020)

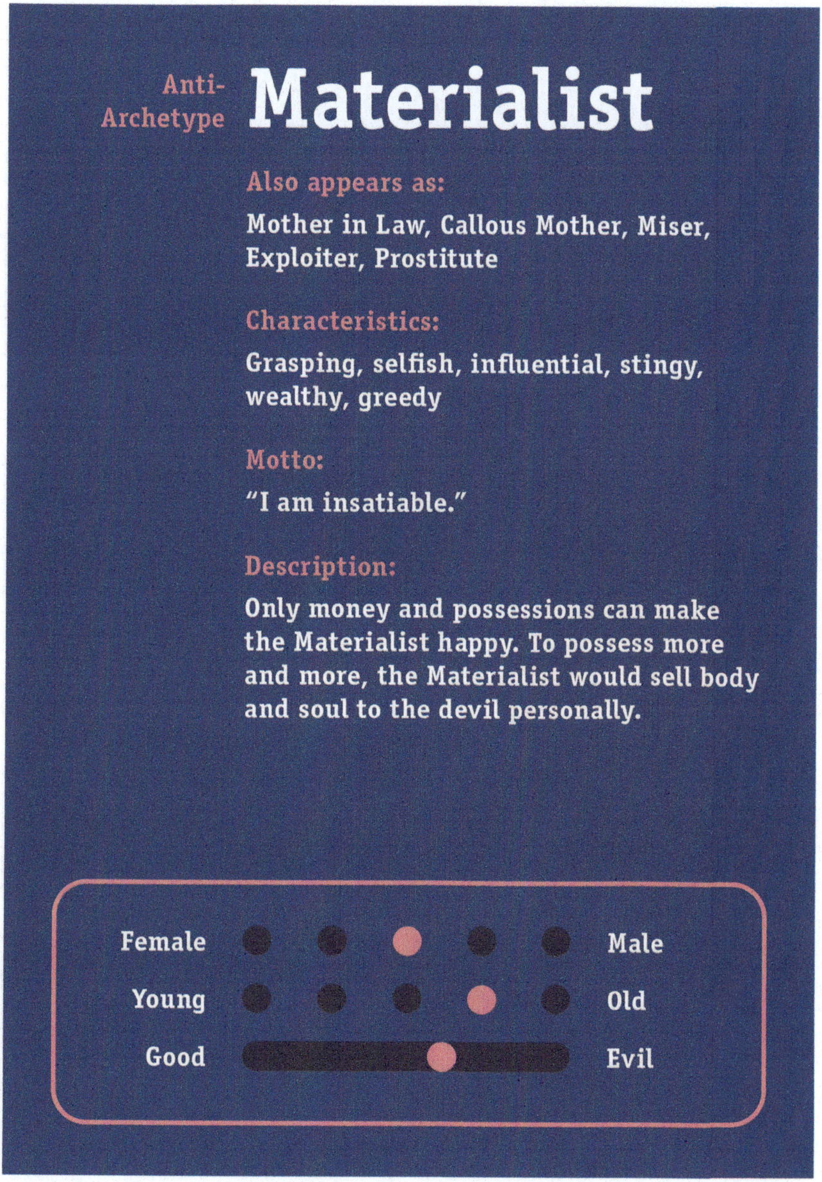

Fig. 9.31 Profile of the anti-archetype materialist. Source: Pätzmann (2020)

Fig. 9.32 Symbolical representation of the anti-archetype traitor. Source: Pätzmann (2020)

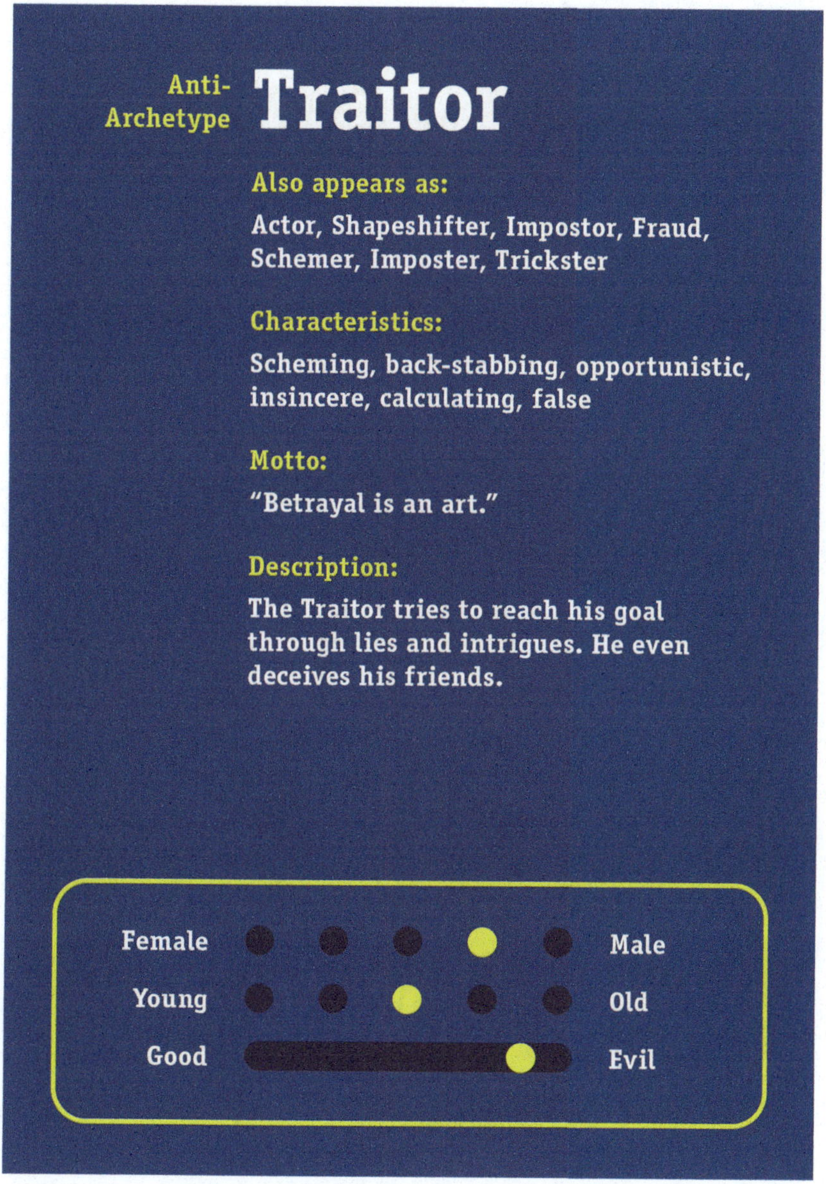

Fig. 9.33 Profile of the anti-archetype traitor. Source: Pätzmann (2020)

Fig. 9.34 Symbolical representation of the anti-archetype diva. Source: Pätzmann (2020)

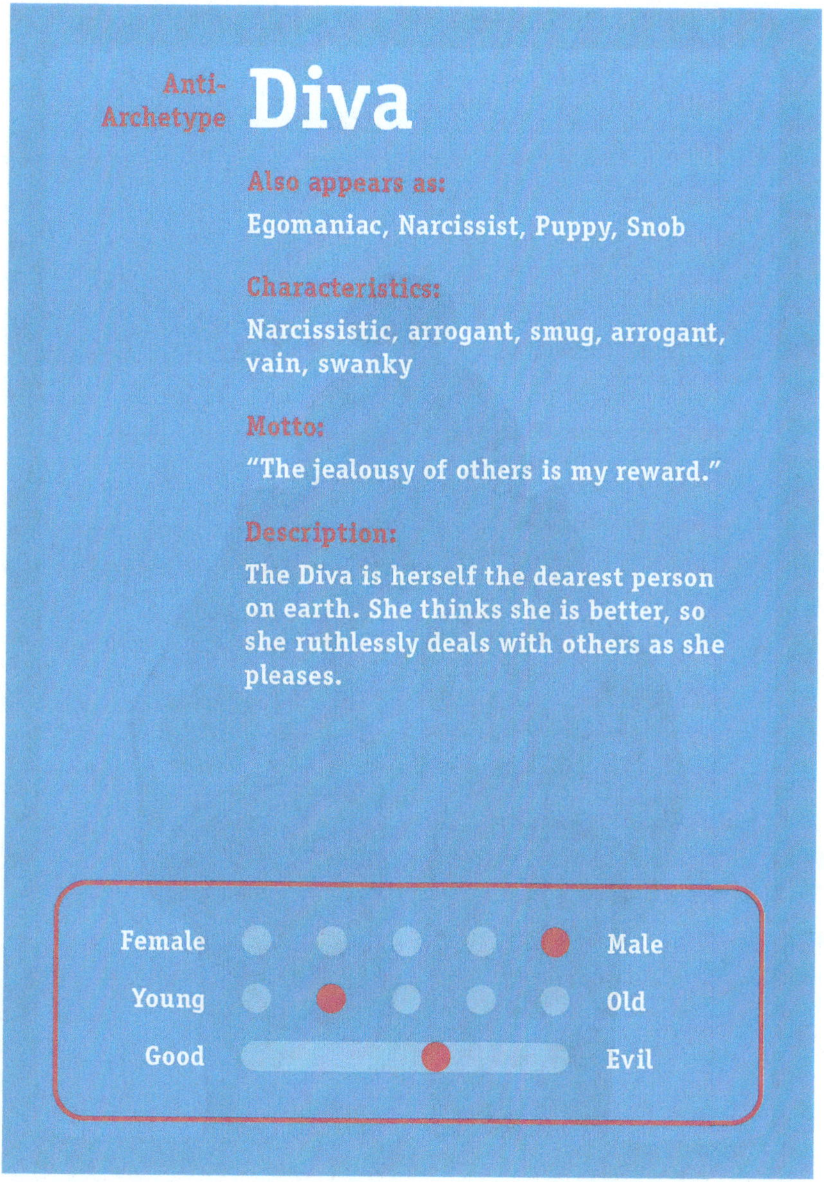

Fig. 9.35 Profile of the anti-archetype diva. Source: Pätzmann (2020)

Fig. 9.36 Symbolical representation of the anti-archetype coward. Source: Pätzmann (2020)

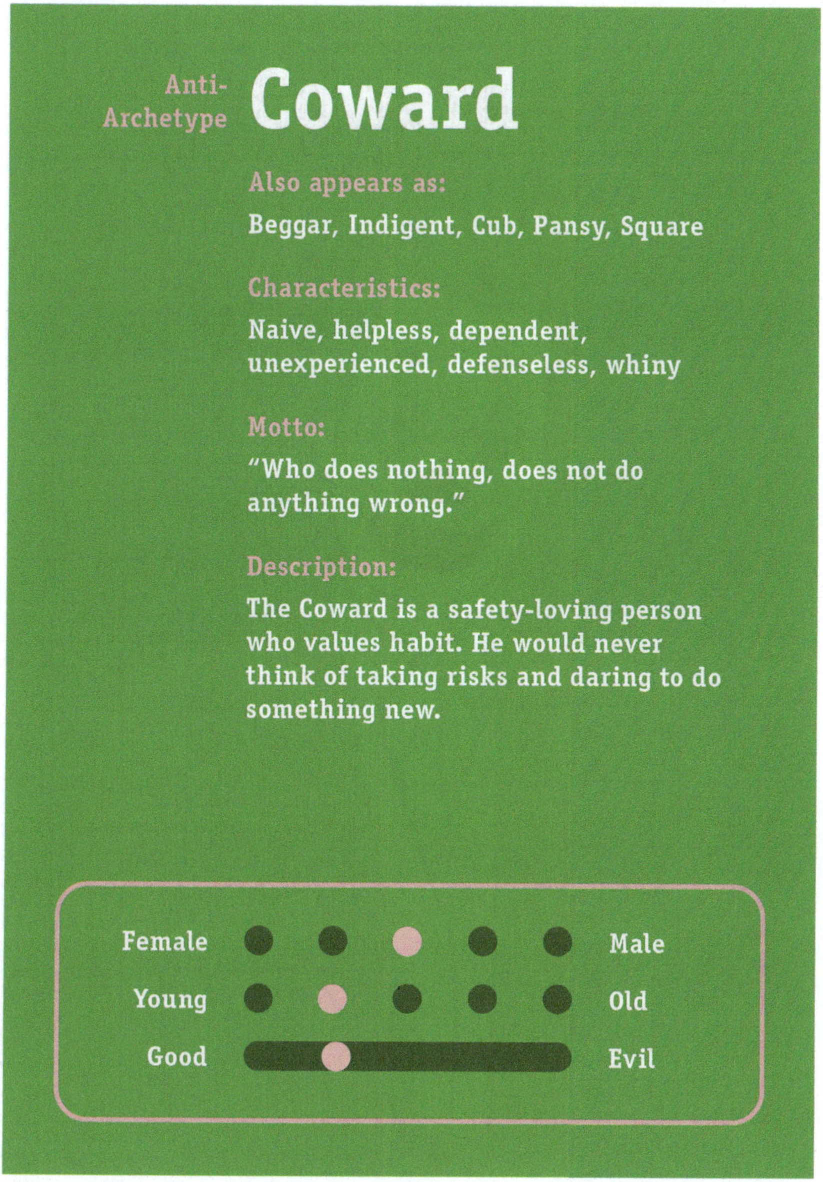

Fig. 9.37 Profile of the anti-archetype coward. Source: Pätzmann (2020)

Fig. 9.38 Symbolical representation of the anti-archetype psychopath. Source: Pätzmann (2020)

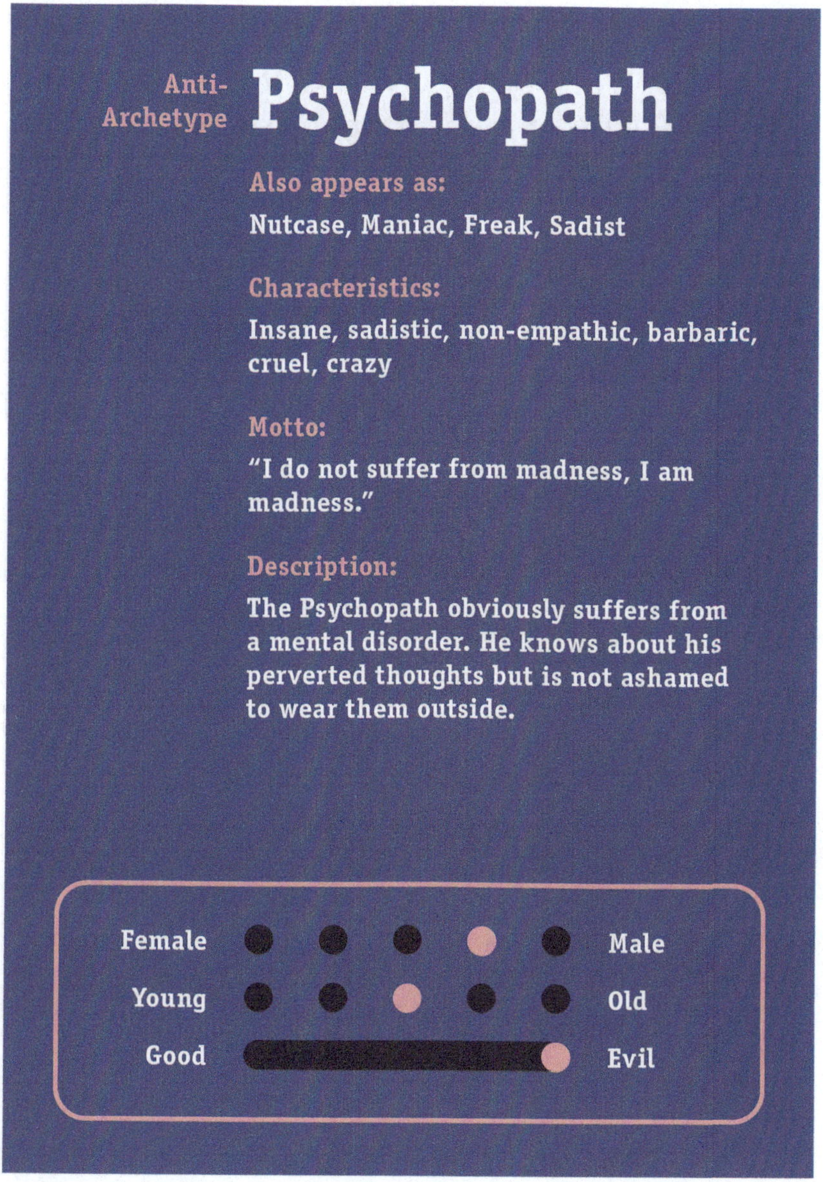

Fig. 9.39 Profile of the anti-archetype psychopath. Source: Pätzmann (2020)

Fig. 9.40 Symbolical representation of the anti-archetype femme fatale. Source: Pätzmann (2020)

Anti-Archetype

Femme Fatale

Also appears as:

Seductress, Slut, Siren, Casanova

Characteristics:

Irresistible, manipulative, seductive, fateful, unfeeling, torturous

Motto:

"Let me be your drug."

Description:

The Femme Fatale uses her beauty like a bait: she seduces a man until he succumbs to her. Then she strikes to reach her true goal.

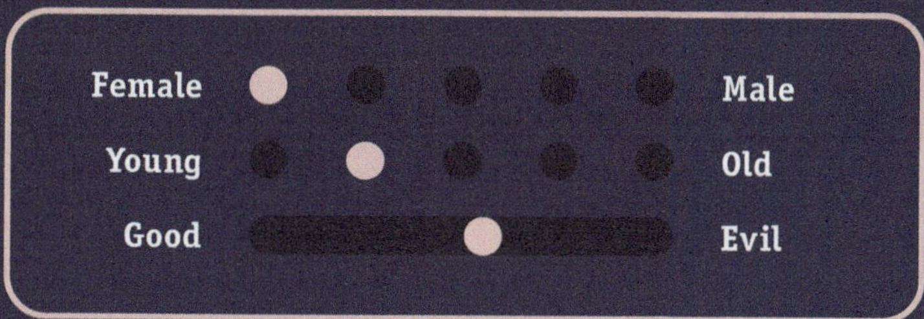

Fig. 9.41 Profile of the anti-archetype femme fatale. Source: Pätzmann (2020)

Fig. 9.42 Symbolical representation of the anti-archetype victim. Source: Pätzmann (2020)

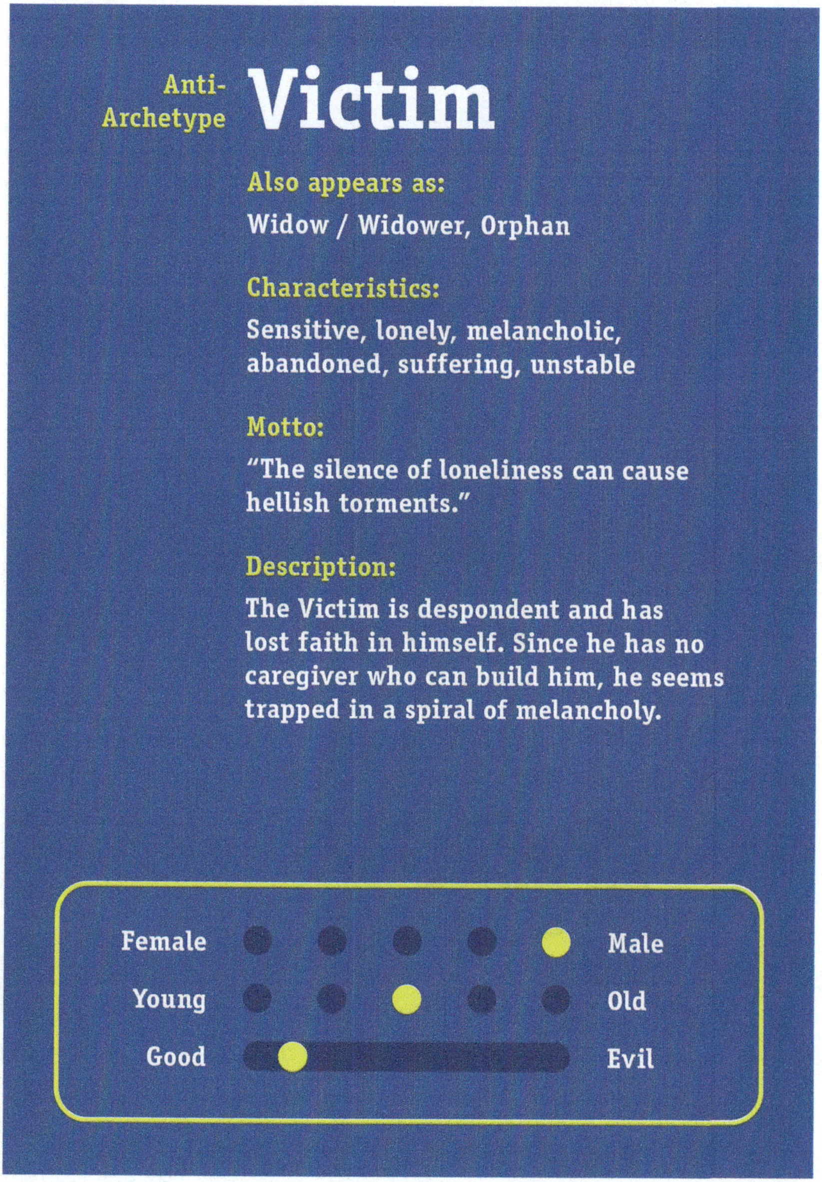

Fig. 9.43 Profile of the anti-archetype victim. Source: Pätzmann (2020)

Fig. 9.44 Symbolical representation of the anti-archetype lazar. Source: Pätzmann (2020)

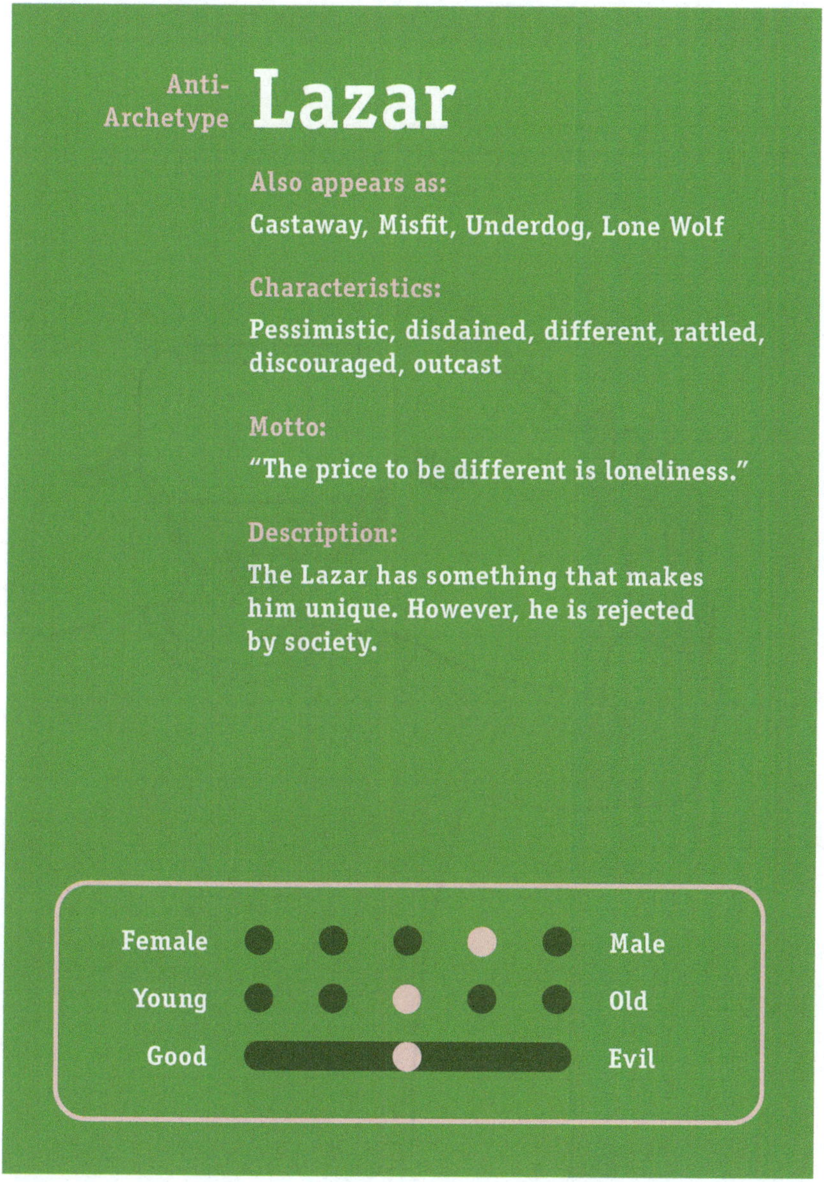

Fig. 9.45 Profile of the anti-archetype lazar. Source: Pätzmann (2020)

Fig. 9.46 Symbolical representation of the anti-archetype idiot. Source: Pätzmann (2020)

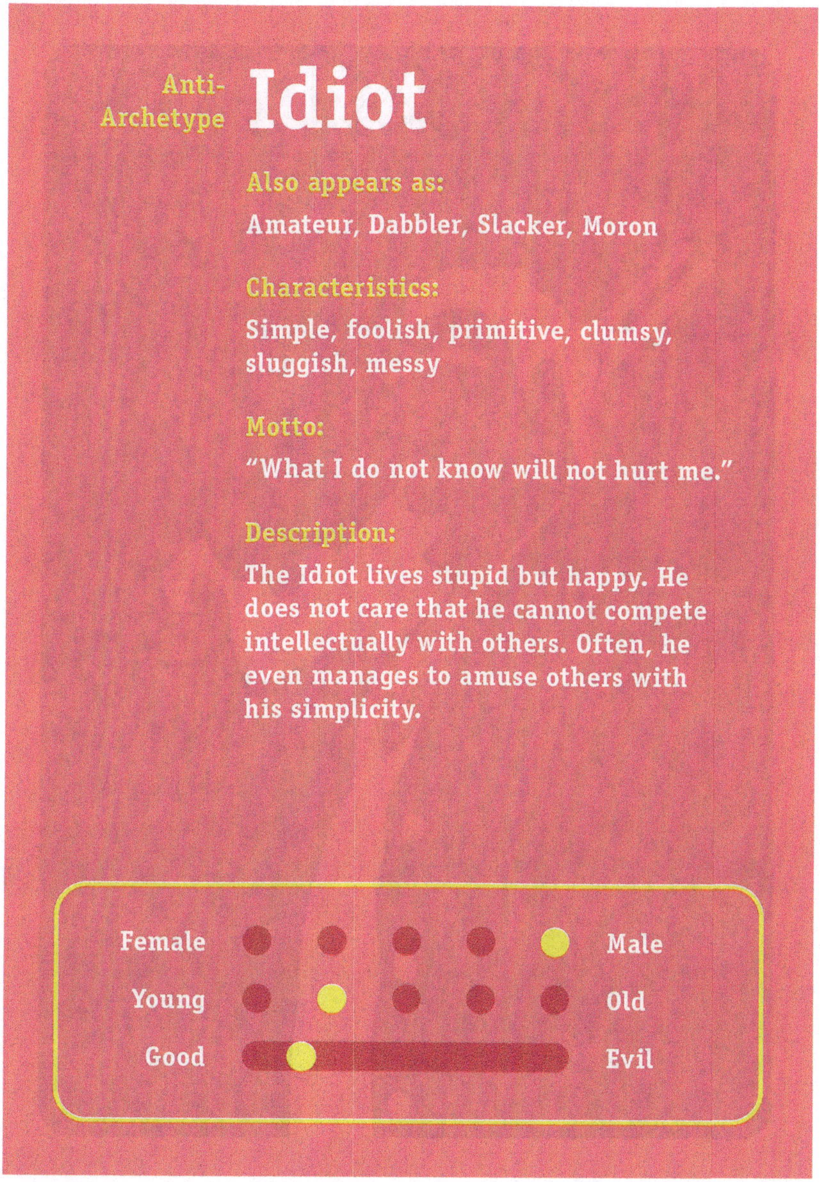

Fig. 9.47 Profile of the anti-archetype idiot. Source: Pätzmann (2020)

Fig. 9.48 Symbolical representation of the anti-archetype avenger. Source: Pätzmann (2020)

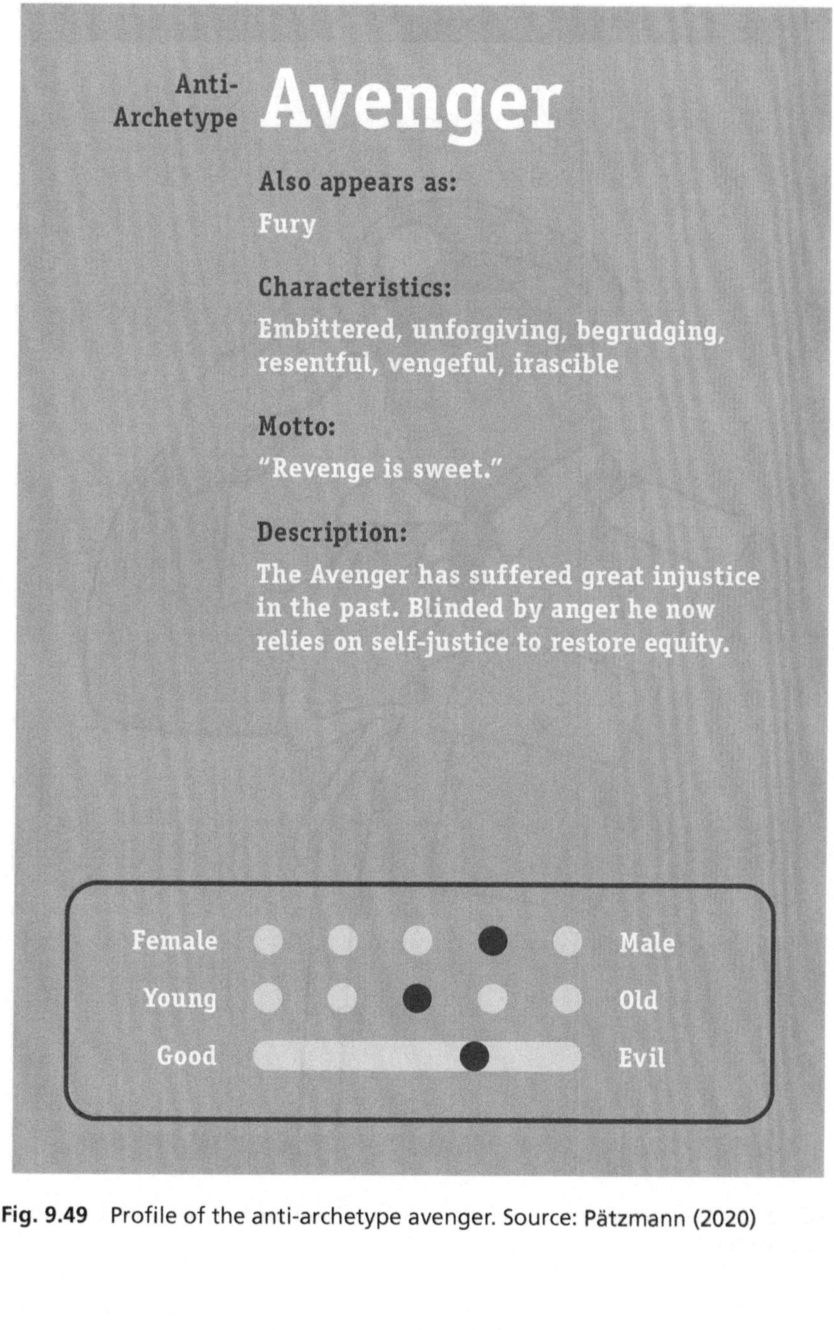

Fig. 9.49 Profile of the anti-archetype avenger. Source: Pätzmann (2020)

Fig. 9.50 Symbolical representation of the anti-archetype tyrant. Source: Pätzmann (2020)

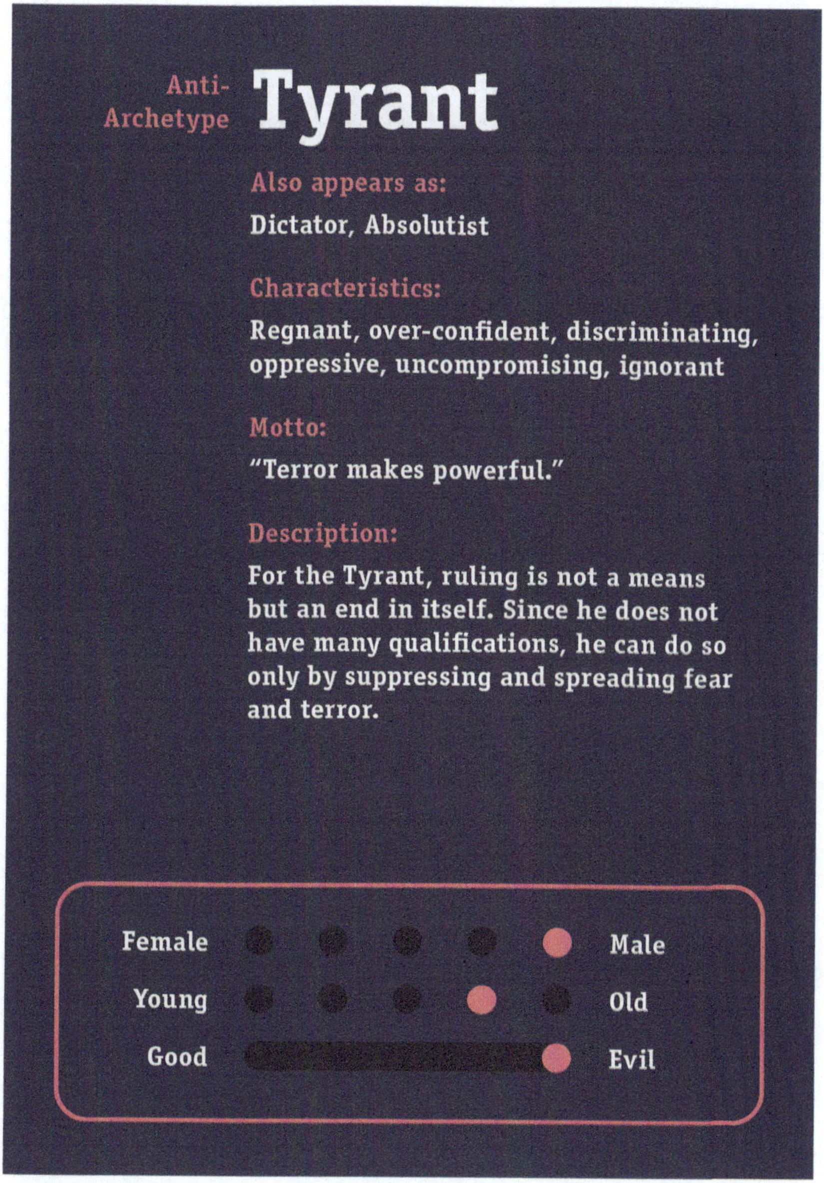

Fig. 9.51 Profile of the anti-archetype tyrant. Source: Pätzmann (2020)

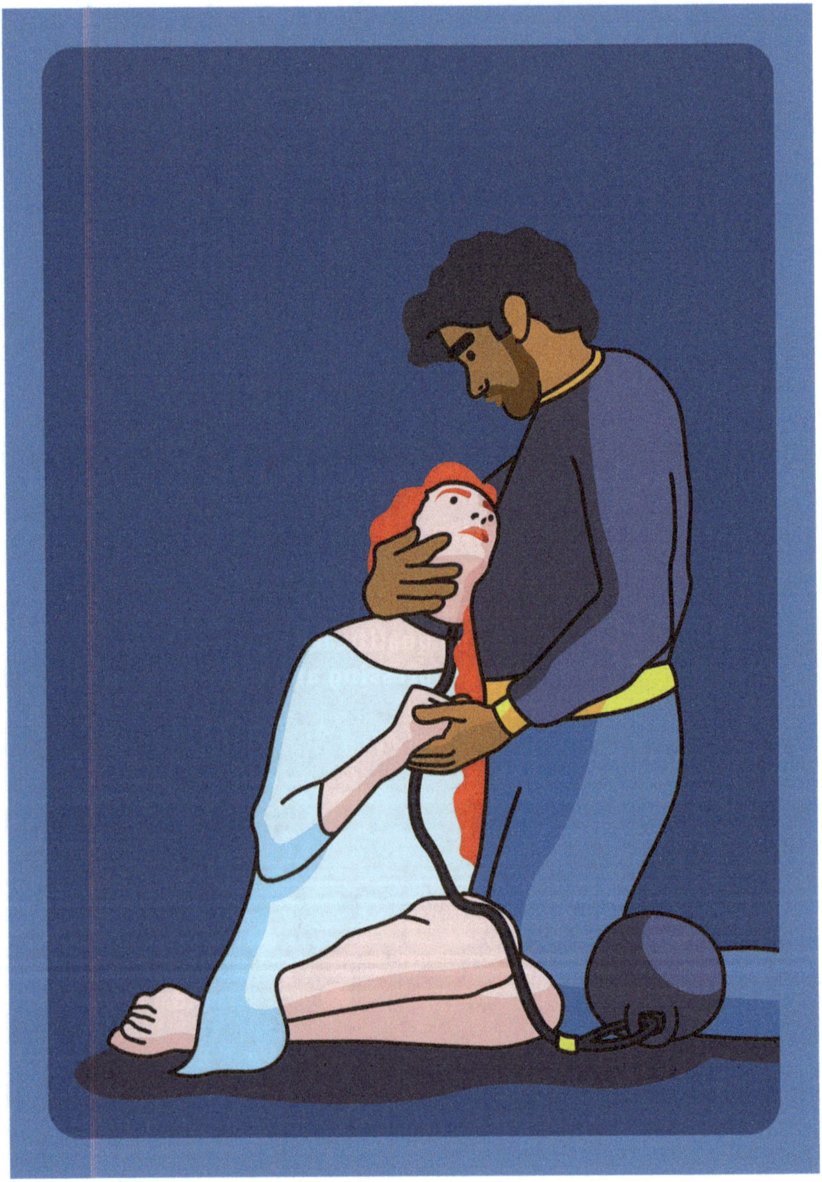

Fig. 9.52 Symbolical representation of the anti-archetype slave. Source: Pätzmann (2020)

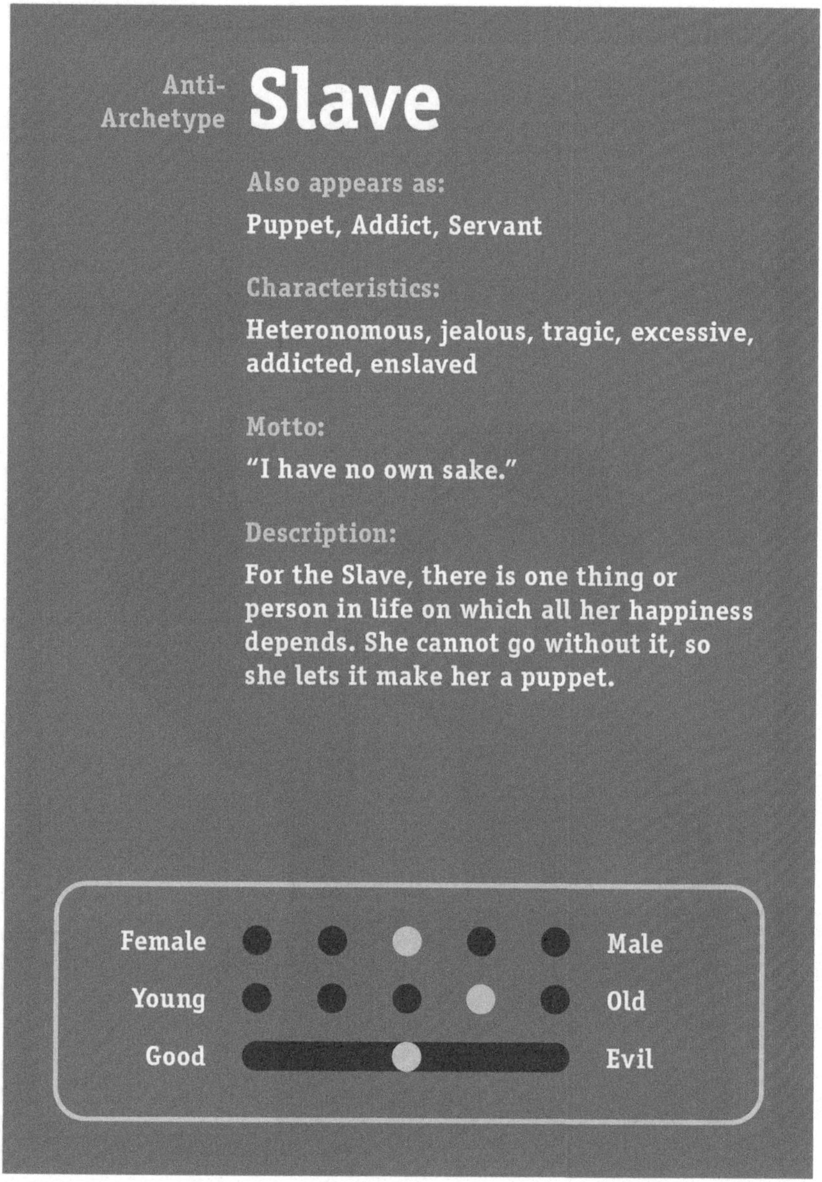

Fig. 9.53 Profile of the anti-archetype slave. Source: Pätzmann (2020)

Fig. 9.54 Symbolical representation of the anti-archetype rebel. Source: Pätzmann (2020)

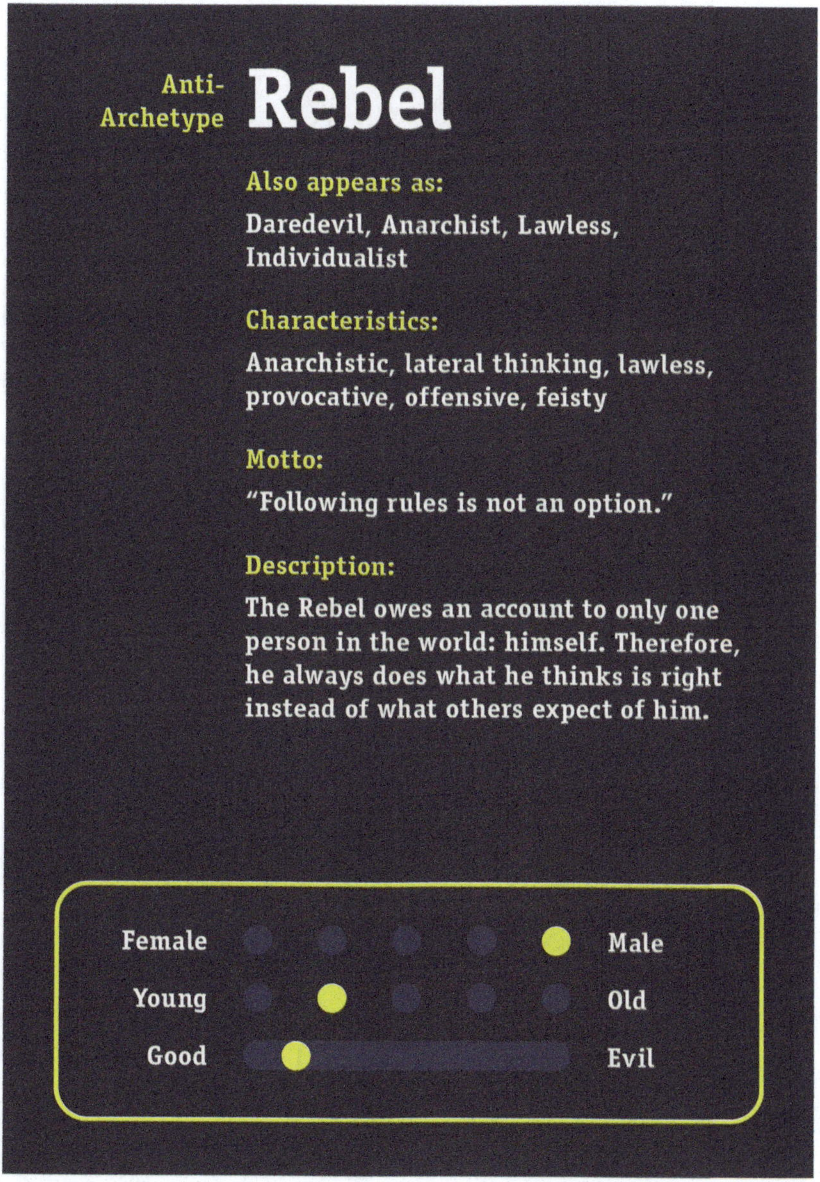

Fig. 9.55 Profile of the anti-archetype rebel. Source: Pätzmann (2020)

Fig. 9.56 Symbolical representation of the anti-archetype destroyer. Source: Pätzmann (2020)

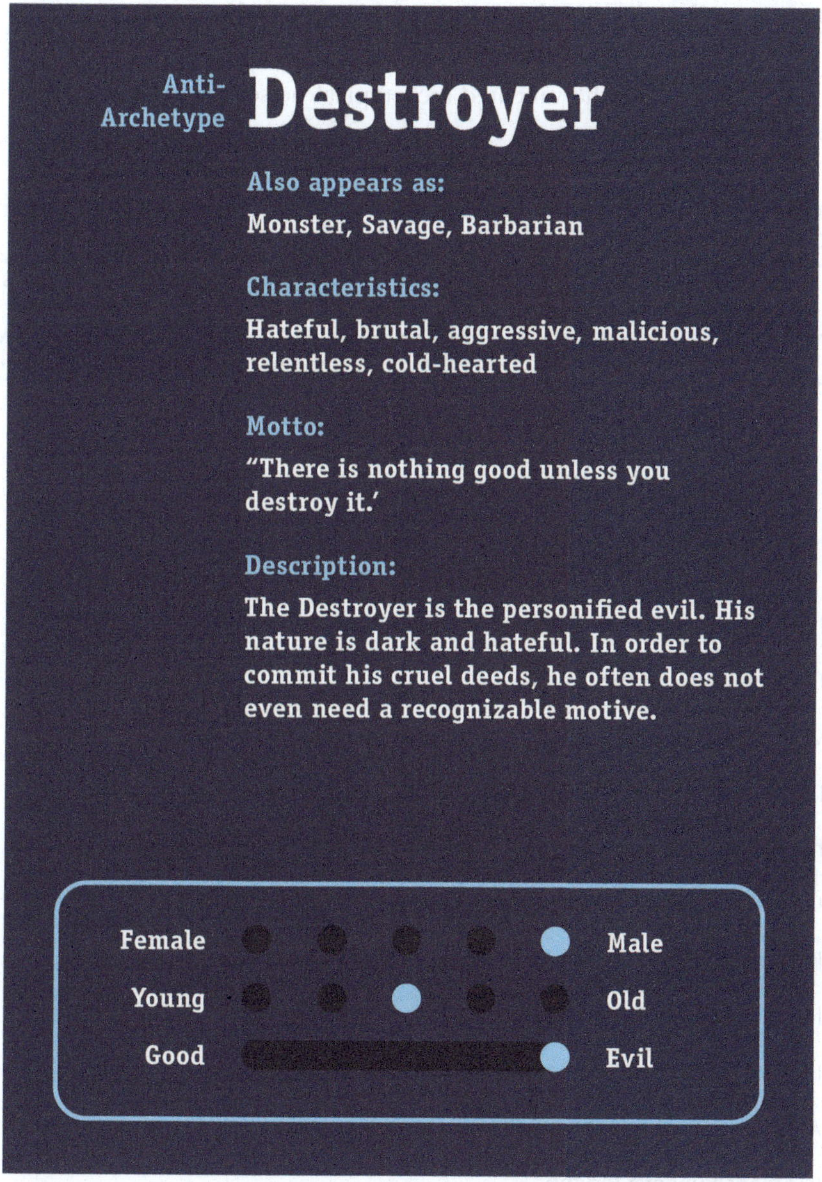

Fig. 9.57 Profile of the anti-archetype destroyer. Source: Pätzmann (2020)

9.2 Fillable Archetypical Personality Test

Table 9.1 presents the validated archetypical personality test in a fillable version.

Table 9.1 Test template for the validated archetypical personality test. Source: Own representation

	Applies fully	Applies essentially	Applies partly	Applies less	Does not apply at all
I would like to find answers to fundamental questions about the world, about humankind and its relationship to its environment					
In my eyes everything is subject to a certain logic, coincidence plays a subordinate role					
I get to the bottom of things in every detail					
I think in terms of the grand scheme of things					
With my experience, I help others to become better					
I think in terms of future scenarios and their long-term effects					
I understand how to reconcile people and their goals					
I lead the way when things need to be done					
I react confidently and thoughtfully in all situations					
I always make independent decisions					
I do not allow myself to be pushed into any role					
A certain pressure encourages me to perform at my best					
In order to understand the complexity of things, I obtain a sound overview through research					

(*continued*)

Table 9.1 (continued)

	Applies fully	Applies essentially	Applies partly	Applies less	Does not apply at all
I handle tasks that arise with great vigor and enthusiasm					
I like when everything is in its proper place					
I like to take care of the needs of others					
I stand up for the weak					
In my opinion, everyone deserves a second chance					
I always have an open ear for problems					
I keep my promises					
I tell the truth					
I consider every individual on Earth to be valuable					
I always look for balanced solutions					
I can mediate well between different people					
I have never done anything evil before					
I can easily put myself in other people's position					
I lead an exemplary life					
I am unconventional					
I enjoy trying out new approaches					
I am open-minded about unknown and different things					
I sense emotions intensely					
I devote myself fully to one thing when I am convinced of it					
Others turn to look at me when I enter a room					
I do not allow myself to be ruffled					
I can make people laugh					

(continued)

Table 9.1 (continued)

	Applies fully	Applies essentially	Applies partly	Applies less	Does not apply at all
Even if unexpected problems arise, I never lose confidence					
I long to constantly try new things					
I want to explore the world with my own eyes					
I can easily be won over by new ideas					
Additional tasks are no problem for me, if I can achieve improvement for everyone					
I am convinced that far-reaching changes can only be achieved with the necessary readiness to take risks					
I have a strong inner drive to put into practice what I have said					
In some situations I feel clumsy					
Banal things often amuse me					
Often I simply act without bothering to think					
I hold the view that life is unjust					
I have difficulties forgiving when I experience injustice					
I have difficulty acknowledging the success of others					
I like to be in command					
I often set myself overambitious goals					
I exclude other people when they do not share my opinion					
I adopt values from my superiors without critically questioning them myself					
I feel worthless and fear losing what I love					
I bear a heavy burden					

(continued)

Table 9.1 (continued)

	Applies fully	Applies essentially	Applies partly	Applies less	Does not apply at all
I do not fit into any system					
The further I move away from routines, the more new things emerge for me					
I break existing rules according to my own discretion					
If others have more than I have I want to catch up with them					
I always act in such a way that no disadvantage arises for me					
I can steer people and processes to further my interests					
To achieve my goals, I play other people off against each other					
I disguise my true intentions					
I adjust my position on critical issues to achieve a general consensus					
I cannot pass a mirror without looking at myself					
I always remain in the memory of others					
I think that I am better than the rest					
I am gullible and always follow others uncritically					
I find it difficult to cope with unexpected situations					
I always make decisions after consultation with a person close to me					
My thoughts disturb normal people					
I enjoy the misfortune of others					
I feel little sympathy for the fate of others					
Others would prefer to spend their time exclusively with me					

(continued)

Table 9.1 (continued)

	Applies fully	Applies essentially	Applies partly	Applies less	Does not apply at all
I am aware of my effect on others and use it skillfully					
I can get others to do things for me in a charming way					
I think about past conversations often and for a long time					
I find it difficult to establish social contacts					
I think about the meaning of life and my individual place in society					
I have fears about the future					
I take it upon myself not to be accepted by society					
Others think I am strange					
I detest most people in my environment					
I sanction the misconduct of others ruthlessly					
I quickly become irritated when things do not go according to my plan					

Table 9.2 Likert scale coding. Source: Based on Pätzmann and Genrich (2020, p. 28)

Applies fully	Applies essentially	Applies partly	Applies less	Does not apply at all
1	0.75	0.5	0.25	0

Test takers rate the applicability of each statement on the Likert scale. To generate the test results, the levels of agreement with the statements are coded using Table 9.2 and converted to percentile norms. The coded values are totaled according to their assigned (anti-)archetype (see Table 5.2) and divided by three, the number of motifs. The result is the percentile rank of the respective (anti-)archetype as an expression of the average value of the motifs on which it is based (ibid). For a graphical representation of the archetypical personality profile, a spiderweb diagram like Fig. 6.1 is suitable. The authors are planning the development of a website and app to facilitate digital test taking.

References

Pätzmann, J. (2020). Of Heroes & Destroyers.. Hochschule Neu-Ulm.

Pätzmann, J., & Genrich, R. (2020). *Employer branding mit Archetypen.* Springer Gabler.

Pätzmann, J., & Hartwig, J. (2018). *Markenführung mit Archetypen.* Springer Gabler.

10

Methods for the Entrepreneurship Ecosystem

An obvious way of employing the archetypical personality test for startup teams is to ask (potential) team members to respond to the test items and to identify their archetypical personality profile. This yields a nuanced spider web profile, revealing to which extent the 28 (anti-)archetypes are pronounced in somebody's personality profile. This renders comparable results and makes it possible to discover archetypes missing or overrepresented in the startup team. Such insights can enable the conscious handling of the personality setup or targeted recruitment of new members to add missing aspects.

Such an approach would, however, have considerable downsides:

1. Matching the archetypical profiles of several team members is complex and difficult to interpret.
2. Archetypical personality profiles include many (anti-)archetypes which are of secondary importance to startup teams and hence add an unnecessary level of complexity.
3. Such an approach does not respect the archetypes which perform best if they appear on the team level, like the hero and the friend.

V. Miller, J. U. Pätzmann, *Archetypical Roles in Startups*, Business Guides on the Go,
https://doi.org/10.1007/978-3-031-22253-5_10

4. It excludes external team members from the assistance network who might only contribute temporarily or very specifically but sometimes constitute the missing link.
5. It disregards that archetypes can and should be shifted according to situational needs.
6. It fosters prejudice and stereotypes among the team members.
7. It does not do justice to group interaction, as individuals behave differently from teams, for example, in decision-making (Brattström et al., 2020, p. 4).

The easy understandability of archetypes, one of the key strengths of working with them, is also their weak spot: they may be taken too literally. It must be clear that no real person can be equated with any given archetype. These are personality dimensions or roles enacted by somebody in a certain context or projected onto them. The archetypes are crafted as personifications, but they are not always manifested in individual team members; they can also appear on the team level or as themes that influence the nature of the teamwork. Moxnes and Moxnes (2016) ask for caution when working with archetypical roles: groups like illusions which can lead to stereotyping and self-fulfilling prophecies. When a group member follows the archetype projected onto them by the group, they are other-controlled (Moxnes & Moxnes, 2016, p. 1534). This is not helpful for trusting and cohesive group work. Furthermore, personalities undergo life-long development (Carducci, 2009, p. 149), so an archetypical personality profile must not be understood as static. Personalities are multi-faceted and evolve constantly.

The model is stylized into 14 positively connotated archetypes and 14 corresponding or contrasting negatively connotated anti-archetypes. In startup teams, however, each archetypical role has its light and dark sides. Teams must learn to manage them purposefully. As Jung suggests: the shadow needs to be integrated. What holds true for individuals, is also relevant for organizations. They, too, create shadows that must be integrated (Kociatkiewicz & Kostera, 2010, p. 66, 2012, p. 258). Stereotyping by looking at only the good or the bad sides should be avoided (Fuchs, 2018, p. 179; Ritter, 2008, p. 10). Belbin (2010) understands the downsides of a personality as "allowable weakness" instead of "development areas"; rather than being worked on, these weaknesses must be accepted and integrated: "for it is a fair trade-off" for the strengths on the other end (p. 55). The archetypical model can alert startup teams to the dark sides of each archetype.

As outlined in Chap. 2, research about startup team diversity already showed that knowing one's own personality as well as appreciating and accommodating others' is key for managing heterogeneous teams. Similarly, the interviews revealed that teams should deliberately foster their ability to manage heterogeneity. Respondent D_Fou_G emphasized that teams usually assemble "naturally" instead of approaching team member selection strategically. This makes awareness and careful management of the team role constellation, not only functional roles, even more important to harvest the benefits of the creativity bred by heterogeneous mindsets. This is in line with extant findings that self-reflection and mutual understanding are strategies to deal with the imminent risk of affective conflict, which is most likely to arise by individuals with vastly similar or largely opposite archetypical roles (Chowdhury, 2005, p. 742; Pearson et al., 2002, p. 366). The importance of self-awareness is even greater in unbalanced teams with an overrepresentation of a certain archetype, as Belbin's work about team roles suggests (2010, p. 52). Careful attention to the team dynamics can overcome shortcomings in its composition.

Alternative modes of application use the archetypical personality test as an abstract framework: (1) *as a research tool*, as exemplified in this book; (2) *through storytelling*, which looks at archetypical themes and roles on a group level. The archetypical profiles for startups can be a great tool for moderating team dynamics and coaching startups, especially with the help of a neutral external party. In this capacity, the model is useful for team member recruitment, but also for improving team dynamics and group work in an existing team. The archetypes can also be understood similarly to de Bono's *Six Thinking Hats* (1999) which recommends to consciously switch between different styles of thinking. Depending on the situation, an archetype embodying a certain way of thinking must be brought to the fore. Archetypical group hero storytelling, as described by Hall (2016), can be used to build a cohesive, collaborative, and committed team.

Kociatkiewicz and Kostera (2012) apply the *narrative collage methodology*. The researchers collect fictive narratives from a group about a relevant topic. Respondents are asked to write a story inspired by a provided illustration or suggested beginning. The researchers identify archetypical themes when interpreting the data. This is a way to uncover hidden archetypical themes which lie in the unconscious. This methodology has been applied in organizational studies for studying areas in the imagination. It has also been further developed into a tool for consulting (Kociatkiewicz & Kostera, 2012, p. 869). This methodology can be adapted by startup mentors to uncover a founding team's hidden archetypes.

Aurelio (1995) applied the *interactive projective test*, which is similarly built on storytelling. The researcher displays illustrations from mythology to small groups of organizational members in focus group sessions. The reactions are recorded and transcribed. The researcher then analyzes them for the selected archetypes using content analysis. This is another qualitative approach to uncover unconscious group dynamics. It combines Jung's method of active imagination with contemporary projective methodologies (Aurelio, 1995, p. 354). Aurelio applies it to uncover the hidden aspects of a hospital's organizational culture. She triangulates it against other methods and confirms that the interactive projective test yields robust results. Both methods could be adapted and combined with the findings of the research presented in this book. This will create a powerful methodology for uncovering team dynamics in startup teams and inciting positive change. Teams can be invited to imagine their own archetypical startup tale or to rewrite theirs as a group hero story. Mentors can frame the coaching process as an archetypical group hero journey.

References

Aurelio, J. M. (1995). Using Jungian archetypes to explore deeper levels of organizational culture: Facing your organization's psyche. *Journal of Management Inquiry, 4*(4), 347–368.

Belbin, R. M. (2010). *Team roles at work* (2nd ed.). Routledge.

Brattström, A., Delmar, F., Johnson, A. R., & Wennberg, K. (2020). A longitudinal project of new venture teamwork and outcomes. In *Research handbook on entrepreneurial behavior, practice and process* (pp. 309–334). Edward Elgar Publishing. https://doi.org/10.4337/9781788114523.00023.
Carducci, B. J. (2009). *The psychology of personality* (2nd ed.). Wiley-Blackwell.
Chowdhury, S. (2005). Demographic diversity for building an effective entrepreneurial team: Is it important? *Journal of Business Venturing, 20*(6), 727–746.
De Bono, E. (1999). *Six thinking hats (rev. and updated ed.)*. Little, Brown and Company.
Fuchs, W. T. (2018). *Crashkurs Storytelling* (2nd ed.). Haufe Group.
Hall, C. (2016). The group hero: An archetype whose time has come. In S. B. Schafer (Ed.), *Exploring the collective unconscious in the age of digital media* (pp. 214–231). IGI Global.
Kociatkiewicz, J., & Kostera, M. (2010). Experiencing the shadow: Organizational exclusion and denial within experience economy. *Organization, 17*(2), 257–282.
Kociatkiewicz, J., & Kostera, M. (2012). The good manager: An archetypical quest for morally sustainable leadership. *Organization Studies, 33*(7), 861–878. https://doi.org/10.1177/0170840612445124
Moxnes, P., & Moxnes, A. (2016). Are we sucked into fairy tale roles? Role archetypes in imagination and organization. *Organization Studies, 37*(10), 1519–1539. https://doi.org/10.1177/0170840616634135
Pearson, A. W., Ensley, M. D., & Amason, A. C. (2002). Understanding the dynamics of new venture top management teams: Cohesion, conflict, and new venture performance. *Journal of Business Venturing, 17*(4), 365–386.
Ritter, L. (2008). *Erfolgreich werben mit Archetypen–Helden und Narren in der Werbung*. VDM Verlag Dr. Müller.

11

Applying the Archetypical Personality Test in Other Areas

Entrepreneurship is not the only application field, where the archetypical personality test can be of great use. This chapter explores how it can be applied to the recruitment of new employees, the training of brand ambassadors, and further areas like life coaching, consulting, and customer segmentation.

Hiring of New Employees Pätzmann and Genrich (2020) describe the archetypical personality test as a tool in the recruiting process of new employees (p. 27 ff). Potential candidates complete the archetypical personality test to determine their preferences for each archetypical motif. The levels of agreement to the test statements are coded and converted to percentile norms as explained in Chap. 9. The individual test results of the potential candidate are compared with a predefined ideal profile.

To generate the ideal profile, representatives from the human resource department and the functional department form a team of experts (+/- six experts as a rule of thumb) and determine the archetypical ideal profile for the vacant position (Pätzmann & Genrich, 2020, p. 30). They take the archetypical personality test rephrased to the third person (the ideal candidate) with their expectations of a candidate ideally suited to fill

V. Miller, J. U. Pätzmann, *Archetypical Roles in Startups*, Business Guides on the Go,
https://doi.org/10.1007/978-3-031-22253-5_11

the vacancy. For a cumulative archetypical profile, the percentile ranks per motif of the (anti-)archetype are formed by dividing the cumulative test scores according to the coded Likert scale by the number of test scores and multiplying this expression by 100 at first (Pätzmann & Genrich, 2020, p. 27). Subsequently, the resulting values are totaled according to their assigned (anti-)archetype and divided by three to generate the percentile rank of each (anti-)archetype (ibid). In this way, the anti-archetypical tolerance profile is also determined, i.e., which negative motifs are considered to be still tolerable, which are not acceptable?

By comparing the ideal profile and the candidate's profile, the gaps can be identified. Separate profiles are created for the candidate's archetypical and the anti-archetypical preferences. In the first step, the fit of the basic archetypical personality profile is analyzed before the benchmarking of the top 3 archetypes follows. The GAP detection of the benchmarking is performed according to a traffic light system: The individual expression of the archetypical personality is considered positive (green traffic light) if it deviates positively from the defined ideal profile, i.e., is more pronounced than required. Hence, the traffic light turns yellow if the individual test value is up to 25 evaluation points below the ideal profile. If the deviation is even greater, the red traffic light indicates a clear lack of fit between the archetypical personality of the candidate and the vacancy (Pätzmann & Genrich, 2020, p. 29). The benchmarking of the anti-archetypical personality profile behaves exactly the opposite way. Here, a negative deviation from the ideal profile is advantageous if the individual test value lies within the defined tolerance range (Pätzmann & Genrich, 2020, p. 30).

The objective analysis of the personality-oriented fit between employee and functional area with the help of the test can be used for a more targeted development of the employer brand (Pätzmann & Genrich, 2020, p. 31). The insights gained into the implicit motifs of personality traits mean a better understanding of what fundamentally drives employees, which is useful for employer branding. On this basis, the employer value proposition can be aligned along the common purpose in order to successfully attract new employees and retain existing ones via the value congruence between employer and employee. To compensate for any deficits, personnel development measures can be used, e.g., coaching on team skills if, for example, an anti-archetype like the diva is overrepresented (Pätzmann & Genrich, 2020, p. 31).

Training of Brand Ambassadors The test can also be used to train existing employees to become brand ambassadors (Pätzmann & Genrich, 2020, p. 31). Basically, the evaluation logic is based on that of recruiting new employees, but the collected parameters differ. The archetypical ideal profile is not defined for a functional area but for the corporate brand, whereby a cross-functional team of brand ambassadors assesses the company using the test. Depending on the size of the company, there should be no less than 25 people (1/3 top management, 1/3 middle management, and 1/3 employees without personnel responsibility). In this way, the archetypical overall personality of the company is worked out on as broad a basis as possible without focusing too strongly on the preferences of individual departments. The overriding guiding question during the entire assessment is: "Which characteristics describe the company brand most accurately?" This is followed by a comparison (benchmarking) of employees from the functional areas with the ideal profile of the corporate brand (Pätzmann & Genrich, 2020, p. 32).

The insights into the implicit motifs of the employee personality generated by means of the personality test are compared with the archetypical personality of the corporate brand (Pätzmann & Genrich, 2020, p. 35). The insights gained in this way with regard to employee brand fit are subsequently used for targeted personnel development measures. The overriding goal of these is to align employees with the corporate brand, i.e., to establish a fundamental congruence of values between the employee, the functional area, and the corporate brand. This is the basis for intrinsically motivated employees who subsequently act as brand ambassadors. An employer value proposition that is actively communicated to the outside world in this way sustainably increases the credibility of the employer and corporate brand (Pätzmann & Genrich, 2020, p. 36). Employees with a strong archetypical fit to the brand profile are best suited to represent the company externally, for example, at trade fairs, in sales, and similar.

Archetypical Life Coaching Along the Hero's Journey There are already examples of the successful application of archetype theory for coaching (life counseling with regard to potentials, goals, and dreams).

For example, the Pearson-Marr-Archetype-Indicator is available as a website with online tests for coaching purposes (Purchase the PMAI®, n.d.). Lindemann (2016) also offers coaching and has his coachees develop systemic hero's journeys for their own destinies.

People seeking guidance fill out the archetypical personality test. Ideally, a constructively critical second person, perhaps a relative or a good friend, also fills out this test for the person concerned (about him or her), so that self-image and external image can be compared. Coaching techniques are then used to work on closing the gaps.

Alternatively, the coachee first fills out an archetypical personality test to determine the status quo and then establishes his or her own ideal image. Then he or she is taken on a hero's journey to get closer to this ideal image, for example, in the form of playing cards or software (Pätzmann & Genrich, 2020, p. 37).

Political Consulting/Top Manager Consulting Pätzmann and Benzing (2018) have made a first attempt to apply archetypes to politicians. In an empirical study, they identified the ideal image of a chancellor and then the profiles of Angela Merkel and the SPD's candidate for chancellor at the time, Martin Schulz. Angela Merkel came very close to the ideal chancellor, sometimes even surpassing the ideal image.

In the study at the time, only the external image was determined. Now that the archetypical personality test exists, one can also analyze the self-image, compare both, and try to close the gaps through suitable image profiling measures (Pätzmann & Genrich, 2020, p. 37). A third variable would be the ideal image, so that one can develop communicative strategies that take into account self-image, external image, and ideal image. The same applies to top managers who are in the public eye and want to control and manage their image, or other personalities of public interest (Pätzmann & Genrich, 2020, p. 37).

Target Group Segmentation and Media Planning There are a number of different ways to segment target groups. The most common method up to now has been to proceed according to sinus milieus. For years, there has been criticism that the sinus milieus are too rough (Pätzmann &

Genrich, 2020, p. 37). The archetypical model of Pätzmann and Hartwig (2018) consists of 14 archetypes and 14 anti-archetypes, which can be represented in a spiderweb diagram to show very differentiated target group segmentations and personas. To do this, a given population would have to be quantitatively measured using the archetypical personality test. This is doable but costly. The archetypes would then have to be linked to standard market media studies (e.g., AWA and B4P) and media usage studies (e.g., MA and AGOF). This would yield a tool that reflects the motivational experience of consumers in terms of consumer behavior and media usage in a differentiated way (Pätzmann & Genrich, 2020, p. 38). Jens Pätzmann is open for cooperation in this regard.

Team Composition and Coaching The present book explored the application of the archetypical personality test to better understand the dynamics in startup teams. Similar studies can be conducted for teams in other settings, for example, in established organizations, schools, or even families. The archetypical personality test can either be used to identify ideal team compositions or to uncover hidden social roles and improve their mutual understanding and collaboration. The methods described in Chap. 9 can also be applied to those contexts.

References

Lindemann, H. (2016). *Die große Metaphern-Schatzkiste–Band 2: Die Systemische Heldenreise* (Vol. 2).

Pätzmann, J., & Benzing, T. (2018). Das tool: Archetypen zur Persönlichkeitsanalyse von Politikern. *Markenbrand, 6*, 8–10.

Pätzmann, J., & Genrich, R. (2020). *Employer branding mit Archetypen.* Springer Gabler.

Pätzmann, J., & Hartwig, J. (2018). *Markenführung mit Archetypen.* Springer Gabler.

Purchase the PMAI®. (n.d.). Retrieved Aug 15 2021 from https://www.storywell.com/purchase-the-pmai.htm

12

Conclusion

The research presented in this book adds to the literature in two thematic areas: archetype theory and insights about personalities in startup teams. It shows that archetypes and in particular the archetypical model developed by Pätzmann and Hartwig (2018) are relevant for the study of personality setups in teams. Based on the findings presented in the preceding chapters, the research question "Can archetypical roles be a useful instrument for startup team formation?" can confidently be affirmed. Table 12.1 summarizes the research sub-questions and where they are answered in this book.

The (anti-)archetypes mentor, leader, friend, hero, artist, rebel, and femme fatale have been identified as being of the greatest relevance (sub-questions 1 and 2). The expert interviews revealed that in the context of startups, the manager is an additional role of importance. Research phase three provided the answers to sub-questions 3, 4, and 5 as presented in Chaps. 7, 8, and 10. Each (anti-)archetype has its distinct contribution to the startup team and throughout the development process. They need to counterbalance each other to avoid harmful predominance of a single archetype.

V. Miller, J. U. Pätzmann, *Archetypical Roles in Startups*, Business Guides on the Go,
https://doi.org/10.1007/978-3-031-22253-5_12

Table 12.1 Overview of research questions and answers. Source: Own representation

Research question	Answer
Can archetypical roles be a useful instrument for startup team formation?	Yes
Sub-question 1: Which archetypes are most relevant for startup teams?	Leader, mentor, artist, friend, hero (manager)
Sub-question 2: Which anti-archetypes are most tolerable in a startup team?	Rebel, femme fatale
Sub-question 3: What is the role of the identified (anti-)archetypes in a startup team?	See Chap. 7
Sub-question 4: How do archetypical team roles interact within a startup?	See Chap. 8
Sub-question 5: Which practical relevance does the archetypical model have for the entrepreneurship ecosystem?	See Chap. 10

This publication also shows that the archetypical model by Pätzmann and Hartwig (2018) can usefully be applied on an international scale. It was easily understood by the interviewees from Israel and Kenya, not only from Germany. The beauty of working with archetypes as opposed to abstract personality models is how they lend themselves to storytelling, imagination, and uncovering hidden themes. Group hero stories as described by Hall (2016) are particularly apt for startups: in a startup, team members with very different personalities can collaborate effectively, if they overcome individual quarrels and know which archetype to evoke in which situation.

The research findings provide valuable insights for practitioners from the entrepreneurship ecosystem: Founders are guided on how to choose and collaborate with their team members and which personality traits need to come to the fore in which stage of founding. Investors know what builds a winning team. Mentors know-how to coach and support a startup team to success. Incubators can design programs using the archetypical profiles presented in Chap. 7. Awareness of one's own team role helps to create efficient teams (Belbin, 2010, pp. 23, 48, 51). Knowledge about archetypical team roles can help individuals and their colleagues to develop better self- or mutual understanding. Working with them can be a way for entrepreneurs to arrive at decision-making processes that take different perspectives into account, being aware of their advantages and downsides, as suggested by Chowdhury (2005). When looking for cofounders or hiring employees, applying archetype theory can help to search for the missing piece instead of building an overly homogeneous team in terms of thinking and working styles. Mentors can support founders to follow the archetypical startup journey described in Sect. 8.2. They can point to the light and dark sides of both archetypes and anti-archetypes and create awareness of the pitfalls of overrepresentation of a certain archetype. These findings are relevant for any innovative team; thus, they can also be applied to intrapreneurship. Furthermore, the validated archetypical personality test can also be applied as a research tool for other team constellations.

Although the research presented in this book has yielded valuable results, it is not without limitations. Research phases one and two relied on quantitative surveys. These are often not fully reliable because the answers depend on the context (Silverman, 2017, p. 397), which in this case cannot be assessed. Furthermore, so far only content validity of the archetypical personality test has been validated in the German language with German respondents. According to Mummendey (2008), construct validity, the most advanced form of validity, should be confirmed for personality tests (p. 106 f). Thus, further validation steps of the English version may be necessary if the archetypical personality test is to be used on a broader international scale.

Research stages two and three are based on experts' know-how. This must be considered a secondary source that is filtered by individual preferences, attitudes, and experiences. It is not a fully objective and unbiased source of data. Following Miles et al.' (2020) statement about the validity of qualitative research, validity of the results of stage three is mainly ensured by its comprehensibility and the plausibility of the systematic qualitative content analysis methodology (p. 9). Generalizations can only be drawn with care and without neglecting the context of data collection (Schreier, 2012, p. 22). The selection of cases from three different countries plus four different categories of expertise from various industries increases the breadth of data collection and consequently the robustness of the results. The research identified patterns that can be validated in further studies.

The samples of both research phases display very poor gender balances: male respondents clearly outweigh females in terms of numbers. This has been reported in other studies and likely mirrors the entrepreneurship ecosystem itself. Brattström et al. (2020), for example, discovered that male attitudes are favored in incubators (Brattström et al.). For this reason, we must assume that the findings presented in this book and the archetypical startup role profiles are strongly influenced by masculine values and behaviors. The findings cannot be automatically transferred to female entrepreneurs.

In addition, most of the literature reviewed in part I relied on data from the United States, some from Germany or Scandinavia. Therefore, it is not sure how far these findings, which served as an interpretive frame for research stage three, apply in Germany, Israel, and Kenya. Culture may influence factors like the propensity for founding alone or in teams, whom to hire, how to split roles, power distance, collectivism, and more (Brattström et al., 2020, p. 18; Wasserman, 2012, p. 365). Yet, this research did not control for cultural dimensions. Since the experts interviewed had different functions and came from different industries, no clear differences between the three target countries could be identified, apart from minor variations. However, the research findings largely coincide with major findings of extant literature, so validity across cultural boundaries is probable.

This research is exploratory in nature. It has opened the field of archetypical team research in the area of startups. The results can inspire further interesting research about startup teams. A quantitative approach could inquire whether startups with a certain archetypical personality setup are more successful than others in reaching their goals. An experimental design could look at how startups, incubators, or investors work with the adapted archetypical profiles for startup teams. A qualitative study could identify archetypical themes present in actual startup teams as opposed to relying on secondary expert experiences. Such a study might take advantage of the narrative collage methodology described in Sect. 9.1. Case study research with selected startup teams would be useful to answer in-depth how and why questions (see Lee, 2017; Yin, 2018). This could be done at an incubator. Longitudinal case study research would be very helpful to generate findings about a startup's evolution over time. A reverse research approach would be to look at personality traits that are *not* desirable in a startup team. For example, this could be realized by conducting in-depth interviews on the most weakly rated (anti-)archetypes and finding out which personality types often *are* present in startup teams but with destructive effects. This could provide valuable results which help founders to circumvent these pitfalls.

This research did not discover substantial differences between the three target countries Kenya, Israel, and Germany, only marginal variations. A further study can build on these results with a stronger comparative approach to find out whether there are significant differences or not. As this research is of exploratory nature, it did not limit data collection to a specific entrepreneurial environment. However, it is very likely that results would vary depending on the circumstances. Upper echelons theory already affirmed the importance of the context in which a top management team operates (Jin et al., 2017, p. 745). Similarly, Fauchart and Gruber (2011) showed how founders' identity, goals, and values influence their effect on their firm. Other researchers have asked for a stronger focus on temporal aspects in team dynamics (Brattström et al., 2020, p. 16; Vanaelst et al., 2006, p. 267). For this reason, further studies should be conducted that focus on specified contexts, e.g., stage of founding, industry, founder characteristics, degree of novelty of the business model or products, organizational structure, economic environment, and others. Contextual research will make it possible to see the nuances and to give more guided advice.

References

Belbin, R. M. (2010). *Team roles at work* (2nd ed.). Routledge.

Brattström, A., Delmar, F., Johnson, A. R., & Wennberg, K. (2020). A longitudinal project of new venture teamwork and outcomes. In *Research handbook on entrepreneurial behavior, practice and process* (pp. 309–334). Edward Elgar Publishing. https://doi.org/10.4337/9781788114523.00023.

Chowdhury, S. (2005). Demographic diversity for building an effective entrepreneurial team: Is it important? *Journal of Business Venturing, 20*(6), 727–746.

Fauchart, E., & Gruber, M. (2011). Darwinians, communitarians, and missionaries: The role of founder identity in entrepreneurship. *Academy of Management Journal, 54*(5), 935–957.
Hall, C. (2016). The group hero: An archetype whose time has come. In S. B. Schafer (Ed.), *Exploring the collective unconscious in the age of digital media* (pp. 214–231). IGI Global.
Jin, L., Madison, K., Kraiczy, N. D., Kellermanns, F. W., Crook, T. R., & Xi, J. (2017). Entrepreneurial team composition characteristics and new venture performance: A meta-analysis. *Entrepreneurship Theory and Practice, 41*(5), 743–771. https://doi.org/10.1111/etap.12232
Lee, B. (2017). *Conducting case study research*. Sage.
Miles, M. B., Huberman, A. M., & Saldana, J. (2020). *Qualitative data analysis* (4th ed.). SAGE.
Mummendey, H. D. (2008). *Die Fragebogen-Methode* (5th ed.). Hogrefe.
Pätzmann, J., & Hartwig, J. (2018). *Markenführung mit Archetypen*. Springer Gabler.
Schreier, M. (2012). *Qualitative content analysis in practice*. SAGE.
Silverman, D. (2017). *Doing qualitative research* (5th ed.). SAGE.
Vanaelst, I., Clarysse, B., Wright, M., Lockett, A., Moray, N., & S'Jergers, R. (2006). Entrepreneurial team development in academic spinouts: An examination of team heterogeneity. *Entrepreneurship Theory and Practice, 30*(2), 249–271.
Wasserman, N. (2012). *The founder's dilemmas: Anticipating and avoiding the pitfalls that can sink a startup*. Princeton University Press.
Yin, R. K. (2018). *Case study research and applications* (6th ed.).

The manufacturer's authorised representative in the EU is Springer Nature Customer Service Centre GmbH, Europaplatz 3, 69115 Heidelberg, Germany. If you have any concerns regarding our products, please contact ProductSafety@springernature.com

Printed and bound by CPI Group (UK) Ltd, Croydon, CR0 4YY

28/09/2026

02224075-0001